D0886867

Multinationals from the Second World

Growth of Foreign Investment by Soviet and East European Enterprises

Carl H. McMillan
Professor of Economics
Carleton University, Ottawa

St. Martin's Press, New York

for the
Trade Policy Research Centre, London

For my parents

First published in the United States of America in 1987

Printed in Great Britain

ISBN 0-312-55253-X

Library of Congress Cataloging-in-Publication Data
McMillan, Carl H.
Multinationals from the Second World.
Bibliography: p.
Includes indexes.
1. Investments, East European—Developing countries.
2. Investments, East European.   3. Investments, Russian—
Developing countries.   4. Investments, Russian.
5. East-West trade (1945-   ).   6. Competition,
International   I. Title.
HG5993.M38   1987   332.6'7347   86-10095
ISBN 0-312-55253-X

Trade Policy Research Centre

The Trade Policy Research Centre, based in London, was established in 1968 to promote independent analysis and public discussion of international economic policy issues. The Centre is managed by a Council, set out below, which represents a wide range of international experience and expertise.

As a non-profit organisation which is privately sponsored the institute has been developed to work on an international basis and serves as an entrepreneurial centre for a variety of activities, including the publication of a quarterly journal, *The World Economy*. In general, the Centre provides a focal point for those in business, the universities and public affairs who are interested in the problems

of international economic relations – whether commercial, legal
financial, monetary or diplomatic.

The principal function of the Centre is the sponsorship of research
programmes on policy problems of both national and international
importance. Conferences, seminars, lectures and dinner meetings
are also convened from time to time.

Publications are presented as professionally competent studies
worthy of public consideration. The interpretations and conclusions
in them are those of their respective authors and do not purport to
represent the views of members of the Council, staff and associates
of the Centre, which, having general terms of reference, does not
represent a consensus of opinion on any particular issue.

Enquiries about membership (individual, corporate or library) of
the Centre, about subscriptions to *The World Economy* or about the
Centre's publications should be addressed to the Director, Trade
Policy Research Centre, 1 Gough Square, London EC4A 3DE,
United Kingdom.

Contents

List of Tables

List of Figures

Biographical Note

Carl H. McMillan has been Professor of Economics at Carleton University, Ottawa, in Canada since 1980. At the University, which he joined in 1968, he has been since 1973 the Director of the East–West Project, having been Director of the Institute of Soviet and East European Studies in 1975–82. In 1974–75, Professor McMillan was a Visiting Research Associate at the Institute of Comparative Economic Studies, in Vienna, and in 1982 he was a Visiting Research Professor at the Institut Universitaire de Hautes Etudes Internationales, University of Geneva.

After graduating in 1952 from Yale University, in the United States, Professor McMillan obtained a masters degree in international relations from the same university and afterwards served, as a commissioned officer, in the United States Navy (1953–57). He then joined the Department of State, in the United States Administration (1957–64), and held posts in the American embassies in Manila and Moscow, having studied at the United States Army Institute of Advanced Russian Studies. Later, Professor McMillan was a Visiting Scholar at the Russian Research Centre at Harvard University in 1966–67, before moving to Carleton University. In 1972, he obtained his doctorate in economics from Johns Hopkins University, Baltimore.

In his research and writing, Professor McMillan has specialised in comparative international economics, with particular reference to the external relations of the centrally planned economies. He is the co-author of *Joint Ventures in Eastern Europe: a Three Country Comparison* (1974), edited *Changing Perspectives in East–West Commerce* (1974) and co-edited *Partners in East–West Economic Relations* (1980). His published articles and papers have been addressed principally to questions of Soviet foreign trade, East European economic integration and East–West relations.

Preface

Over the last decade and a half the Soviet Union and its six East European partners in the Council for Mutual Economic Assistance (Comecon), emerging from comparative isolation, have been increasing their economic relations with countries in the rest of the world economy. There has been a marked increase in East–West trade and also a marked increase in foreign direct investment by Comecon state enterprises in Western countries and the Third World. Over six hundred companies of Comecon origin have been established in developing countries and in twenty-three, of the twenty-four, countries belonging to the Organisation for Economic Cooperation and Development (OECD). By contrast, Western equity participation in enterprises operating within the Comecon countries has been far more limited.

Who and what are these multinational enterprises from the Second World, these 'red multinationals', as some Western journalists have called them? What challenges do they pose to host countries and to international business competitors? These are the questions addressed here in Carl McMillan's study. Professor McMillan assesses the phenomenon, describing its nature, establishing its quantitative dimensions and explaining its motivations and limitations, as well as identifying its more significant directions.

The growth of state-socialist investment in the market-oriented economies of the OECD and the Third World has received little serious academic attention until now. Professor McMillan's study has drawn on a unique data base on Soviet and East European foreign investment which has been built up over a period of ten years by a research team, under his direction, at Carleton University in Ottawa. Using this statistical information, and using illustrative case-study analyses, Professor McMillan has traced the growth of Comecon direct investment outside the Second World's domain, setting out the range of Comecon investment activities and the kinds of problems encountered by individual Soviet and East European companies in their operations abroad.

With the rapid integration of the world economy since World War II, the growth of multinational enterprises has assumed dimensions which, for many, have challenged the sovereignty of nations – as if the growing interdependence of national economies was not in any case blurring the meaning of national interest, national power and national sovereignty. In developing and developed countries some have queried whether the operations of multinational enterprises serve the goals of stable growth, industrialisation, employment security, and so on. A number of instances of questionable political activity by multinational enterprises have stimulated the public debate. Multinational enterprises *per se* have been a controversial issue.

The study elaborates on these issues by addressing four more issues, namely (i) how the activities of multinational enterprises might be regulated through an international code of conduct, (ii) whether foreign direct investment by Comecon state enterprises poses a special threat to the economic interests of host countries, (iii) whether they undermine the national security of host countries, and (iv) whether direct investments increase the power of foreign leverage for the Soviet Union and East European countries.

The Comecon countries, as state-socialist economies, maintain that their enterprises are not geared primarily to making profits and are necessarily distinct from multinational enterprises which originate in the private sector of market-oriented economies. This is the argument put forward by the Comecon countries in the United Nations and in other inter-governmental discussions on the perceived abuses by Western multinational enterprises. Ideology apart, the Comecon countries are in effect arguing for their exemption from any international regulation of the behaviour of multinational enterprises.

If the external investment activities of comecon enterprises are not geared to profits, what, it may be asked, is their primary objective and what are the implications for host countries? Is there not a danger, it is asked, that they will be used, as have Comecon trade missions in the past, for espionage and subversion?

The evidence presented by Professor McMillan in this study indicates that Comecon subsidiaries adhere to familiar commercial norms and in fact are principally concerned with profits (or at least hard-currency turnover). Professor McMillan finds that their operations do not appear to differ significantly from the practices of other foreign-owned firms.

Professor McMillan concludes that Soviet and East European investment activities are of considerably more qualitative than quantitative significance. They represent, in the first place, an important new element in the external activities of the Soviet and East European economies, indicating a continued commitment to increased participation in the world economy. In the second place, they constitute a form of 'state investment' (by 'state-trading' countries) in which the parent state enterprises are subject to a relatively high degree of control by central governmental authorities in the home countries.

As usual, it has to be stressed that the views expressed in this study are those of the author and do not necessarily reflect the views of the Council, staff or associates of the Trade Policy Research Centre which, having general terms of reference, does not represent on any particular issue a consensus of opinion. The purpose of the Centre is to promote independent analysis and public discussion of international economic policy issues.

HUGH CORBET
Director
Trade Policy Research Centre

London
May 1986

Acknowledgements

The original data on which this study for the Trade Policy Research Centre is based were assembled over a number of years with the assistance of a succession of young researchers in the East–West Project at Carleton University in Ottawa. Without their dedication, the work could not have been done; and without their enthusiasm, it would have been far less enjoyable. For this I should like to thank Bruce Morgan, Reid Henry, Michel Goffin, Frank ter Borg, Barbara Darnowska, François Cadieux, Peter Egyed and especially Agnieszka Warda, who provided general research assistance in writing. The work also owes much to the co-operation of many of the companies themselves and to a number of officials in the home and host countries. I am indebted, as well, to several colleagues who have given their help and advice throughout, in particular to Patrick Gutman and Jeanne Laux.

At the Trade Policy Research Centre in London, thanks are due in particular to Janet Strachan, the Administrative Director, for coping patiently with the various stages of the project, and to Annabel Huxley for preparing the typescript for publication.

I should like to acknowledge the financial support of the Social Sciences and Humanities Research Council of Canada in the initial stages of the research and a grant from the Dean of Social Sciences at Carleton University which greatly facilitated the preparation of the final manuscript. Tara McCreery ably processed the final drafts.

A section of Chapter 8 is based in part on a paper, 'Soviet and East European Participation in Business Firms and Banks Established in the West', which was presented to the 1983 NATO Colloquium, published as *External Economic Relations of the CMEA Countries* (1983). Lastly I am grateful to the Economics Directorate of the North Atlantic Treaty Organisation for permission to use this material.

CARL H. McMILLAN

Ottawa
January 1986

CHAPTER 1

New Dimensions to Multinational Enterprise

Unquestionably one of the most important developments in the world economy during this century has been the spread of multinational enterprise. Firms increasingly have conducted their international operations through foreign branches, subsidiaries and other affiliates acquired or established by the processes of direct investment. Especially in the second half of the century, the growth of this phenomenon has assumed dimensions which have challenged the sovereignty of nations. The developed countries have shown concern over the impact of multinational operations on their pursuit of stabilisation policies; the developing countries have questioned whether multinational activities have served the interests of their industrialisation goals. Several widely publicised instances of questionable political activity by multinational enterprises have added to the concern. As a result, 'multinational enterprise' has become a controversial issue of international political economy, posing major questions of policy for both host and home countries, and attracting increasing attention and debate within the framework of multilateral institutions.[1]

The more recent evolution of the multinational phenomenon has witnessed the rise of international flows of direct investment from potentially important new sources, in terms both of geography and type of institution.[2] The near monopoly of American firms in the period following World War II has been eroded by the growth of foreign direct investment not only from other industrially advanced countries (the member states of the European Community, Canada and Japan) but also from Third World countries (especially the more developed among them). This geographic diversification has contributed to a second trend. Private multinational firms have increasingly been joined by state-owned enterprises, thus casting the state in a new, direct role in the multinational sphere.

These two trends have been reinforced by the emergence of direct investment from yet another source: the planned, state-socialist economies of the Soviet Union and Eastern Europe, which constitute

1

the European membership of the Council for Mutual Economic Assistance (CMEA or Comecon).[3] In their present state of development, the foreign investments of the Comecon countries remain comparatively limited; many investments abroad are tiny by international standards and the multinational activities of most Comecon state enterprises are still in their infancy. By the early 1980s, Soviet and East European direct investments abroad had nevertheless developed sufficiently to add a significant new dimension to the rise of state enterprises in international business generally and in multinational investment activity in particular. They had themselves begun to pose difficult policy questions for host countries and to claim the serious attention of international organisations in their deliberations on the global challenges posed by the growth of international investment.[4]

PHENOMENON OF COMECON FOREIGN DIRECT INVESTMENT

The purpose of this study is to explore the phenomenon of foreign direct investment from the Comecon countries and to assess its implications. The exploration follows a dual analytical approach, centred around two major hypotheses.

The first is that when examined in comparative perspective, Comecon foreign investment can be seen in fundamental respects to resemble that from other sources:

(a) the foreign investment activities of Comecon-based enterprises are undertaken in response to the same conditions of world economy which have prompted the rise of multinational enterprise generally;

(b) the nature of their foreign investment response is analogous; and

(c) their activities are pursued in circumstances similar to those in which multinational enterprises originating in other systems operate so that multinational enterprises from Comecon countries compete directly, and occasionally collaborate, with other multinationals.

While it is understood that Comecon-based multinational enterprises are not only state-owned, but are also controlled by administrative agencies of states espousing ideologies and embracing socio-economic systems which set them apart from the rest of the world, it is as a result of the factors outlined above, rather than the nature of the system in which they originate, which have served as the primary determinants of the multinational organisation and behaviour of Comecon-based enterprises.

The second hypothesis is that foreign direct investment represents an important development in the external economic policy and relations of the Comecon countries. It must, therefore, be viewed in the light of the evolution of their centrally-planned economic systems and associated state-trading mechanisms. Foreign investment activities are one manifestation of a pragmatic search by these countries, especially since the mid–1960s, for more effective means of participation in the world economy – a search which has resulted in a number of important changes in their foreign trade regimes.

In the area of foreign capital investment, as in other areas, this pragmatism has come into conflict with orthodox ideology. The ideological context has, as will be seen, both conditioned and retarded the approach to foreign investment by state agencies in Comecon countries.

Lenin, in 1919, characterised as the highest 'imperialist' stage of capitalism, that in which 'the dominance of monopolies and finance capital has established itself; in which the export of capital has acquired pronounced importance; in which the division of the world through international trusts has begun, in which the division of all territories of the globe among the greatest capitalist powers has been completed'.[5] Lenin's concept has since been employed by analysts in the Comecon countries to condemn as 'exploitative' the activities of Western multinational enterprises, especially in the Third World.

Western observers have remarked on the consequent irony that, in their drive to establish new links to Western technology and markets, Soviet and East European countries have revealed a marked preference for partnerships with large Western multinational enterprises.[6] Perhaps even more ironic is that state-owned monopolies in the Comecon countries should have increasing recourse to strategies of foreign direct investment which bear so many of the attributes of Western multinational enterprise.

The gap between traditional ideology and present reality has acted as a brake on the pursuit of foreign investment goals. Ideological impediments and associated political factors have by no means, however, been the sole restraints on the growth of foreign investment activity. The Comecon countries face more severe economic obstacles, both internal and external, to the development abroad of a marketing and production infrastructure through which to realise their external-policy objectives. These will be examined in subsequent chapters.

STRUCTURE OF THE ANALYSIS

This book falls into three parts. The initial chapters are of a general, introductory nature. The second chapter sets the broader policy context within which Comecon foreign investment activities have been pursued, particularly since the mid-1960s. The third chapter describes the forms of organisation and, in quantitative terms, outlines the current dimensions of Comecon foreign investment. The absence of comprehensive official statistical data has made it necessary to develop an independent data base, which is drawn upon throughout the book. The nature of this data base and the methodology employed in its compilation are described in the Appendix to this book. The fourth chapter examines the processes of investment decision-making in the Comecon countries and explores the motivations which have given rise to foreign investment activity in individual countries. There then follow chapters which deal with investments in specific sectors of foreign economies and which use a case-study approach to analyse the experience encountered in specific host countries. The concluding chapter summarises past trends in the external investment activity of Comecon countries, discusses policy issues to which they give rise and evaluates their longer-term significance.

The analysis in this book is directed to the investment activities of the Comecon countries in the West and the South. It deals exclusively with the extra-regional investment activities of the Comecon countries, because the concept of foreign direct investment does not apply to relations among them. Within the CMEA, member states have engaged in joint investment projects and have formed a handful of joint enterprises, but these have taken the form of contractual ventures, without the direct equity investment of one Comecon state in the economy of another.[7] The nature of the economic systems involved, and the ideologies underlying them, have dictated that the kinds of international business activities and the forms of partnership undertaken by Comecon enterprises with each other differ significantly from those employed with the rest of the world.

NOTES AND REFERENCES

1. For these reasons, a voluminous literature on the topic was developed. See *Bibliography on Transnational Corporations*, ST/CTC/4 (New York: United Nations, for the Commission on Transnational Corporations, 1979).

2. See *Transnational Corporations in World Development: A Re-examination*, UN E.78-II-A.5 (New York: United Nations, for the Commission on Transnational Corporations, 1978) and K. Kumar and M. G. McLeod (eds), *Multinationals from Developing Countries* (Lexington, Mass.: D. C. Heath and Company, 1981).

3. The Council for Mutual Economic Assistance (CMEA or Comecon) set up in 1949 is an international organisation consisting of six East European countries: Bulgaria, Czechoslovakia, the German Democratic Republic, Hungary, Poland, Romania and the Soviet Union, together with three non-regional members: Mongolia, Cuba and Vietnam.

   The terms 'CMEA', 'Comecon' and 'East European' will be used interchangeably to designate the six East European Comecon countries and the Soviet Union and their multinational investment activity.

4. The United Nations Centre for Transnational Corporations, the Organisation for Economic Cooperation and Development (OECD) and the International Chamber of Commerce have all addressed the question in this context.

5. V. I. Lenin, *Imperialism, the Highest Stage of Capitalism*, revised translation (New York: International Publishers, 1939) pp. 88–9.

6. G. Lauter and P. Dickie, *Multinational Corporations and East European Socialist Economies* (New York: Praeger, 1975); J. Wilczynski, *The Multinationals and East–West Relations* (London: Macmillan, 1976) and, in a more polemical vein, C. Levinson, *Vodka-Kola* (Paris: Stock, 1977).

7. See M. Lavigne, *Le programme du Comécon et l'intégration socialiste* (Paris: Editions Cujas, 1973) and H. Brzezinski, *Internationale Wirtschaftsplanung im RGW* (Paderborn: Ferdinand Schöningh, 1978).

CHAPTER 2

Comecon Countries and the World Economy

Most of the foreign investment activity of state enterprises in the Comecon countries has developed since the late 1960s. A few Soviet investments that were established before World War II – those concentrated in timber, oil and banking – survived the war. The Communist regimes which came to power in Eastern Europe after World War II inherited some foreign assets when they nationalised large capitalist firms with foreign branches and affiliates. By the 1960s, however, these and a few additional investments constituted only a handful of cases and could be regarded as exceptional, even anomalous, in terms of the priorities of contemporary policy.

The rise of foreign direct investment by the Comecon countries must, therefore, be understood in the context of more recent trends. As noted in Chapter 1, it was but one manifestation of a more general opening up of the Comecon economies to greater and more diverse interaction with the world economy. This chapter will review the principal developments in the external policies and relations of the Comecon countries which accompanied, and inevitably conditioned, the growth of their foreign investments. An examination of the more specific factors, within this context, which have motivated foreign investment decision-making and policy-making will be left until Chapter 4.

ORIGINS AND EVOLUTION OF THE NEW ORIENTATION OF EXTERNAL POLICY

In the course of the 1960s, the Comecon countries perceived an increasing need to break out of their regional isolation and to engage more actively in the mainstream of international economic relations. Accordingly, there emerged in all seven countries by the end of the decade new approaches in policy to the conduct of relations with extra-regional partners. These continued to evolve over the 1970s to become important new dimensions in the economic relations of Comecon countries with the rest of the 'non-socialist' world.

The Comecon countries envisaged these trends as part of a desirable process of integrating their economies into the world economy. The 'international socialist division of labour', which previously had been given emphasis, was now subsumed under a broader concept. Relations with socialist and non-socialist partners and, within the latter category, with partners from the developed West and developing South, were increasingly approached in a new, 'global' perspective, within the framework of a more general 'international division of labour'.[1] At the same time, this entailed explicit recognition of the increased interdependence inevitably involved in the pursuit of these goals. Spokesmen for this new orientation of economic policy stressed the 'mutuality of interests' involved, the acceptability of the levels of interdependence envisaged and the important benefits expected to ensue from the new relationships.[2]

The Comecon countries had, by the 1960s, reached a stage in their economic development which stimulated interest in more active participation in the world economy. The economic isolation of the Comecon countries in the preceding period had only partially been imposed by the sanctions of the Cold War. It was also the result of a self-imposed, inward orientation, as these countries embarked on programmes of rapid reconstruction and industrialisation, the example for which was set by the Soviet Union. One of the well-known characteristics of the Soviet pattern of development was the establishment of a diversified, domestic industrial base in comparative neglect of foreign trade opportunities. While more reasonable for a country of the size and endowment of resources of the Soviet Union, an industrial strategy of this nature could not indefinitely be maintained by the smaller, East European countries.

The traditional pattern of development (referred to as 'extensive growth' in Comecon terminology because of its emphasis on the extensive mobilisation of labour and capital in the development drive) had been broadly successful in laying the industrial foundations of the Comecon economies, but its comparative disregard for scarcity of resources could not be tolerated in the long run, even by the Soviet Union.[3] Nor, especially in the smaller Comecon countries, could its neglect of external opportunities. The result was the emergence of a new 'intensive' strategy for growth, which shifted attention from quantitative goals to qualitative improvements in both industrial products and processes.[4] Further development would therefore have to be based on more efficient use of resources, in both internal and external economic relationships, and on the introduction of new technology.

Extensive growth with its emphasis on a high rate of investment had left the consumer as a residual claimant on resources. An intensive growth strategy, in this regard, was to permit a more balanced pattern in the allocation of resources. The issue of the priority of consumer demands was to be raised, after long years of enforced saving.

In the late 1950s and early 1960s, these considerations had prompted interest in greater specialisation among the East European countries, within the framework of the CMEA. Progress was slow, however, and impeded by economic and political controversies and institutional weaknesses in its regional organisation.[5] In particular, regional sources of new technology and associated equipment were found inadequate to the needs of the modernisation programmes of Comecon industries.

As a result, pressure mounted to take advantage of a broader international division of labour, through more intensive development of relations with non-socialist countries, both developed and developing. This, however, was not intended to be mounted at the expense of continued efforts to advance regional integration – the two objectives were regarded not only as compatible but also as mutually reinforcing. Integration of the Comecon countries would facilitate their integration into the world economy as a whole and, conversely, extra-regional linkages would stimulate increased specialisation in production processes among the Comecon members.[6]

The intensive growth strategy required not only new priorities but also new organisations and procedures. Accordingly, it set off a wave of institutional change, or 'reform', in the Comecon countries. The nature of the changes instituted in the different countries in the 1960s, and the course which the reforms subsequently took, are complex subjects which cannot be pursued in any detail here. The measures taken ranged from more modest attempts to streamline and update the traditional institutions of central economic administration (this happened, for example, in Bulgaria, the German Democratic Republic, Romania and the Soviet Union) to more ambitious efforts to substitute market forces for detailed plan directives and to restrict central planning to the definition of broad goals and their implementation by means of indirect policy instruments (which occurred at various times in Czechoslovakia, Hungary and Poland).[7]

These varied attempts at institutional change have had one thing in common. They have all run into major obstacles – political, social, and economic – which, for the most part, they failed to overcome. As a result, the reform initiatives gradually lost momentum. Only in Hungary (and there, too, not without serious difficulties and setbacks) did the reforms succeed in bringing about substantial change in the traditional system.

The difficulties encountered in pursuing intensive growth strategies through domestic reform stimulated the regimes to rely all the more heavily on external solutions, thus clarifying the need for external measures such as those which are the subject of this book. At the same time, it has increasingly been recognised that the intensive growth strategy requires a two-pronged approach and that, if they are to succeed in the longer run, the new external initiatives must be backed by domestic changes. The search for a viable course of economic reform has, therefore, continued, in varying intensity, in all the Comecon countries under consideration.[8]

The emergence of the Comecon countries in more recent years was the result not only of their growing need to derive all possible advantage from more active engagement in international economic relations but also of the greater scope afforded them to do so. The heightened competition and rapid technological progress in world markets, which marked the period of boom in the West from the late 1950s through to the early 1970s, raised the cost of isolation to the Comecon countries. Economic prosperity also made more attractive to the West the concept of a relaxation of the political tensions of the earlier Cold War period and gave rise to a new emphasis on unexplored areas of mutual economic interest where there was potential for East–West co-operation. The normalisation of Soviet and East European relations with the Federal Republic of Germany, and the improvement of relations with the United States, had established by the 1970s a favourable political climate in which the new external economic strategies of the Comecon countries could be pursued.[9]

A drive to import Western capital goods and technology formed a major element of the strategy to raise industrial productivity and inject a new, dynamic efficiency into Comecon industry.[10] Given priority in this regard was the expansion and modernisation of new or underdeveloped industries, such as the automotive, chemical and electronics industries. Especially in the Soviet Union, Poland and Romania (but, to some extent, in all the Comecon countries)

Western technology and capital were also seen as important factors in the further development of resource-intensive industries, such as mineral fuels and metals.

The import drive was linked as well to the new consumption goals. With the development of the automotive industry, for example, were envisaged rapid increases in capacity to produce private as well as industrial vehicles; and the Soviet licence agreement with Fiat in the mid-1960s to build a giant automobile complex at Togliattigrad, was one of the major signposts of the new external course. Western technology and know-how were subsequently used to diversify consumer manufactures on a broad front, from soft drinks to razor blades and blue jeans, and imports of plant and equipment to boost the capacity of the chemical fertiliser industry (as well as massive direct imports of grain) have been fundamental to achieving improved levels in the consumption of meat, which, as incomes rose, was one of the first priorities of households in the Comecon countries.

In the immediate term, the Comecon countries found little difficulty in obtaining Western financing for their import drive. At the official level, financing was facilitated by the political atmosphere of *détente*. At the unofficial level, it was favoured because of the liquidity of major Western commercial banks which had resulted from the flood of petro-dollars earned by the oil-exporting countries after 1973. Trade and banking officials in the Comecon countries nevertheless recognised (much earlier, it would seem, than many of their Western counterparts) that trade imbalances could not indefinitely be financed and that, in the longer run, a sounder basis for the growth of East–West trade had to be established.

An essential part of the new external strategy was therefore to improve the structure of Comecon trade with the more advanced industrial countries. The modernisation of Comecon industries through trade and co-operation with the West was intended, in part, to result in the development of an export structure more reflective of the level of industrialisation attained by the Comecon economies. For these countries, then, 'integration into the international division of labour' meant not only more effective links to international flows of industrial technology but also the use of those new links to develop more widely competitive export industries.

While the interest in forging new, extra-regional economic links was focused principally on the advanced industrial economies, it also extended to the developing economies of the Third World. As the

Comecon countries entered what they perceived as a new phase of their industrialisation, they sought new approaches to their economic relations with the South as well as with the West.[11] It is generally argued that, for the mid-1960s, they increasingly saw their interests in the Third World to lie in the direction of more pragmatic, less ideologically determined, policies and deeper, more stable and more mutually advantageous economic ties with the developing countries. As a consequence, priority was shifted from politically-tied, economic aid projects to more businesslike, commercial relations. Not only was support no longer reserved for Marxist, or even 'progressive', Third World regimes, but some of the Comecon countries' most active economic partners were countries whose governments could easily be called 'reactionary' and which pursued domestic policies opposed to Communist ideology.

From the perspective of economic developments in the Comecon countries, the new course of policy with regard to the Third World can, as in the case of Comecon policy towards the West, be linked to the imperatives of the new industrialisation strategy. Rapid industralisation under the extensive growth strategy, and inefficiency in the use of resources fostered by systems of over-centralised, 'command' planning, had created a voracious demand for raw materials within the Comecon countries. The mounting dependence of Eastern Europe on imports of Soviet raw materials and the rising cost of exploitation and transport within the region were increasingly recognised as posing serious, long-term problems for the Comecon countries.[12] As the relative scarcity of intra-regional supplies of industrial raw materials grew, the search for external sources extended with increasing urgency to the Third World. Although the efficiency goals of the new intensive growth strategy, and the systemic changes which accompanied it, sought to relieve pressure on regional sources of supply, they could at best only modify the mounting requirement for extra-regional sourcing.

Perhaps the most striking example was in petroleum. As regional surpluses eroded, the East European countries had, by the end of the 1970s, to import oil from the Organisation of Petroleum Exporting Countries (OPEC) in order to meet a growing share of their requirements.[13] Third World sourcing of raw materials was by no means limited to petroluem, however, and, even for the Soviet Union, included such commodities as bauxite, nickel, copper, rubber and phosphates.

The developing countries also formed a market where industrial output from the Comecon countries proved to be competitive with Western products. The bulk of the Comecon exports to the Third World were the industrial products and technology that were linked with the 'heavy' industries to which the Comecon countries had given priority in their own industrialisation drives. These were often supplied in the form of complete plants, sold on a 'turn-key' basis, with associated technical assistance provided in the run-in period. In many cases the industrial products of the Comecon countries proved to be of acceptable quality for Third World uses. Their simplicity and durability outweighed the lack of the sophisticated features of Western alternatives, which sported features more appropriate to the high-income and high-labour-cost economies for which they had been developed than to the purposes of Third World countries. Moreover, Comecon enterprises often proved willing to provide more generous technical assistance and training for longer periods of time than were private firms from Western Europe. The competitiveness of Comecon capital goods exports was also enhanced by their lower prices, more favourable terms of credit and the possibility of soft-currency settlements made under bilateral clearing arrangements.[14]

The international economy which the Comecon countries sought to break into through these new approaches in the West and the South, was one characterised by rapid technological change in their leading sectors, accompanied by increased product and functional specialisation and sharpened commercial competition. These conditions had contributed to the rapid growth of foreign direct investment by Western firms in the period following World War II.[15] Anxious to extend and improve their own participation in the world economy, the Comecon countries recognised that the successful strategy of North American and West European firms entailed the direct exploitation of their commercial and technical advantages over rival firms through the establishment of subsidiaries within foreign markets. It is scarcely surprising, therefore, that, like other industrial exporters late in arriving on the international scene, the Comecon countries should decide that their own international success depended on the pursuit of a similar strategy.

EXPANSION OF EXTRA-REGIONAL TRADE

These new external policies, and the measures implemented as a result, brought about rapid growth in the extra-regional trade of the

Comecon countries. Real growth was concentrated in the late 1960s and early 1970s, before the effects on the world economy of the two oil price shocks and related difficulties (inflation, unemployment, protectionism and debt) had made themselves felt. The impact of the subsequent slow-down was differential, however, affecting in various degrees the geographic and commodity structure of Comecon trade with the rest of the world.

The overall trend in trade with the West is revealed in Table 2.1, which presents the nominal and real growth of East–West trade between 1965 and 1980. It shows evidence of a burst of growth over the first years, followed by a slow-down after 1974 and stagnation by the end of the decade. Overall, however, the entire period between 1965–80 is one of roughly balanced expansion of trade, measured in current prices, as the growth of East European imports from the West were reined-in after 1976, in response to the large deficits which had then opened up in East–West trade.

In reality, this balance of trade did not exist. Eastward flows grew much more rapidly between 1965 and 1980 than did westward flows,

Table 2.1   Growth of East–West trade, 1965–80[a]

Year	Westward flows			Eastward flows			Share of world trade
	Nominal	*Real*	*Index*	*Nominal*	*Real*	*Index*	
1965	4,110	4,110	100	4,080	4,080	100	2.2
1970	7,032	6,572	160	6,938	6,250	153	2.6
1972	8,941	7,269	177	10,199	8,094	198	2.3
1974	19,878	5,846	142	21,037	11,131	273	2.2
1976	23,753	6,729	164	29,055	13,876	340	2.5
1978	29,300	7,325	178	34,453	13,150	322	2.3
1980	48,690	6,887	168	46,592	13,875	338	2.1

[a] Merchandise trade between Developed Market Economies and CMEA-7. Nominal and real figures in millions US dollars. Index (1965 = 100) indicates growth of real flows in constant 1965 dollars. Shares of world trade also express relationships in real terms. Real values derived by employing price indices of relevant world export categories.

Sources: For exports of CMEA-7 and Developed Market Economies: *UN Yearbook of International Trade Statistics*, (New York: United Nations, 1969 and 1980) Special Table C.
For price indices, 'World Trade of Market Economies, Index Numbers by Region, Exports', Special Table B, *UN Monthly Bulletin of Statistics*, New York, various issues.

although both declined at the end of the 1970s from peaks in 1976–78. (Preliminary data indicate even more striking real declines in the early 1980s.) Nevertheless, East–West trade either outstripped or approximately kept pace with the growth of world trade throughout the period.

The striking divergence between the flows in nominal and in real terms has its roots in the structure and terms of East–West trade. Indeed, the chronic imbalances in East–West trade flows shown in Table 2.1 reflect their imbalanced structure. The industrialisation drive to modernise the Comecon countries produced an appetite for increasingly sophisticated Western machinery, equipment and technology. At the same time, primary products continued to predominate in westward trade flows. The East European countries were, as a group, able to maintain relatively high nominal earnings from a comparatively low real base, largely because of the dramatic rise in the value of energy products (principally from the Soviet Union, the dominant economic force in the group) which make up an important share of Comecon exports to the West.

The comparatively limited role which manufactures play in the exports of Comecon countries to the West is demonstrated in Table 2.2. The share of manufactures in the exports of the seven Comecon countries to the developed market economies remained below 30 per cent at the end of the 1980s. For some of the more industrialised of these countries, such as Czechoslovakia and the German Democratic Republic, the share of manufactures was more than twice this average, although declining. The Soviet share (and hence the regional share) was pulled down by the rapid rise in the relative prices of energy exports. At the same time, there was notable growth of manufactured exports in real terms for all countries, but especially the Soviet Union, Hungary, Poland and Romania. The data in Table 2.2 imply an average annual real growth of Comecon manufactured exports to the West of 7 per cent over the decade.

Nevertheless, it can safely be asserted that the role of manufactures in Comecon exports is generally not commensurate with the level of industrialisation of the Comecon countries. Expansion has been impeded by a number of important factors. These include not only discriminatory trade barriers and the rise of the general level of protectionism in Western Europe; but also deficiencies in quality, supply and marketing on the East European side – problems to which the discussion will turn in later chapters.

Not surprisingly, in view of geographical proximity and of

Table 2.2   Trends in Comecon exports of manufactures to the West, 1970–80[a]

	Value[b] (in million constant US 1970 dollars)			Percentage of total exports to West[c]		
	1970	*1975*	*1980*	*1970*	*1975*	*1980*
Bulgaria	75.2	84.0	125.9	31.3	42.0	40.3
Czechoslovakia	473.5	574.4	628.3	65.4	65.3	62.1
East Germany	313.5	371.6	449.4	76.5	70.1	68.0
Hungary	219.0	326.1	510.7	40.9	51.1	57.6
Poland	307.5	529.1	594.3	29.0	32.7	40.4
Romania	201.6	370.3	523.6	36.4	43.7	47.5
Soviet Union	372.7	573.2	940.0	14.6	13.2	12.6
Total	1,963.0	2,828.7	3,772.2	32.3	31.1	29.4

[a] Manufactures are defined here as SITC categories 5 to 8.
[b] Figures in 1970 dollars derived by deflating 1975 and 1980 values by a unit value index in US dollars for manufactured exports of European countries.
[c] Exports of manufactures to the West as a percentage of total exports, in current values.

Sources: Derived from Working Party of the OECD Trade Committee on East–West Trade, *The Commodity Structure of East–West Trade, Statistical Annex*, TC/WP(82)41 (Paris: OECD Secretariat, 1982); and *UN Monthly Bulletin of Statistics* (New York, March 1981).

historical and cultural ties, the Comecon countries' principal trading partners among the developed countries are in Western Europe. Here the large economies (the German, French, Italian and British) account for the bulk of trade, but some of the smaller West European countries (such as Austria, Finland, Sweden and Belgium) have also been important. Japan has become an increasingly significant factor in East–West trade, with its growing role in Siberian resource development and with its expanding commercial presence in East Europe. Among the Comecon countries, while the Soviet Union dominates because of its size, several East European countries (Hungary, Poland and Romania) have accounted for a share of East–West trade substantially greater than their relative weight in total Comecon output.

East–West trade is far more important for the Comecon countries than it is for their Western trading partners. For most of the latter, trade with East European economies is well under 10 per cent of their total trade. Conversely, the share of trade with the member countries of the Organisation for Economic Cooperation and Development (OECD) as a percentage of the total trade of the Comecon countries ranges from 25 to nearly 40 per cent.[16] For some individual sectors of the OECD economies, however, dependence on Comecon markets, or on Comecon raw materials, is considerably higher than these aggregate shares suggest.

Comecon trade with the developing countries has also grown rapidly in the past decade and a half, although the relative importance of trade with these countries remains well below that of Comecon trade with the West.[17] Table 2.3 shows both the rate of growth of East–South trade and its share in the total trade of the seven Comecon countries. It is apparent that their degree of involvement varies significantly, with Romania and the Soviet Union the most active and the German Democratic Republic the least active.

The structure of East–South trade has been the reverse of that of Comecon trade with the West, reflecting the intermediate level of development of the Comecon economies between the two groups of partners. Thus the East tends to export manufactures (especially machinery and equipment, including military arms) to the South, in exchange for primary products (typically minerals and metal ores, but also grains). There are, however, significant exceptions to this overall pattern, and the Arab OPEC countries have provided growing markets for the food, as well as machinery, exports of the East European countries, in particular of the Balkan countries and Hungary.

Partly in consequence of this structure, the Comecon countries have generally enjoyed trade surpluses with the developing countries. In the 1970s, however, the combination of increasing East European imports of oil from the Middle East (especially by Romania) and the rise in the price of crude oil served to weaken trade balances with major OPEC partners. As a result, the East European countries have had to step up exports and cut back oil imports in trade with these countries.[18]

Although Comecon commercial relations have been developed with a wide spectrum of Third World partners, they nevertheless reveal a distinct geographic pattern, as Table 2.4 shows. Trade has been concentrated in the band of countries stretching across the Middle East and North Africa, a concentration which is explicable

Table 2.3   Growth of East–South trade, 1970–80[a]

Country		1970	1975	1980
Bulgaria	Turnover	195	541	1,165
	Index	100	277	597
	Share	5.6	7.2	8.2
Czechoslovakia	Turnover	511	855	1,434
	Index	100	167	281
	Share	7.6	7.0	7.1
East Germany	Turnover	343	697	1,716
	Index	100	203	500
	Share	4.0	4.4	6.7
Hungary	Turnover	272	570	2,128
	Index	100	210	782
	Share	6.3	6.6	10.3
Poland	Turnover	431	1,113	2,359
	Index	100	258	547
	Share	6.7	6.5	9.5
Romania	Turnover	283	1,476	n.a.
	Index	100	522	n.a.
	Share	8.2	18.5	26.2[b]
Soviet Union	Turnover	2,981	6,305	11,961
	Index	100	212	401
	Share	13.5	12.4	12.7

Trade of individual CMEA countries with developing countries. Turnover (exports plus imports) expressed in million current rubles. Index (1970 = 100) indicates growth of turnover. Share (trade with developing countries in country's trade) expressed in per cent.
Estimate derived from data on Romanian exports by country, *Anuarul statistic al Republicii Socialiste Romania* (Bucharest: Directia Centrala de Statistica, 1982).

Source: Except where indicated, all data from *Statisticheskii Ezhegodnik Stran-Chlenov Soveta Ekonomicheskoi Vzaimopomoshchi* (Moskva: Finansy i Statistika, various years).

in terms of strategic, geo-political factors as well as complementary commercial interests. Certain major partners account for much of Comecon trade with other regional groups: Nigeria in sub-Saharan Africa, India in Asia, and Mexico and Brazil in Latin America.

Since 1980, the slow-down in Comecon extra-regional trade

Table 2.4   Geographic distribution of East–South trade, 1979[a] (percentage

Developing countries of:	Soviet Union			CMEA-6		
	Exports	Imports	Turnover	Exports	Imports	Turnov
Asia	15.3	33.6	21.4	9.3	9.3	9.3
Africa	11.0	29.4	17.2	30.0	19.8	25.0
Latin America	1.2	16.2	6.2	5.5	23.8	14.4
Middle East	27.6	19.9	25.0	35.0	37.0	36.0
Unallocated[b]	44.9	0.9	30.2	20.2	10.1	15.3
Total	100.0	100.0	100.0	100.0	100.0	100.0
OPEC Countries	23.1	25.8	24.0	32.1	41.6	36.7

[a] Trade between Central Planned Economies of Europe and Developi
Market Economies (United Nations categories), excluding Cuba.
[b] Share of trade with Developing Market Economies not allocated by count
in reported national statistics and hence not contained in the above.

Source: Derived from 'External Trade of Countries with Central Planne
Economies, Special Table C', *UN Monthly Bulletin of Statistics*, (Ne
York, July 1981).

experienced in the late 1970s has been reinforced by domestic an
international developments. Among the domestic developments
the continued decline in growth in all seven Comecon countries (
decline rooted more in structural than cyclical factors) and th
accompanying constraints on supply felt in certain traditional expo
industries (for example, Soviet and Romanian oil, Polish coal an
agricultural products). Among international developments wer
adverse trends in the terms of trade (including East European term
of trade with the Soviet Union which forced the redirection
exports to the Soviet economy), debt crises and weak foreig
markets for industrial raw materials as well as for manufactures.

GROWTH AND DIVERSIFICATION OF EXTERNAL FINANCING

Increased recourse to extra-regional sources of industrial technology
capital goods and raw materials posed unprecedented problems
trade financing for the Comecon countries. Their responses to thes
problems formed part of the new orientation in their overall extern
economic policy and stimulated the rapid development of a relativel
uncharted area of Comecon economic relations with the rest of th

'orld. The emergence of new forms of financing was especially
onounced in East–West relations.

The Comecon import drive was in part financed by the expansion
f traditional exports of primary and semi-processed goods to the
Vest. Rapidly rising export prices for some of the most important of
iese (especially petroleum and other energy products, as well as
old) improved the terms of trade with the West of some of the
omecon countries, notably the Soviet Union and Poland. The
thers suffered adverse trends in their terms of trade, and efforts to
nance imports through increased export of manufactures generally
ncountered obstacles to both supply and demand which will be
xamined in Chapters 4 and 5. While the Comecon countries
njoyed some earnings from invisible exports (tourism and transport,
or example), these formed a relatively small element in their
urrent accounts and were increasingly offset by the cost of servicing
heir debts.

On the whole, the increased pressure to import, in the 1970s, far
xceeded the capacity to export, and the difficulties the Comecon
ountries had traditionally encountered in balancing their trade with
he West now escalated. In the circumstances, they abandoned their
raditional conservatism with regard to external borrowing, and
mbarked on a course of extensive balance-of-payments financing
hrough credits negotiated with both public and private foreign
enders. First Romania, and later Hungary, carried their more active
articipation in the international financial system so far as to join
he International Monetary Fund (IMF) and the World Bank.[19] The
ew course was aided, and even abetted, by the favourable political
nd financial climate in the West, as already noted.[20]

The volume, structure and form of borrowing varied substantially
mong Comecon countries. On the whole, however, given the
ndustrial strategy behind the import drive, much of it was medium-
erm or long-term. It included tied credits from Western official
ending agencies as well as general-purpose loans raised privately on
he Eurocurrency markets through Western commercial banks.
Some of the latter were wholly or partly owned by Comecon
ountries, as will be seen in Chapter 5.) Project loans by Western
ommercial banks and supplier credits from Western exporters
ypically formed a smaller share of private lending.

In the absence, in most cases, of official statistics from the debtor
ountries, the size and structure of the Comecon debt to the West
as had to be estimated, and Western estimates vary.[21] While the

magnitudes cannot be determined with precision the trends nevertheless, are clear. There was a very rapid build-up of the Comecon external debt in the mid-1970s, followed by generally successful efforts to slow its growth in the late 1970s and even to reduce it in the early 1980s.

Owing to the uneven term structure of the debt, the burden of servicing was particularly heavy in the early 1980s. Combined with weak export markets, worsening terms of trade and a retractive international financial climate, this resulted in some of the Comecon countries experiencing severe problems in the repayment of their debts.

The Comecon countries most seriously affected were Poland and Romania which, in 1981–82, were forced to reschedule their debt when they were unable to meet payments on time. Hungary and the German Democratic Republic also struggled under a severe debt financing burden. Least affected were Czechoslovakia and Bulgaria, owing to the more conservative policies of their debt-management and the Soviet Union, whose rich endowment of natural resources added special strength to its balance of payments.

By 1983, new lending by the Western economies to the Comecon countries had come virtually to a standstill. This was the result of the pre-occupation of lenders in the West with the problems of the larger debtor-countries, especially those in Latin America, as much as their concern over the financial difficulties of the Comecon economies. At the official lending level, it also reflected the political tensions in East–West relations.

Like other countries with payments difficulties, the Comecon countries have sought to improve their trade balances by linking together their export and import operations through various methods. These arrangements fall under the generic heading of 'countertrade', and they range from short-term barter deals to long-term product-payback agreements.[22] The latter, for which the term 'compensation' is also frequently employed, have been especially significant. The form has been widely used in trade relations within the Comecon framework, as well as in extra-regional trade relations.

Compensation involves the transfer from one country to another of resources (including technology embodied in machinery and equipment, as well as know-how) for a capital-development project and the eventual repayment of those resources (with interest) through return deliveries of a share of the output of the completed facilities. Compensation not only relieves short-term pressure on the balance of payments, but allows a form of foreign investment without equity participation. The 'investor' shares in the risks of the venture and receives in return a stake in the results, with the possibility of a variable return on his investment, if the pricing of the compensatory deliveries in kind is flexible. (Often a minimum price is set in advance.) There may be some involvement of the foreign partner in the operations of the venture beyond the initial phase of construction when the arrangement provides for quality control, but such involvement is minimal in the case of standardised production (such as natural resources) where external quality control is not essential. The degree of foreign involvement with the host economy through compensation arrangements is nevertheless generally far less than in the case of direct investment.

If, in East–West financing, the Comecon countries have been the recipients of export credits, in East–South financing, they have more typically been the source of such credits.[23] This reflects the inverse structures of trade flows in the two instances. In the East–South case, with the Comecon countries serving as the exporters of capital goods, they have had to assume the role of furnishers of related credits at low nominal rates of interest.

Short-term credit has also been provided through the mechanism of bilateral clearing. Whereas by the end of the 1960s, East–West trade was almost exclusively settled in convertible currencies, East–South trade continued to be conducted largely in the framework of bilateral payments agreements. Since the Comecon countries traditionally found themselves in surplus in their trade with Third World partners, they were obliged under these arrangements to provide financing to the latter in the form of 'swing' credits.[24]

More recently, however, there has been a trend towards harder terms of settlement in East–South trade and bilateral clearing has become increasingly rare. Unfortunately for the Comecon countries, this coincided with the weakening of their trade position *vis-à-vis* certain partners in the South, as they grew more dependent on Third World supplies of raw materials, especially petroleum. They have even become the recipients of credits, both short-term and long-term, from some of the oil-exporting countries. This was not carried to the point, however, where the Comecon countries lost their overall net-creditor position with the developing countries.

Compensation has also been widely employed as a means of financing in East–South relations. Here again the Comecon role has been the reverse of that assumed in the East–West context.

Compensation agreements have been used to help developing countries finance the purchase of Comecon capital goods and services for industrial projects. They have also been employed to improve Comecon access to natural resources in the Third World.

INTEGRATION INTO THE INTERNATIONAL DIVISION OF LABOUR

The growth of Comecon links to the world economy, and in particular to the sphere of international production, also took more direct forms than the expansion of trade and its related financing. Relations at the production level were encouraged in the form of industrial co-operation agreements between East European enterprises and foreign firms.[25] A network of bilateral agreements concluded at this time with foreign governments was intended to establish the institutional framework for inter-firm ties and to encourage their development.

International industrial co-operation can take a variety of forms.[26] According to the broad definition put out by the United Nations, it may range from ventures based on the compensation format described in the preceding section to the establishment of mixed equity companies. It thus covers equity and non-equity relationships between partners. Firms are provided with a choice of institutional arrangements through which jointly to pursue international goals.[27]

From the perspective of East European planners, the objective of these inter-firm relationships is to bring about a more effective integration of the Comecon economies into a changing international division of labour. Through the acquisition of new capital and technology, increased production specialisation and improved export competitiveness, this integration is intended to make a significant contribution to the growth of productivity in the Comecon economies. Industial co-operation with foreign firms has been regarded as a key element in the Comecon countries' intensive development strategy.

The new Comecon development strategy and its external manifestations coincided with the emergence of a complementary international investment strategy among potential foreign partners.[28] West European and Japanese firms, backed by their governments, were challenging the dominance of American multinational enterprises. The new opportunities for co-operation with Comecon state enterprises thus arose at a time when major Western firms were actively seeking ways to increase their shares of world markets. The Comecon economies were attractive, especially for the West Europeans, being not only a neighbouring and historic market area, but one in which American restrictions on East–West economic relations gave them an edge over their American competitors. The various forms of industrial co-operation appeared to afford avenues for expanding a Western partner's exports to the East, especially of capital goods and technology, while allowing it to take advantage of the industrial capacity of Eastern Europe, as a cost-effective and convenient source of inputs to its international production and marketing system.

In industrial co-operation with the Third World, as in trade with the developing countries, the role of Comecon enterprises was analogous to that of Western firms in East–West relations. Partnerships with developing partners seemed a promising means of expanding Comecon industrial exports in order to increase market shares, as well as an attractive channel for the sourcing of raw materials and intermediate products.[29] For the developing countries, Comecon enterprises offered an alternative to Western multinational enterprises as a mechanism for the acquisition of needed capital and technology.

Industrial co-operation between Comecon enterprises and Western firms has been concentrated in non-equity partnerships, designed to promote inter-firm production contracting and specialisation between firms, co-operation in third markets and technical collaboration.[30] The principal object has been the expansion and modernisation of Comecon industry. East–South industrial co-operation has primarily taken the form of compensation deals, sometimes extending to joint-equity arrangements.[31] These have focused on industrial development projects in Third World economies.

In addition to these various types of partnership with foreign firms, Comecon enterprises have undertaken unilateral expansion of their international activities, through the establishment of representative and branch offices abroad and more significant forms of foreign direct investment. These are the principal subject of the present study, and will be described and analysed in subsequent chapters.

Direct business operations by foreign firms within the Comecon economies, however, have been possible only within severely circumscribed limits. In all seven countries, foreign firms and banks may with special approval open representative offices, and in four countries (Bulgaria, Hungary, Poland and Romania) may enter into limited types of equity partnerships with local enterprises. Participation is restricted to minority holdings in all but exceptional cases, and operational control is constrained by the planned nature of the Comecon economies.[32]

DECELERATION IN THE 1980s

This chapter has described the broadening and deepening which occurred in the Comecon countries' relations with the rest of the world over the 1960s and 1970s. It has also analysed the considerations of policy which have supported these trends. At the beginning of the 1980s, however, there was a marked deceleration in the expansion of extra-regional Comecon relations, especially with the West.

The East European Comecon countries had tended for the most part to precede the Soviet Union along the new external path. With their smaller economies and consequently greater dependence on foreign trade, it is hardly surprising that they should have tended to lead the way in terms of innovative external policies in this area.

Too much should not be made, however, of the Soviet lag. The evidence does not indicate that the Soviet Union either disapproved of or abstained from the new external course, nor that the subsequent slow-down in the expansion of extra-regional relations was the result of Soviet opposition to them. If the differences with respect to dependence on foreign trade (determined by domestic resource endowment and market size) are borne in mind, the Soviet Union's demonstrated interest in Western technology, Third World resources and extra-regional markets for its industrial products was not disproportionate to that of its East European allies. The Soviet Union also encouraged the latter to look outside the region for additional sources of key industrial raw materials, notably petroleum, in order to reduce their dependence on increasingly scarce, and high-cost, Soviet supplies.

The growth of the extra-regional relations of the Comecon countries, particularly dynamic in the period 1965–75, began to lose momentum in the second half of the 1970s. As it became evident that the Soviet Union and the United States had failed to reach a broader accommodation, and as they increasingly confronted each other in areas of conflict in the Third World, the climate of *détente*, favourable to the development of economic relations, began rapidly to erode. The second oil price shock in 1979–80 served to deepen the economic crisis in the West and much of the South, and to destabilise the international financial system. These developments found the Comecon economies beset by mounting internal structural problems and external imbalances.[33] The deterioration in the markets for their exports, and pressures induced by balance of payments difficulties to cut hard-currency imports, resulted in a decline in the volume of their trade with the West, which was especially severe in the case of the six East European countries.

The 1980s, then, began as a time of troubles and, as the middle of the decade approached, the outlook for the trends with which this chapter has been concerned remained clouded. In real terms, peak levels in the turnover of extra-regional trade attained in the late 1970s had been recovered only by the Soviet Union. The Comecon countries nevertheless showed little sign of abandoning the external policy orientation pursued in the 1970s, although their short-term ability to develop extra-regional relations further (and even in some areas to maintain them at their current levels) remained severely limited. If the current domestic and international climate for the continuation of past policies was uncertain, the fundamental economic pressures for them remained strong. It seemed likely that the long-term process of integration of the Comecon countries into the world economy would resume, once more stable conditions were restored.

NOTES AND REFERENCES

1. See E. Valkenier, 'The USSR, the Third World and the Global Economy', *Problems of Communism*, Washington DC, July–August 1979.
2. See, for example, O. Bogomolov, 'East–West Economic Relations: Economic Interests of the Socialist and Capitalist Countries of Europe', in F. Nemschak (ed.), *World Economy and East–West Trade* (Vienna– New York: Springer-Verlag, 1976) pp. 66–77; and N. P. Shmelyov, 'Scope for Industrial, Scientific and Technical Cooperation between East and West', in N. Watts (ed.), *Economic Relations between East and West* (London: Macmillan, 1978) pp. 211–21.
3. The East European countries, including the Soviet Union, had experienced adverse trends in economic performance in the 1960s, manifested most significantly by decelerating rates of growth in their national incomes and rising capital–output ratios.

4. These contrasting development concepts were clearly defined by G. Kohlmey in his article, 'From Extensive Growth to Intensive Growth', *Czechoslovak Economic Papers*, No. 6, 1966.

5. See. M. Kaser, *Comecon: Integration Problems of the Planned Economies* (London: Oxford University Press, 1965).

6. This was recognised in *The Comprehensive Programme for the Further Extension and Improvement of Cooperation and the Development of Socialist Economic Integration by the CMEA Member Countries* (Moscow: CMEA Secretariat, 1971) Ch. I. See also C. McMillan, 'The Council for Mutual Economic Assistance: A Historical Perspective' in R. Nyrop (ed.), *Czechoslovakia: A Country Study* (Washington, DC: US Government Printing Office, for Foreign Area Studies, The American University, 1981) pp. 251–76.

7. For details, see G. Schroeder, 'Soviet Economic "Reforms": A Study in Contradictions', *Soviet Studies*, July 1968; M. Bornstein, 'Economic Reform in Eastern Europe', in *East European Economies Post-Helsinki* (Washington, DC: US Government Printing Office, for the Joint Economic Committee, US Congress, 1977), pp. 102–34; and K. Thalheim, 'The Balance Sheet', in H. Höhmann *et al.* (eds), *The New Economic Systems of Eastern Europe* (London: C. Hurst, 1975) pp. 529–68.

8. See the discussion in Bornstein *et al.* (eds), *East–West Relations and the Future of Eastern Europe* (London: George Allen and Unwin, 1981).

9. On the interaction of politics and economics in the development of East–West relations see C. Friesen, *The Political Economy of East–West Trade* (New York: Praeger, 1976); and A. Stent, *From Embargo to Ostpolitik, the Political Economy of West German–Soviet Relations 1955–1980* (Cambridge: Cambridge University Press, 1981).

10. Philip Hanson carefully traces the evolution of Soviet policy in this area in his *Trade and Technology in Soviet–Western Relations* (New York: Columbia University Press, 1981) Part II. More generally on evolving East European perceptions of the need to import Western technology, see E. Zaleski and H. Weinert, *Technology Transfer between East and West* (Paris, OECD Secretariat, 1980) especially Chs 1 and 4.

11. Valkenier traces this policy evolution in Chapter 1 of her *The Soviet Union and the Third World: An Economic Bind* (New York: Praeger, 1983). See also R. Lowenthal, *Model or Ally? The Communist Powers and the Developing Countries* (New York: Oxford University Press, 1977). For the parallel policy development in East Europe, see M. Radu (ed.), *Eastern Europe and the Third World* (New York: Praeger, 1981), especially the contribution by Radvanyi.

12. See I. Dobozi, 'Problems of Raw Materials Supply in Eastern Europe', *The World Economy*, Vol. 1, No. 2, January 1978.

13. See J. Hannigan and C. McMillan, 'CMEA Trade and Cooperation with the Third World in the Energy Sector', in NATO Economic and Information Directorates (eds), *CMEA: Energy, 1980–1990* (Newtonville, Mass.: Oriental Research Partners, 1981) pp. 215–37.

14. On these various points, see D. Nayyar (ed.), *Economic Relations between Socialist Countries and the Third World* (London: Macmillan, 1977); Dobozi (ed.), *Economic Cooperation between Socailist and Developing Countries* (Budapest: Hungarian Scientific Council for World Economy, 1978); and P. Desai, 'Transfer of Technology from Centrally Planned and Market Economies to the Developing Countries', report prepared for the UN Association of the United States of America, New York, August 1979, mimeograph.

15. See J. Stopford *et al.*, *The World Directory of Multinational Enterprises* (London: Macmillan, 1980) pp. xviii–xix.

16. These shares are for 1980, and range among the Western countries from under one per cent for America, through to around 5 per cent for the Federal Republic of Germany and Italy to 11 per cent for Austria; and among the East European countries from lows of 18 and 25 per cent for Bulgaria and Czechoslovakia to highs of 36 and 38 per cent for the Soviet Union and Hungary.

17. The developing countries of the Third World in the usage here and throughout this study include the non-OECD countries of Africa, Asia, Latin America and the Middle East, with the exception of Mongolia, Vietnam and Cuba (members of the CMEA) and the centrally planned economies of China, Cuba, Mongolia, North Korea and Vietnam.

18. See McMillan, 'Eastern Europe's Relations with OPEC Suppliers in the 1980s' in *European Economies: Slow Growth in the 1980s* (Washington, DC: US Government Printing Office, for the Joint Economic Committee, US Congress, 1985) Vol. I, pp. 368–82.

19. Poland applied for membership in 1982 but, as of the end of 1983, its application was still under consideration.

20. The conditions which favoured East European borrowing have been analysed by R. Portes, in 'East Europe's Debt to the West: Interdependence is a Two-way Street', *Foreign Affairs*, July 1977.

21. The methodological problems are discussed in detail by K. Melson and E. Snell in 'Estimating East European Indebtedness to the West' in *East-European Economies Post-Helsinki, op. cit.*, pp. 1369–95. Western estimates of the total net indebtedness by 1981 of the seven CMEA countries of Europe ranged from $72.4 to $80.7 billion ('Problems of Assessing the Present Financial Situation of the East European Countries' (OECD Secretariat, Paris, June 1982)).

22. For a detailed description of these arrangements, see *East–West Trade, Recent Developments in Countertrade* (Paris: OECD Secretariat, 1981).

23. See Nayyar, *op. cit.*; J. Diambou, 'Faiblesses et qualités des relations Est–Sud' in Lavigne (ed.), *Stratégies des pays socialistes dans l'échange international* (Paris: Economica, 1980) pp. 119–32; and US Department of State, *Soviet and East European Aid to the Third World, 1981* (Washington, DC: Department of State Publication 9345, February 1983).

24. That is credits, typically at low rates of interest, extended to cover imbalances on account under bilateral clearing agreements.

25. F. Levcik and J. Stankovsky, *Industrial Cooperation between East and West* (White Plains, New York: M. E. Sharpe, 1979).
26. On these, see D. St Charles, 'East–West Business Arrangements: A Typology' in McMillan (ed.), *Changing Perspectives in East–West Commerce* (Lexington, Mass.: D. C. Heath and Co., 1974) pp. 105–24; and D. Barclay, 'USSR: The Role of Compensation Agreements in Trade with the West' in *Soviet Economy in a Time of Change*, Vol. 2 (Washington, DC: US Government Printing Office, for the Joint Economic Committee, US Congress, 1979) pp. 462–81.
27. McMillan, 'The International Organisation of Inter-Firm Cooperation' in N. Watts (ed.), *Economic Relations between East and West, op. cit.*, pp.171–91, and compare M. Casson, *Alternatives to the Multinational Enterprise* (London: Macmillan, 1979).
28. J. Laux, 'Eastern Europe in a Changing International Division of Labor' (Paper presented to the International Studies Association 24th Annual Convention, Mexico City, April 1983).
29. On these latter points, see Dobozi, 'Economic Interaction between East and South – the Mineral Resource Dimension', *Raw Materials Report* (Vol. 2, No. 2, Stockholm, 1983) and 'Arrangements for Mineral Development Cooperation between Socialist Countries and Developing Countries, in *Natural Resources Forum* (New York, October 1983). Dobozi stresses the need to penetrate world markets for raw materials dominated by major Western firms.
30. See UN Economic Commission for Europe, *East–West Industrial Cooperation* (New York: United Nations, 1979).
31. I. Grosser and G. Tuitz, *Structural Change in Manufacturing Industries in the European CMEA Area and Patterns of Trade in Manufactures between CMEA and Developing Countries* (Vienna: UNIDO document ID/WG.375/5, January 1982) pp. 122ff.
32. See A. Tiraspolsky, 'Les investissements occidentaux dans les pays de l'Est', *Le Courrier des Pays de l'Est* (Paris, April 1979); and T. Suzuki, 'Joint Venture Corporations in Socialist Countries', *Digest of Japanese Industry and Technology*, No. 144, 1980.
33. See J. Vanous, 'East European Economic Slowdown' in *Problems of Communism*, July–August 1982, and the contributions to *East European Economic Assessment*, 2 vols (Washington, DC: US Government Printing Office, for the Joint Economic Committee, US Congress, 1980/1981). See also J. Drewnowski (ed.), *Crisis in the East European Economy: The Spread of the Polish Disease* (New York: St Martin's Press, 1982).

CHAPTER 3

Profile of External Investments by the Comecon Countries

The new orientation of the external policies of the Comecon countries has given rise to a proliferation of foreign direct investments by Soviet and East European state enterprises. By the early 1980s, these investments had spread on a global scale across a broad spectrum of countries and activities. This chapter will take a comprehensive view of the nature and extent of social multinational enterprise as it appeared after a period of growth of more than two decades, before embarking on more detailed analyses, by sector and by country, in subsequent chapters. A note on the data and methodology underlying the analysis is presented in an Appendix to this book.

ORGANISATIONAL FORMS AND STRUCTURE OF OWNERSHIP

Comecon direct investments typically take the form of equity in a locally-incorporated, joint stock company (see Glossary). Other forms, such as limited liability partnerships, are more rarely employed, being regarded as less flexible and enjoying fewer privileges under local laws and regulations.

A subsidiary company abroad is generally preferred to a foreign branch by parent enterprises in the home, Comecon countries. The branch form, when directly employed, has tended to be reserved for banks and insurance companies. Branches, domestic and foreign, have not infrequently been established by the foreign subsidiaries of East European parent enterprises.

The choice of form depends in the first instance on the nature of the activity to be pursued and the degree of autonomy which is required. In general, the subsidiary, as a legal entity established abroad, limits the parent's liability and enjoys the advantages of operating as a domestic firm, within the local legal framework. Branches, as foreign firms, are often subject to more strict legal conditions in the host country, especially with regard to taxation. Moreover, they have the disadvantage of involving the foreign parent directly in local affairs and of being more closely associated in the public mind with a foreign company. These latter considerations have been of particular importance in the case of Comecon investment (especially Soviet investment in some major Western economies), where the investing enterprise is an agency, albeit a legally independent one, of what a significant segment of potential clients in the host country may regard as a 'hostile foreign state'.[1]

Subsidiaries, however, often establish their own branches, usually in the country where they are themselves headquartered, but occasionally in other countries. Some have even opened branch offices in the home countries of their parents.

A number of representational and sales offices have been set up abroad, especially by East European state airlines, transport companies, tourist agencies and banks. In some cases, these have been established as separate juridical persons under host country law.

Direct investment by Comecon enterprises may follow a number of organisational paths. Frequently it results in the creation of a new company, wholly or jointly owned, sometimes on the base of the assets of a previously existing company. It may also be employed to gain an interest in an established company or may be undertaken in partnership with another, home-based, enterprise. It is not unusual for investment to be channelled through an already established foreign subsidiary of the parent; and several foreign subsidiaries of enterprises based in a given Comecon country may join forces to invest in the same, or another, foreign market. The ownership structure of some companies can therefore be highly complex. Joint investment by the enterprises of more than one Comecon country is, however, extremely rare.

Most investments by Comecon enterprises are in companies which are not only joint stock companies but are owned jointly with foreign (usually host-country) partners. Something less than a quarter of the companies in the West with Comecon capital participation, in which the ownership structure could be determined, were found to be wholly owned by the Comecon country (see Table 3.1). Wholly owned companies in the South are much rarer, representing under 10 per cent of cases where the basic equity structure could be established (Table 3.2).

The equity split between the Comecon and foreign partners can vary considerably, however, as Table 3.1 shows. While all Comecon

Table 3.1   Ownership structure of Comecon investments in the West, end-1983[a] (percentages)

East European country	100% Eastern equity	Majority Eastern ownership	50–50 ownership split	Minority Eastern ownership	Equity split un-determined[b]	All
Bulgaria	14.6	12.2	17.1	12.2	43.9	100
Czechoslovakia	48.6	18.9	8.1	8.1	16.2	100
East Germany	31.0	24.1	13.8	10.4	20.7	100
Hungary	25.5	15.4	36.3	14.7	8.1	100
Poland	18.9	31.1	8.9	10.0	31.1	100
Romania	5.9	11.8	76.4	5.9	0.0	100
Soviet Union	20.8	55.7	7.5	5.6	10.4	100
All	22.8	30.3	21.2	9.8	15.9	100

[a] Based on data for those instances where at least basic equity structure known (over 90 per cent of 484 identified cases).
[b] Cases where joint equity with Western partner established, but exact equity split undetermined.

Source: Comecon Foreign Investment Data Bank, East–West Project, Carleton University, Ottawa.

Table 3.2   Ownership structure of Comecon investments in the South, end-1983[a] (number of instances)

East European country	100% Eastern equity	Joint equity with local partner[b]	Total
Bulgaria	1	16	17
Czechoslovakia	1	19	20
East Germany	0	1	1
Hungary	3	25	28
Poland	1	22	23
Romania	2	42	44
Soviet Union	3	15	18
Total	11	140	151

[a] Based on data for those companies where basic equity structure known (64 per cent of 236 identified cases).
[b] Includes 11 cases where Western equity participation also involved.

Source: Comecon Foreign Investment Data Bank, East–West Project, Carleton University, Ottawa.

countries are occasionally observed to take a minority position, the more usual pattern is for the Comecon partner, or partners, to hold a majority of the equity and, in many cases, the local equity interest is in fact no more than a token holding. There is also considerable variation among the Comecon countries in their preferred structure of ownership, with the Soviet Union, Czechoslovakia and the German Democratic Republic showing most clearly a preference for sole or majority ownership.

The structure of ownership is determined not simply by the predilection of the investor but also by the nature of the activity in which the investment is made. Analysis shows that sole, or majority, Comecon ownership structures are associated with investments in retailing, technical servicing and production, as well as in banking and transport. These are operations which by their nature or organisation tend to require clear control. In smaller agency firms, with simple import-marketing functions, allowance of a more significant role for the foreign partner is expedient and equal partnerships, or a minority stake by the Comecon investing enterprise(s), are common. This helps to explain the unique pattern of ownership of Romanian investment in the West, which is concentrated in small importing firms, as well as in several joint venture banks.

Regardless of the extent of its equity holding, it is usually not difficult for the Comecon partner to exercise effective control. It is the functional, as much as the organisational, structure of most companies that justifies their designation as the foreign 'subsidiaries' of multinational Comecon 'parent' enterprises. In a typical marketing venture, the tangible assets involved are of secondary importance, and it is the Comecon partner, as the principal source of supply of the goods marketed, which provides the *raison d'être* of the joint company. In many instances, the terms on which these goods are supplied provide crucial leverage. Even in the case of joint companies in production, the Comecon partner is usually the source of the specific technology, and often, as well, of specialised capital equipment and important component parts upon which the venture's manufacturing operations are based. The Comecon partner's key role as the source of technology, capital and other major inputs to the operation provides in most instances the basis for its controlling influence, regardless of the degree of its formal ownership.[2]

On the other hand, the local partner often plays an important role in at least the day-to-day management of marketing operations, even though its equity share may be minor. This is not surprising, since a principal Comecon objective is to obtain through such partnerships direct access to foreign commercial expertise, local contacts and knowledge of domestic markets, as well as native understanding of the political, social and legal environment of the host country. It can, therefore, be desirable to allow sufficient equity to local partners to ensure their active involvement and interest in the success of the venture.[3] Even wholly-owned subsidiaries are most often locally staffed, with host country nationals frequently occupying senior executive positions.

Effective control in joint companies is also fundamentally affected by the asymmetry between the partners, which asymmetry is frequently observed.[4] The East European partner, as will be seen in Chapter 4, is typically a large state enterprise, either a foreign trade organisation with operations world-wide or a major production enterprise whose scale of operations has earned it direct foreign trade and investment rights. The Western partner is most often a small firm (often an agency firm under single proprietorship), or even an individual, who may serve as a member of the executive of the joint company.[5] In the South, however, the asymmetry tends to be reduced or eliminated, with the local partner itself frequently a state-owned enterprise, in a joint venture arrangement negotiated on an inter-governmental basis.

The small size and relative obscurity of the typical Western parties to East–West equity partnerships located in the West contrast with the multinational scale and prominence of Western participants in many joint (equity and non-equity) ventures in the East.[6] This is largely explicable in terms of the difference in purpose of these associations. In the West, they serve primarily as the marketing arms of Comecon producing and exporting enterprises, where Western partners are required primarily for their commercial know-how. In the East, where they serve as major channels for the acquisition and assimilation of more advanced industrial technology, those Western partners are sought which are capable of making strong technical and financial contributions to the expansion and modernisation of productive capacity.

GEOGRAPHIC AND FUNCTIONAL DISTRIBUTION

The geographic distribution of Comecon investments is very broad. In the more industrially-advanced (OECD) economies, nearly 500

Table 3.3 Geographic distribution of Comecon investments in the West, end 1983 (number of instances)

Host Country	Investing country							
	Bulgaria	Czechoslovakia	East Germany	Hungary	Poland	Romania	Soviet Union	Total[a]
Australia	0	1	0	0	4	0	4	9
Austria	2	1	3	23	8	3	4	44
Belgium	2	3	7	1	8	0	13	34
Canada	2	5	0	1	4	2	5	19
Denmark	0	0	1	2	1	0	2	6
Finland	0	0	1	2	1	0	9	13
France	4	5	3	7	8	0	12	46
West Germany	13	6	1	28	17	7	11	83
Greece	2	0	0	1	1	2	2	8
Ireland	1	0	0	0	0	0	0	2
Italy	6	3	1	6	2	5	8	31
Japan	3	1	0	1	1	0	1	7
Liechtenstein	0	0	0	1	0	0	0	1
Luxembourg	0	0	0	1	0	0	1	2
Netherlands	1	1	2	3	3	1	3	14
New Zealand	0	0	0	0	1	0	3	4
Norway	2	0	0	1	1	0	3	7
Portugal	0	0	0	0	1	0	0	1
Spain	1	1	0	3	2	1	6	14
Sweden	1	3	2	3	7	0	5	21
Switzerland	2	2	0	2	3	2	4	15
United Kingdom	6	10	9	10	13	5	15	68
United States	0	2	1	10	16	1	5	35
Total	48	44	31	107	102	36	116	484[b]

[a] Row totals indicate numbers of companies with Comecon equity participation in designated Western countries. Row sums may exceed these figures because of equity participation by several Comecon countries in some individual companies.
[b] Of these 484 cases, 48 were known to be no longer operational as of end-1983.

companies with equity participation by state enterprises in the seven
Comecon countries could be identified as having been established by
the end of 1983. Table 3.3. shows the distribution of this cumulative
total across twenty-three Western economies. The principal
investment targets have been those West European economies
(Austria, the Benelux countries, France, the Federal Republic of
Germany and Italy) with which the Comecon countries have
developed the most intensive commercial relations. The importance
of London as a financial and commercial centre has served to raise
the number of investments in the United Kingdom. Investments in
Japan have been constrained by strict foreign investment regulations,
while uncertainties in the political sphere have slowed the growth of
investments in the United States. Canada, in the latter circumstances,
has served as a springboard to the North American market,
attracting a disproportionate share of Comecon investments (see
Chapter 7).

In the developing economies, a sample of well over 200 instances
of Comecon direct investment revealed a similarly broad coverage.
Although investments were spread over some seventy-five Third
World countries, a definite pattern emerges (Table 3.4). Africa is
the target of twice as many Comecon investments as any other area,
with Latin America, the Middle East and Asia sharing more equally
in the remaining investments. Within these regions, key countries
often attract much of the investment activity. Thus Nigeria and
Morocco (in Africa), India and Singapore (in Asia), Lebanon and
Iran (in the Middle East) and Mexico and Peru (in Latin America)
together accounted for nearly half of the Comecon investments in
Third World countries. As argued in the following chapters, these
locations would appear to have been chosen as much for pragmatic,
economic reasons as on political or ideological grounds.

Comecon investment in the developed Western economies has
been undertaken primarily in support of exports to those markets.
As Table 3.5 shows, the principal object of the large majority
(almost 70 per cent) of Comecon investments in the OECD countries
has been export-marketing. Most remaining investments have been
directed to the provision of other services, especially financial and
transport services. Relatively few companies (thirty-four in all) have
been established directly in the sphere of material production,
although their share of the total value of investment is considerably
greater (see following section).

Export promotion is a secondary aim in the developing countries.

Table 3.4 Geographic distribution of Comecon investments in the South, end-1983 (number of instances)

Location of investment	Investing country							
	Bulgaria	Czechoslovakia	East Germany	Hungary	Poland	Romania	Soviet Union	Total
Africa[a]								
Total	15	8	0	13	20	33	13	102
of which:								
Nigeria	6	4	0	8	10	4	1	33
Morocco	1	1	0	0	2	3	3	10
Libya	2	0	0	1	0	4	0	7
Egypt	1	0	0	2	1	1	0	5
Asia								
Total	6	3	0	6	8	3	9	36
of which:								
India	2	2	0	1	3	1	0	10
Singapore	2	1	0	0	2	0	6	11
Latin America								
Total	1	24	2	11	6	8	1	52
of which:								
Peru	0	3	0	3	2	3	0	11
Mexico	0	5	1	1	0	1	0	8
Venezuela	0	6	0	1	1	0	0	8
Brazil	0	2	0	2	3	0	0	7

Middle East[b]								
Total	12	3	0	14	3	10	4	46
of which:								
Lebanon	5	1	0	4	2	5	1	18
Iran	2	1	0	5	1	2	2	13
Kuwait	4	0	0	3	0	0	0	7
Total South	34	38	2	44	37	54	27	236[c]

[a] Including Malta.
[b] Including Cyprus.
[c] Of these 236 cases, 23 were known to be no longer operational as of the end of 1983.

Source: Comecon Foreign Investment Data Bank, East–West Project, Carleton University, Ottawa.

Table 3.5 Distribution of Comecon investments in the West by activity, end-1983 (number of instances)

Principal activity	Investing country							
	Bulgaria	Czechoslovakia	East Germany	Hungary	Poland	Romania	Soviet Union	Total[a]
Commerce								
Import-export operations and some related marketing functions	25	24	19	63	59	27	23	240
Marketing, including retailing	1	2	0	5	13	0	13	34
Marketing, retailing and servicing[b]	9	14	7	0	8	1	24	63
Material production								
Extraction and processing of raw materials	0	0	0	0	2	0	5	7
Assembly and manufacturing	4	0	0	14	3	0	6	27

Other services

Financial services	1	1	0	5	4	5	12	28
Transport services	5	1	3	5	10	1	26	51
Technical services	1	1	0	7	1	1	6	17
Consumer services	2	1	2	8	2	1	1	17
Totals	48	44	31	107	102	36	116	484[c]

[a] Row totals indicate numbers of companies with Comecon equity participation in designated Western countries. Row sums may exceed these figures because of equity participation by several Comecon countries in some individual companies.

[b] Including product modification in some cases.

[c] Including 42 companies no longer active.

Source: Comecon Foreign Investment Data Bank, East–West Project, Carleton University, Ottawa.

Table 3.6 Distribution of Comecon investments in the South by activity, end-1983[a] (number of instances)

Principal activity	Investing country							Total
	Bulgaria	Czechoslovakia	East Germany	Hungary	Poland	Romania	Soviet Union	
Material production								
Mining, incl. ores and minerals processing	4	0	0	3	0	12	1	20
Agricultural production incl. animal husbandry	1	0	0	2	0	7	0	10
Forestry and wood processing	1	0	0	0	0	2	0	3
Fishing and fish processing	2	0	0	0	5	1	8	16
Assembly and manufacturing, incl. related marketing functions	6	14	1	17	12	9	0	59
Total	14	14	1	22	17	31	9	108

Services

Import–export operations and related marketing functions	4	18	0	11	9	11	7	60
Financial services	3	0	0	0	2	1	3	9
Transport services	7	0	0	5	3	4	7	26
Construction services	3	2	0	0	1	3	0	9
Exploration, engineering and technical services	2	2	0	5	5	3	0	17
Business and management services	0	0	0	0	0	0	1	1
Consumer services	1	0	0	0	0	0	0	1
Total	20	22	0	21	20	22	18	123
Grand total	34	36	1	43	37	53	27	231[b]

[a] Distribution of known cases; 5 cases in sample of 236 engaged in unidentified activity.
[b] Including 23 companies no longer operational.

Source: Comecon Foreign Investment Data Bank, East–West Project, Carleton University, Ottawa.

There, the establishment of production facilities and related infrastructure, or participation in resource-development projects, providing access to raw materials in return for Comecon industrial technology, have been the primary functions to which equity investments have been directed. A majority of Comecon companies in the Third World are therefore engaged in resource exploitation, construction and engineering. Table 3.6 shows the breakdown of a sample of Comecon investments in the Third World. Detailed examples of the multinational activities of Comecon state enterprises, in both the West and South, will be presented in subsequent chapters.

SCALE OF OPERATIONS

The substantial number and broad geographic and functional distribution of Comecon foreign direct investments provide some measure of the extent and impact of socialist multinational enterprise. They do not, however, tell much about the scale of operations to which these investments have given rise. For this purpose other measures of investment activity are required.

Systematic data on the level of employment in the foreign affiliates of Soviet and East European state enterprises are difficult to assemble. Employment data for a third of the 484 cases of investment in the West, summarised in Table 3.3, indicate that the typical firm has 10–50 employees; only 8 per cent have over 100 employees, and none more than 500. Soviet affiliates are larger, on average, by this measure than are those of East European-based enterprises. Only scattered data are available for operations in the developing countries, but these suggest that the average level of employment in affiliated companies there is somewhat higher than in the West.

Because of the variety of foreign investment activities in which Comecon state enterprises have engaged, no single value measure is appropriate. In this and subsequent chapters, therefore, three different measures of the size of business firms and banks abroad with equity participation by Comecon state enterprises will be employed: (i) the authorised value of invested capital; (ii) the value of financial assets held by banks and other financial companies; and (iii) the value of sales turnover.

In all cases the figures are estimates, based on information obtained from annual reports and business registries for some, but by no means all, companies involved. (See the discussion of methodology in the Appendix.) Data in foreign currencies have been converted into American dollars at current rates of exchange (rates effective at the end of the calendar year in question). Value data for Comecon direct investment in the Third World are far less complete than for investment in the developed West. At best they provide some idea of the range, by category, of basic activities.

The aggregate value of equity capital invested in companies in the West with Soviet or East European capital participation is estimated at almost $550 million at the end of 1983. This figure includes some $385 million invested in banks and other financial companies. Comecon entities are believed to have contributed over 80 per cent of this figure, with the balance provided by Western investors. Table 3.7 shows the distribution of total estimated capital invested, by country and by sector.

The average value of capital invested in the companies primarily engaged in marketing which make up the great majority of Comecon companies based in the OECD economies is somewhat under £300,000. The actual invested capital in individual companies ranges widely, however, from under $10,000 for some small agency firms to nearly $10 million for a few large distributing and servicing companies with extensive distributing and servicing operations. Companies engaged in assembly or manufacturing operations are typically larger, with an average value of invested capital close to a million dollars.

In developing countries, some production operations are quite large. The capitalisation of companies engaged in production (the extraction of resources, processing and manufacturing), which constitute some 60 per cent of Comecon investments in the South (Table 3.6), is estimated to range from under $1 million to over $20 million. The Comecon capital share is probably under half the total in most cases.

It is more difficult to obtain information on the value of fixed assets of the companies concerned. These, too, range widely, from negligible (in the case of a small agency firm with only office equipment to purchase) to substantial (for a mining company or manufacturing firm). Even in the Third World, however, Comecon subsidiaries and affiliates are, at most, medium-sized by international standards. The largest firms in either the West or South which have been identified have fixed assets in the range of $20–30 million.

Table 3.7 Estimated value of authorised capital invested in companies in the West with Soviet and East European equity participation, end-1983 ($US thousand)[a]

Principal activity	Investing country							
	Bulgaria	Czechoslovakia	East Germany	Hungary	Poland	Romania	Soviet Union	Total
Import–export	2,040	2,843	5,327	6,974	12,653	2,073	7,755	39,665
Marketing/retailing	657	2,657	0	446	2,888	0	11,739	18,387
Marketing, retailing and servicing	2,757	2,489	1,541	0	2,825	419	18,345	28,376
Assembly and manufacturing	10,737	0	0	7,957	321	0	6,258	25,273
Extraction and processing of raw materials	0	0	0	0	262	0	1,092	1,354
Financial services	73	4,175	0	22,450	31,207	29,085	299,137	386,127
Transport services	152	15	108	1,241	646	193	18,385	20,740
Technical services	430	0	0	165	1,130	367	25,675	27,767
Consumer services	87	0	84	37	84	202	0	494
Total	16,933	12,179	7,060	39,270	52,016	32,339	388,386	548,183

[a] Estimated value of capital invested in 434 companies operative at end-1983.

Source: Comecon Foreign Investment Data Bank, East–West Project, Carleton University, Ottawa.

In general, Comecon companies abroad tend to be under-capitalised. This is particularly true of the Western marketing subsidiaries of the smaller East European countries and is largely attributable, as will be discussed in Chapter 4, to financial constraints imposed by the home governments. To compensate, the Comecon parent enterprises often extend generous supplier credits on favourable terms to their marketing subsidiaries abroad.[7] Hungarian enterprises, for example, are reported to have extended supplier credits to their subsidiaries and affiliates abroad worth three times the total capital invested in them. Like the subsidiaries of Western multinational enterprises, Comecon companies based abroad rely heavily on local capital markets for operating funds.

Total assets are a more relevant measure of the scale of operations of banks and other financial companies (for example, those in insurance or leasing). The combined assets of companies based in the West stood at approximately $10.8 billion at the end of 1980. Soviet banks and insurance companies accounted for much of this total, with the assets of two large Soviet banks (based in London and in Paris) alone constituting over half the total. Comecon banks in the Third World tend to be comparatively small, branch operations.

The estimated aggregate annual value of sales turnover in 1980–82 of the marketing companies in the first four categories of Table 3.4 was $13.5 billion, or 35 per cent of the average value of total exports from the European Comecon countries to the OECD countries in those years. This figure comprises the value of goods sold directly by the companies, as well as commission sales arranged through them. The shares of exports to the West handled by marketing subsidiaries and affiliates abroad were highest for Hungary (41 per cent), Bulgaria (37 per cent), Poland (32 per cent) and the Soviet Union (29 per cent). For Czechoslovakia, the German Democratic Republic and Romania, the shares were around 17 per cent.

By all three value measures, the scale of Soviet investment operations in the West is far greater than that of even the most active East European countries. The annual turnover, for example, of some Soviet marketing companies handling bulk sales of primary products (oil, timber and chemicals, for example) was in the billion-dollar range by 1981. Poland is the second largest investor by these value measures. Investments by Romania and the German Democratic Republic in the West are, on average, by far the smallest of the group.

The value of the stock of foreign direct investment by the Comecon countries would be of considerable interest, especially for the purposes of making comparative analyses. The East European countries, however, have not published figures on which estimates might be based, and from the West the only obtainable relevant information has come from Canada. The Canadian data indicate a relationship of nearly 7 to 1 between the book value of direct investment from the Comecon countries and the authorised value of capital invested in Comecon subsidiaries and affiliates in Canada. The Canadian case is not unrepresentative of Comecon investment activities in the OECD economies, and if used with the data presented in Table 3.7 to arrive at a very rough estimate for the West as a whole, a value of $3–4 billion is obtained. Although there are fewer Comecon investments in the South than in the West, they tend on average to be larger. An educated guess, then, might roughly place the stock of Comecon direct investment in the West and South combined in the range of $4–6 billion. These figures should be treated with caution, however; they are no more than suggestive.

Subsequent chapters will examine in more detail the operating experience of the Comecon-based multinational enterprises, including the profitability of their investment activities. The analysis however will first turn to the investment process in the home Comecon countries and the motivations underlying their increased recourse to foreign direct investment over the last two decades.

NOTES AND REFERENCES

1. Pisar discusses the legal and operational problems which Soviet and East European companies have faced in the United States, where they have customarily been regarded as foreign agents. See S. Pisar, *Coexistence and Commerce* (New York: McGraw-Hill, 1970) pp. 95–6.
2. Recognising that this is generally true of foreign participation in mixed companies, host countries (and many analysts of multinational enterprises) have used a minority share, often as little as 10–20 per cent, as the criterion for determining foreign direct investment.
3. See A. Engibarov, *Smeshannye Obschchestva na Mirovom Rynke* (Moscow: Mezhdunarodnye Otnosheniia, 1976) p. 23.
4. More than one party from each side may take an equity position in a given mixed company. Nevertheless, it is possible to identify a principal Comecon, and a principal Western, partner in most cases.
5. Sufficient information is available to permit some quantification of this point. In a sample of nearly 200 mixed companies with Comecon capital participation operative in the West at the end of 1983, in which the

nature of the principal Western partner could be established, nearly half (48 per cent) involved a private national firm. In 27 per cent of the cases, the principal Western partner was an individual, often an employee or associate of the firm. In nearly as many instances (26 per cent), the partner was a multinational company, but typically privately-owned and small, or its subsidiary. In contrast, some prominent multinational banks have participated in joint financial ventures with East European banking partners (see Chapter 5).

6. See Wilczynski, *The Multinationals and East–West Relations*, *op. cit.*
7. F. Bartha, 'Külföldi közös érdekeltségek helye Magyaroszag kereskedelempolitikajaban', *Külgazdasag* No. 8 (Budapest, 1978) and *Rynki Zagraniczne* (Warsaw, 31 May 1983).

CHAPTER 4

Actors and Strategies

Because of their special political and economic nature, the Comecon countries are a qualitatively new source of foreign direct investment in the world economy. Their unique significance in this regard is not fully revealed by the quantitative measures presented in the preceding chapter. Essentially one-party states, the countries in question are ruled by Communist parties which play a paramount role at all levels of the economy. Espousing public ownership and economic planning as basic principles, they style as 'socialist' their socio-economic systems, and differentiate themselves, in Marxist-Leninist, ideological terms, from the 'capitalist' and 'developing' economies of the rest of the world. In the Western literature of the social sciences, they are often designated as 'state-socialist', to indicate the degree to which their economies are organised and managed by administrative agencies of government, in pursuit of objectives set for the state by the party. Private ownership, producer autonomy and consumer sovereignty play a minor, or distinctly secondary role, in all of these economies.[1]

This book, then, deals with foreign direct investment from sources characterised by an exceptionally high degree of state ownership and control. This chapter addresses two sets of questions which are fundamental to any discussion of the origins of foreign investment from the Comecon countries and to their situation in a broader comparative perspective:

(a) What has been the role of the state in the growth of Soviet and East European foreign direct investment? Can one speak of state 'strategies' for foreign investment?

(b) What is the nature of the Comecon approach to foreign direct investment, and how does it differ from the approaches of non-socialist countries? To what extent have specific conditions and objectives characterised the foreign investment policies and behaviour of individual Comecon countries?

The discussion here of the factors which have given rise to foreign

48

nvestment by the Comecon countries is set against the background
of the review in Chapter 2 of the broader development of Comecon
external policies and relations. Before turning to the determinants
of investment decisions, the organisations and procedures involved
in the decision-making process in the Comecon countries must
be examined.

ACTORS

t must be emphasised that in the Comecon countries foreign
investment is organised exclusively by state enterprises. Foreign
rade and all international financial transactions are a state monopoly.
This Leninist principle, adopted soon after the 1917 Revolution in
he Soviet Union and by the East European countries when they
came into the Soviet orbit after World War II, has been modified
over time only to the extent that a broader range of state enterprises
has been granted the right to engage in external operations. Private
entities have not been granted such authority; and private individuals
and enterprises are obliged to make external deals through vested
state organs.

In the Comecon countries, enterprises are not only state-owned,
they are also subject to very substantial administrative control by
centrally-governed state agencies. While the degree of central
control varies from country to country, Comecon enterprises
generally enjoy far less autonomy than is characteristic of state-
owned enterprises in the developed economies, or for that matter in
the developing ones.

The principle instrument of state control is the national economic
plan, through which the bulk of producer goods and related services
are centrally allocated. The plan is backed by law, and by a complex
system of financial incentives, as well as (by now) the force of
custom and tradition. State enterprises are subordinated to economic
ministries, or to other authorities at ministerial level, which supervise
their operations within the parameters set by the plan.

A relatively detailed foreign trade plan forms part of the national
economic plan and imposes import and export directives (targets) on
state enterprises. Enterprises are told what and how much to trade
and (where bilateral commitments to trading partners exist), even
with whom to trade. Their only autonomy is residual, determined by
the degree of specificity of the plan directives imposed upon them.
Backing up the plan is a strict regime of foreign-exchange control,
administered by the national bank or the state foreign trade bank.[2]

Much of the state's monopoly of foreign trade is vested in th Ministry of Foreign Trade and, through it, in directly subordina foreign trade organisations which enjoy a monopoly of extern operations in a prescribed set of goods or services.[3] These act intermediaries between domestic production enterprises and foreig markets, not only in trade but also in related investment activitie In some East European countries, special enterprises under th ministries of foreign trade have been vested with the authority t undertake trade-related investment activities across a wide range goods and services.[4]

In some East European countries, large production enterprises or groups of enterprises (associations or combines) – with substanti export markets, have been granted the right to engage directly i foreign trade, rather than through the intermediary of specialise foreign trade enterprises. These production organisation subordinate to various industrial, branch ministries, may als undertake foreign direct investments.[5]

Finally, in the case of service-oriented investments (for exampl in banking, insurance, freight and so on), yet other state organs ma be the 'actors'. Thus national and foreign trade banks, insuranc companies, shipping lines and other transport enterprises, engineerin and design institutes and construction firms, among othe organisations in the Comecon countries, have all establishe branches, subsidiaries and affiliates abroad. In sum, the investin enterprises in the home Comecon countries, while always stat enterprises, cover a broad spectrum of economic organisations (se Table 4.1). Moreover, these actors at the 'enterprise' level ar subordinate to a number of different authorities at ministerial level.

This said, it must be added that investment activity is, nevertheles fairly concentrated. The majority of investments from Comeco countries have been made by specialised foreign trade enterprise and associations and, except in the case of Poland and the Sovie Union, less than 40 per cent of all existing foreign trade organisation have engaged in foreign investment activity.[6] Furthermore, 20 pe cent of all the state enterprises of the seven Comecon countrie which have engaged in foreign direct investment, account for 47 pe cent of total investments. These are necessarily organisations wit multiple investments, more specifically enterprises which hav invested in at least five foreign branches or subsidiaries. Some hav invested in considerably more than this number; one Polish foreig trade enterprise has investments in twenty-five foreign companies i the OECD economies alone.[7]

Category	Comecon country						Soviet Union	Totals
	Bulgaria	Czecho-slovakia	East Germany	Hungary	Poland	Romania		
Foreign trade enterprises and associations	12	7	10	19	29	16	41	134 (61.8%)
Production enterprises and associations	1	3	1	8	5	—	—	18 (8.3%)
Banks	—	1	—	4	2	1	4	12 (5.5%)
Insurance companies	1	1	—	1	1	1	1	6 (2.8%)
Transport and freight enterprises	2	2	2	1	6	2	10	25 (11.5%)
Engineering and construction organisations	2	—	—	1	—	—	—	3 (1.4%)
Tourist agencies	1	—	1	1	1	—	—	4 (1.8%)
Others[a]	2	—	—	6	2	3	2	15 (6.9%)
Totals	21	14	14	41	46	23	58	217 (100%)

[a] Research and design institutes, publishing houses, hotel and catering firms, etc.

Source: Comecon Foreign Investment Data Bank, East–West Project, Carleton University, Ottawa.

This, however, is by no means the end of the story. In a numb
of instances, the foreign subsidiaries of Comecon-based enterpris
have in turn established branches or affiliates in other forei,
countries. Thus seven of the twenty-five foreign subsidiaries of t
Polish foreign trade enterprise just cited have themselves undertak
foreign direct investments. Hungary even went so far as to establi
a holding company in Luxembourg as a vehicle for profitable forei,
ventures.[8]

It may be concluded, therefore, that comparatively few (at t
end of 1983, some fifty-four) large, state enterprises account f
much of the multinational activity of the Comecon countries.[9] In
number of cases, these parent enterprises have established extensi
networks of foreign branches and subsidiaries. The parent compani
themselves, however, are subject to control at home by central sta
authorities at a higher level: functional (foreign trade, transpor
and branch (industrial) ministries, as well as national banks. Tab
4.2 lists the most active Soviet and East European multination
enterprises and indicates the areas of their activity.

DECISION-MAKING PROCESS

The Comecon countries thus possess the instruments, in the form
state-owned and centrally-controlled enterprises, through which
pursue national policy in the area of foreign investment. Th
external policy objectives of the state are in fact the princip
determinants of socialist foreign investment decisions.

The broad outlines of the decision-making process with regard
foreign investment in the Comecon countries are as follows. Th
state, having determined that foreign investments are a desirab
means of pursuing certain external policy objectives, establishes th
legal framework for foreign investment by state enterprises (in th
form of special legislation if deemed necessary). Certain enterprise
are officially empowered to undertake foreign investment operation
usually together with the right to engage in foreign trade in relate
goods or services. It may be presumed that the purposes, forms an
limits of foreign investment are further spelled out in internal sta
memoranda for the guidance of ministries and enterprises. Thes
are in turn reflected in officially-sanctioned publications, which serv
to advertise the foreign investment possibility and to educate officia
and managers in its potential.

The state thus sets the parameters of law and policy within whic

Table 4.2 Comecon state enterprises with five or more investments in the OECD economies, end-1983[a]

Enterprise	Product/service	Number of investments
Bulgaria		
Balkancarimpex	materials-handling equipment	9
Machinoexport	industrial machinery	7
Czechoslovakia		
Strojimport	industrial machinery	10
Transakta	commercial transactions	6(2)
Motokov	transport vehicles, agricultural machinery	6(1)
Glassexport	glassware, glassfibre products	6
East Germany		
Carl Zeiss Jena[b]	optical equipment	9(2)
Hungary		
Hungarotex	textiles	10
Tungsram[b]	lighting equipment	8(1)
Monimpex	wines, juices, foodstuffs	7(1)
Medimpex	pharmaceuticals	7
Hungarian Foreign Trade Bank[b]	financial operations	5(1)
Poland		
DAL	commercial transactions	37(12)
Ciech	chemicals	14(4)
Metalexport	industrial machinery	13(5)
Agros	foodstuffs	13(7)
Minex	construction materials, glassware	10(4)
Paged	wood and paper, furniture	10(3)
Textilimpex	textiles	7(2)

Enterprise	Product/service	Number of investments
Animex	livestock and meat products	11(4)
Hortex-Polcoop	foodstuffs	10(6)
Bank PKO S.A.[b]	financial operation	9(2)
Coopexim-Cepelia	folk art and crafts	10(5)
Polimex-Cekop	complete plants, production lines, machinery	5(1)
Rolimpex	agricultural products	6(3)
Hartwig[b]	freight forwarding	6(2)
Metronex	automatic regulation systems	5(1)
Impexmetal	ores and concentrates	8(4)
Romania		
Chimimportexport	chemicals, pharmaceuticals	6(1)
Romanian Bank for Foreign Trade[b]	financial operations	5(1)
Soviet Union		
Gosbank[b]	financial operations	20(15)
Soyuznefteexport	crude oil, petroleum products	18(9)
Vneshtorgbank[b]	financial operations	20(13)
Sovracht[b]	freight forwarding	23(8)
Exportles	wood and paper goods	14(8)
Tractoreexport	agricultural machinery, tractors, road-building equipment	17(7)
Avtoexport	automotive equipment	14(7)
Stankoimport	machine tools	15(8)
Mashpriborintorg	scientific instruments	10(3)
Soyuzchimexport	chemicals	12(6)
Ingostrakh[b]	insurance	6(3)
Soyuzpromexport	ores and concentrates	13(8)

Enterprise	Product/service	Number of investments
Sovrybflot[b]	fishing	8(1)
Techmashimport	textile machinery	11(4)
State Labour Savings Bank[b]	financial operations	12(9)
Energomashexport	hydroelectric power plants	12(8)
Sudoimport	ships and rigs constructions	7(3)
Almazjuvelirexport	jewellery, diamond extraction equipment	5(1)
Machinoexport	mining, metal-working, construction equipment	7(3)
Zapchastexport	spare parts	5(1)
Exportlion	textile raw materials, fabrics	7(6)
Licensintorg	patents, licensing, know-how	5(1)
Promsyrioimport	iron, metal products	8(6)
Soyuzgazexport	natural gas	9(8)
Soyuzkoopvneshtorg	foodstuffs	9(8)
Techmashexport	industrial machinery and equipment	6

[a] Based on the large majority of cases where the ownership structure could be established. Includes indirect investment (investment by a company abroad in which the Comecon enterprise has an equity holding). The number of total investments which are indirect is indicated in parentheses.

[b] Enterprises which are not specialised foreign trade organisations.

Source: Comecon Foreign Investment Data Bank, East–West Project, Carleton University, Ottawa.

individual investment decisions are made. Specific foreign investment projects are usually initiated at the enterprise level, where both the needs and the possibilities are more readily perceived. The administrative organs of the state, however, retain powerful residual controls over the implementation of investment decisions. While there may be no formal process of approval, enterprises cannot undertake foreign investments of any significance without the concurrence and support (with regard to function and geography) of the supervising departments of the ministry (most often the Ministry of Foreign Trade) to which they are subordinate. Perhaps even more powerful a control is the financial one: the necessary allocation of foreign currency must be made by the state bank (whether national or foreign trade), where projects are reviewed and may be rejected. In Hungary, for example, an office within the Trade Promotion Division of The Foreign Trade Bank supervises foreign investments by Hungarian enterprises and helps to formulate the state's foreign investment policy.[10]

The potential for a concerted, national approach to foreign investment thus exists in the planned economies to a greater extent than it does in the market economies. Foreign investment policies are formulated at the level of the government rather than at the level of enterprises, as they are in the market economies, where state attempts at policy control (to the extent that they exist) are extended through regulation rather than directive, and are aimed more at inflows of foreign direct investment than at outflows. This is not to suggest that foreign investments by Comecon state enterprises invariably constitute effective implementation of state policy; the state may provide inadequate policy guidance and errors of judgement in enterprise investment decisions certainly occur. Moreover, the state has played an important role in determining the participation of some of the new capitalist arrivals on the multinational scene, the case of Japanese firms being the most notable example.[11] Nevertheless, the scope for a divergence, much less a clash, of interests between the enterprise and the state in the area of foreign investment is reduced in the Comecon countries in comparison with the more decentralised, Western economic systems.

RATIONALE FOR COMECON INVESTMENT IN THE WEST AND SOUTH

The Comecon countries of Europe are by no means homogeneous in terms of their attained stages of economic development. They range from the older and more advanced industrial economies of Czechoslovakia and the German Democratic Republic to the newly developed economies of Romania and Bulgaria. As a group, however, the Comecon countries hold an intermediate place, in terms of industrial development, between the developed economies of the OECD countries and the developing economies of the Third World. Primarily in consequence of these relationships, the structure of Comecon trade with the two groups differs markedly, as does the pattern of Comecon investment in them. It is therefore appropriate analytically to separate the 'West' and 'South' in any discussion of the motives for the foreign investment activity of Comecon countries.

Differences in levels of development certainly help to explain the pattern of Comecon trade with the OECD countries, which has remained essentially an exchange of primary-product exports (fuels and other raw materials, as well as foodstuffs) for manufactured imports (especially machinery and equipment). As noted in Chapter 2, however, Comecon manufactured exports to OECD markets have not grown at a rate commensurate with the industrial development of the Comecon countries.

The impediments to the expansion of Comecon exports of manufactures to OECD markets have long been recognised.[12] The traditional institutions of the centralised Comecon economies have in many ways discouraged exports. They have not fostered attention to the quality of their products; producers have lacked the incentives and the flexibility to respond to changes in external market demand; foreign trade organisations have been ill equipped to engage in effective marketing and servicing.[13] These problems have been compounded by the difficulties which Comecon exporters have often faced as new entrants on imperfect markets characterised by both formal and informal barriers to entry. Moreover, Comecon exporters have frequently had to contend with special marketing problems created by politically-motivated official and public hostility to their activities.

The external strategy launched in the late 1960s included a major effort to expand manufactured exports to the OECD countries. To this end, institutional modifications were introduced to lessen the restrictive impact of the traditional system.[14] The objective of export promotion has been an important stimulus to economic reform, especially in the smaller, more trade-dependent East European countries.

One of the modifications in the traditional foreign trade system, seen as important to the success of the export drive, has been the establishment through foreign direct investment of a network of marketing facilities abroad. Export promotion has, in fact, been the single most important motivation underlying the growth of Comecon investments in the West. While traditional exports of standardised, primary commodities could for the most part be handled adequately 'at arms length' through official Comecon trade delegations abroad, or through local agents, more effective marketing techniques were needed to expand exports of increasingly diversified and sophisticated industrial products and related services.[15]

Development of a permanent market in the developed West for machinery and equipment and other manufactured goods required not only detailed knowledge of the needs and preferences of the customer, but rapid and responsive servicing of their demands. More often than not officials of trade missions have lacked the specialised knowledge or the time required to cultivate such markets. The alternative – the local agent – has also been criticised as costly and unsatisfactory, with their commissions entailing substantial outlays of precious convertible currencies, and their interests often conflicting with those of their Comecon clients.[16]

One solution to these problems has been to take an agent, or another local firm, as an equity partner.[17] Partnerships also serve to obscure the involvement of the Comecon investing enterprise and, by giving subsidiary activities local colour, help to reduce market hostility. As a result, at the end of 1983, almost 200 of the nearly 500 investments that had been made in the West by Comecon state enterprises were in companies jointly-owned with local partners and engaged primarily in importing, mainly from their home countries, and in directly related marketing operations.

As the Western market share of Comecon exports increases, however, a more elaborate infrastructure of warehouse and support facilities, dealer networks and technical service centres is required. This gives further impetus to direct investment by the parent company, and to increased equity holdings. Nearly one hundred companies operating in the West at the end of 1983 had developed the facilities for direct distribution and technical support of parent exports.

Not only special national tastes, but technical standards and other regulations imposed by governments of the importing countries, can necessitate a considerable adaptation of products for local markets.

This is often most conveniently and effectively performed on site, and necessarily entails expansion of subsidiary facilities as well as operations. When these functions become extensive enough, they merge into low-grade assembly and manufacturing operations. This is the rationale for most of the twenty-seven subsidiary companies in the West so classified in Table 3.5. In other cases, foreign production facilities have been established in order to surmount national tariff barriers or to meet local content requirements.[18]

The governments of host countries offer positive incentives, as well as such negative stimuli, to foreign investment. Such incentives hinge on the potential employment benefits (usually in depressed regions) stemming from the establishment of foreign-owned production facilities, and often take the form of financial inducements as well as administrative measures to facilitate the proposed investment projects. Comecon state enterprises have shown themselves as ready to respond to these incentives, as have Western multinational enterprises.[19]

The transfer of technology – in both directions – also plays a role in Comecon direct investments in the OECD countries. Marketing subsidiaries are typically founded on the technical, as well as commercial, competitiveness of the export product marketed by the Comecon country. There have been investments in plants established abroad to engage in production on the basis of licensed Comecon technology.[20] A foreign subsidiary or affiliate also creates, for its Comecon parent, direct links to the industry in the host country and thereby establishes channels for improved feedback of useful technical and commercial information. Some marketing subsidiaries serve an important secondary function as well-informed, on-the-spot purchasing agents for their parent enterprises.

Access to raw materials has not been a significant motive for Comecon investment in the OECD countries. As noted earlier, the Comecon countries are net exporters of fuels and raw materials to the West. Most of the handful of Comecon companies in the West shown in Table 3.5 as engaged in extraction and processing of raw materials are joint fishing ventures, a number of them prompted by the creation of exclusive off-shore fishing zones by Western coastal states.

Comecon investments in the West have also been directed significantly to services other than marketing and distribution. Foreign-based banks, insurance firms and companies engaged in shipping and freight, as well as in engineering and construction, were originally established in support of East–West trade and, for the most part, have continued to serve this function. The intent was to provide in these areas services otherwise not readily available to those engaged in East–West trade, as well as to earn foreign currency. As East–West trade became more respectable, the former consideration grew less important. At the same time, these enterprises found that they had gained capital and expertise which could profitably be put to more general use. As a result, they have expanded their activities into areas of banking, insurance, transport and construction not directly related to East–West trade. The provision of services through foreign subsidiaries has thus become an important source of foreign currency earnings in its own right. Comecon services are, on the whole, arguably more competitive on Western markets than Comecon goods, and this has probably contributed to the relative growth of direct investments in the service sector.

It is certainly conceivable that the foreign subsidiaries of centrally-controlled state enterprises may be used in pursuit of political as well as economic objectives of the state. While such objectives are never discussed by Comecon countries in their treatment of socialist foreign investment policy and activities, these objectives are often emphasised in the West, especially in Press coverage of the subject. The available evidence indicates, however, that the misuse of Comecon subsidiaries for non-commercial purposes is relatively rare, and suggests that political objectives play a secondary role in any foreign investment strategy established by Comecon countries in the OECD economies.[21]

As was seen in Chapter 2, the growth of investment by the Comecon countries in the developing economies, as in the developed West, has formed part of a new overall policy approach which first emerged in the 1960s and took shape over the 1970s. The Soviet Union and its allies have tended to treat their economic relations with the Third World in less orthodox ideological and political terms, and have increasingly viewed them in the context of interdependent, world economic problems and objectives. Emphasis has shifted from the large-scale and highly-visible, but often economically ill-conceived, aid projects characteristic of earlier relations between Comecon and developing economies, to the development of a broader range of economic links based, more pragmatically, on what is termed a mutually profitable division of labour.

The growth of mixed-equity companies through direct Comecon

investment in the developing economies has been one manifestation of this emphasis on more 'organic' economic ties.

The external investment policies of the Comecon countries envisage three spheres of activity to which investments in the Third World are principally directed: (i) mining, and other forms of the extraction and processing of natural resources; (ii) marketing of machinery and equipment, and the provision of engineering and construction services for development projects; and (iii) manufacturing for both the home and host markets.

As noted earlier, the rapid industrial development of the Comecon countries has created a demand for industrial raw materials which has increasingly outstripped the supply capabilities of domestic, and even intra-regional, sources. The search for external supplies has motivated participation in the development and control of potential sources from the Third World. The traditional device employed for this purpose by the Comecon countries – the compensation agreement – has provided the pattern for more direct investments in the extractive industries of Third World countries. These increasingly serve to ensure the return flows of essential raw materials to the Comecon countries.[22]

It was also noted in Chapter 2, that the developing economies comprised an important export market for industrial equipment and technology from the Comecon countries, which included entire installations sold on a turn-key basis. The creation of subsidiary companies and joint equity ventures has supported the export of capital goods from Comecon to the developing countries, where marketing and installation of industrial equipment, frequently of complete plants, have increasingly required on-site facilities.

Comecon-based enterprises also face, as do Western firms, pressure from host countries to accept an equity stake in full or partial payment for the equipment and technology they supply. What begins as a turn-key project or a compensation agreement (in the extractive or manufacturing sectors) may, as a result, be institutionalised in the form of a mixed equity company.

The shift of labour-intensive manufacturing operations to locations in the lower-wage economies has not been limited to capitalist firms. Access to plentiful, low-cost labour has been a motive for Comecon investments in the Third World and it appears likely to be of growing importance as labour becomes increasingly scarce in the developed Comecon countries. It is often a combination of relatively high wages (including welfare costs to the state) and low productivity, in the Comecon countries, which makes foreign locations attractive. Most often, this has given rise to the establishment of production facilities for intermediate or final processing for the home, Comecon, markets in not-too-distant Third World locations.[23]

In addition to such cost factors, the advantages of market proximity and other considerations, which have similarly motivated Western firms to invest directly in foreign markets, have stimulated the shift of final-stage processing of traditional Comecon exports to locations in the developing economies.[24] Investments have been made on this basis in facilities for the assembly or finishing of imported Comecon components or intermediate products. The end products are then sold within the local-market area.[25]

Frequently alleged is the political nature of the economic objectives which motivate the activities of Comecon countries in the Third World. In the case of direct investments, this allegation is not easily substantiated. These investments evidently contribute to a Soviet and East European 'presence' in the developing countries, and thereby enhance their influence in the area. One does not find, however, that Comecon investments are clearly concentrated in countries which might be regarded as important targets from a political or strategic point of view. This is probably both a reflection of economic pragmatism on the part of Comecon investors, and of the irony that Third World countries of 'socialist orientation' tend to be those which have established the most inhibiting barriers to foreign direct investment from any source.

The differing rationales for Comecon investments in the West and South have indeed produced differing patterns of investment in the two areas. Companies with Comecon equity participation, engaged primarily in marketing, are not only fewer in number but also account for a much smaller share of Comecon investments in the developing countries than they do in the West. This is certainly a reflection of the lesser role Third World markets play in total Comecon exports. Markets in the developing countries are, nevertheless, also served by the more numerous Comecon investments made directly in the sphere of material production, which often perform secondary marketing functions. The structure of Comecon investments in services other than marketing is also quite different from that found in the developed West, and is concentrated in technical (engineering) and construction services which function in support of Comecon capital development projects in the host economies.

INHIBITING FACTORS

The volume and structure of Comecon foreign direct investment is determined by negative as well as positive factors. This section now turns to the reasons why, despite the strong motivations explored above, Comecon foreign investment activity has only recently begun to assume significant proportions.

Because it has been primarily in support of exports, and because it represents a commitment to an intensive and prolonged interaction with external markets, foreign investment by Comecon countries has necessarily tended to follow the growth of trade. Factors (political, economic and systemic) which contributed to the earlier slow growth of East–West trade, and have continued to impede and render uncertain its further development, have therefore also served to retard the growth of investment. Since these factors were reviewed in Chapter 2, the discussion will turn instead to more direct constraints on investment.

The most severe of these constraints is financial. Ambitious domestic industrialisation programmes sharply restricted the volume of investment resources available to the Comecon countries for allocation to external use. The chronic scarcity of foreign exchange reserves has further constrained the funds available for investment, especially funds of convertible currency. While in the long run, foreign investment holds the promise of a positive impact on the balance of payments, it poses an immediate drain on scarce foreign currency reserves.

In these circumstances, therefore, it may seem paradoxical that, measured by flows of direct investment, the Comecon countries are net exporters of capital, even to the OECD countries.[26] But the paradox is superficial. Legal and institutional barriers – reflecting the ideology of state ownership and the reality of state-controlled economic and political systems to which large inflows of foreign direct investment would pose a serious challenge – have severely limited the possibilities for direct investment in the Comecon economies.[27] The large-scale, long-term Western investment which has, nevertheless, occurred has therefore been forced to take other forms: official and commercial credits, for example, in the nature of both general-purpose and project-specific loans, including compensation (product-payback) arrangements. On overall capital account, the Comecon countries are of course heavy net debtors.

The relative scarcity of capital for foreign investment, especially of convertible currency funds, has contributed to several important features of the investment strategy of the Comecon countries. The first is the concentration of investment in activities which are less capital-intensive – marketing and other services, and small-scale manufacturing – and their very gradual extension to large foreign production operations. There is also the Comecon tendency, noted in the preceding chapter, to under-capitalise their investments abroad. While the capital costs of foreign marketing ventures may not be great relative to the capital requirements of major production facilities, they can nevertheless be substantial when the establishment of extensive warehousing, technical servicing and distribution facilities is involved. Moreover, to initial capital costs must be added the requirement for operating capital during what is often a lengthy run-in period, before the subsidiary is able to generate net income.

These circumstances create a strong incentive to enlist foreign capital participation in Soviet and East European ventures abroad. The advantages of this solution have long been officially recognised.[28] But the attraction of sufficient foreign capital to finance larger-scale, foreign investments must be balanced against what may be undesired sharing of control.

Other solutions have also been employed to ease the capital (convertible currency) constraint. Parent enterprises advance inventories on generous terms to alleviate the amount of working capital required by their subsidiaries. The surplus funds of profitable foreign subsidiaries have also been enlisted for investment, even when the latter belong to different parent enterprises in the home country. The Soviet Union has been particularly prone to cross-invest in this manner, suggesting that Soviet foreign investments are subject to a higher degree of central management.[29]

East European sources also complain of a scarcity of managerial personnel to run foreign subsidiaries.[30] This constraint eases as a trained cadre is developed, but can, nevertheless, act as a deterrent to parent enterprises new to the field of foreign investment. It helps to explain the immediate operating losses often incurred and the need to enlist local participation, at least in the short run; points to which the discussion will return in later chapters.

As noted in Chapter 1, direct foreign investment has been regarded, in the Leninist construct of international political economy, as the principal instrument of monopoly capitalism in its final, imperialist stage. In this context, it might seem inconsistent, if not unprincipled, for monopolistic enterprises in the Comecon countries to follow the pattern of foreign investment set by Western multinational enterprises. Comecon representatives have, therefore, sought vigorously to reject, in their presentations to international forums, any association of the foreign investment activity of socialist state enterprises with that of capitalist firms.[31]

Whether this official disavowal is from ideological conviction or political expediency is open to question. In either case, the Comecon regions face the problem of an ever-widening gap between traditional ideology and contemporary reality in this area. Nor, politically, can they afford entirely to disregard the impact of the blurring of socialist and capitalist external behaviour, in the controversial area of multinational enterprise, on their image at home and abroad. Hence, ideological and political considerations have served as a brake which more pragmatic approaches to Comecon foreign investment activity have had to overcome.

The ideological sensitivity of the subject has also been reflected in the relative paucity of its treatment in the East European literature, especially in the more orthodox countries. When it is discussed, it is treated as a new form of international economic co-operation under the heading of 'joint ventures'.[32] The foreign direct investment dimension and analogies with Western multinational enterprises are studiously ignored.[33]

With regard to Comecon investments in the Third World, these various inhibiting factors have operated with differing intensity. Balance-of-payments constraints on capital investments in the Third World are less severe than those which limit the scope of Comecon investment in the OECD economies. For the most part, Comecon countries have traditionally enjoyed a positive balance of trade with the developing countries, and, in the soft-currency areas, surpluses of local currencies held by Comecon countries tend not only to facilitate, but even to motivate direct investment.

Investments in the Third World do, however, raise especially sensitive ideological questions. They even risk undermining efforts by Comecon ideologists and propagandists to establish an identity of interests with the developing countries against the West, lately in terms of demands from Third World countries for a 'New International Economic Order'.[34] More pragmatic approaches to relations with the Third World have led the Comecon countries to enter into new arrangements which closely resemble, and directly compete with, those employed by capitalist firms. Necessity has, moreover, dictated that Comecon investments in the Third World be concentrated in natural resources and manufacturing. Like capitalist firms, and sometimes in partnership with them, they thus find themselves employers of local labour, extracting a profit from an essentially capitalist mode of production.

In these circumstances, writers in the Comecon countries have sought to differentiate the investment activities of enterprises in the Third World from those of Western firms. They have argued that socialist capital participation in Third World ventures is qualitatively different in purpose and nature from the investments of Western firms.[35] They have maintained that it is not geared primarily to monetary gain (profits), nor exploited for political ends, and have played up the mutuality of interests involved, stressing the contribution of Comecon participation in capital projects in the developing economies to shared industrialisation goals.[36] In emphasising the co-operative aspects of Comecon investment activities in the Third World, they have affirmed that: (i) investments take the form of equity partnerships in mixed companies, with Comecon participation usually limited to an equal or minority share and restricted in term; (ii) investments are very often negotiated on a government-to-government basis, in the framework of inter-state agreements; and (iii) Comecon partners in the developing countries are typically state enterprises or medium-sized, national firms rather than the large, private-capital interests preferred by Western multinational enterprises.

In spite of these efforts, Comecon investment activities have by no means been exempt from the cultural and political sensitivities of host countries in the Third World. They have, generally, had to function within the same conditions and uncertainties as have Western multinational enterprises. The multinational operations of the Comecon enterprises in Iran, for example, apparently suffered the disruptive effects of the political and social upheaval that accompanied the Islamic Revolution of 1979, although it is not clear whether all Comecon assets were subject to the same sweeping nationalisation measures as were Western investments.[37]

DIFFERENCES IN ORGANISATION AND APPROACH AMONG COMECON COUNTRIES

The preceding discussion has emphasised the common elements in the foreign investment strategy of the Comecon countries. Differences approach are, however, discernible. They vary among the countries according to external commercial and other foreign policy interests, and reflect more fundamental differences in levels of development, in economic structure and in economic and political systems.[38] An analysis of the differences of approach among the Comecon countries helps to bring out more specific determinants of socialist foreign investment strategy.

Differences among Comecon countries in the level of investment activity (as measured by number of investments abroad and as shown in Tables 3.3 and 3.4 correlate closely with their relative participation in extra-regional trade. The correlation is especially apparent in investments in the OECD economies where, as it has been stressed, the majority of investments are directly related to trade. The relationship is brought out further by the locational pattern of investments, which are concentrated in those Western economies which are the individual Comecon countries' major trading partners. There is, for example, a relatively high concentration of Hungarian investments in Austria.

Soviet writing has treated the foreign investment activities of Soviet enterprises as a manifestation of the new stage in the development of Soviet external economic relations.[39] They link them to the more effective role desired for the Soviet Union in the world economy, and to the need for economic co-operation between partners representing different socio-economic systems.

Consonant with its size, the Soviet Union is the major foreign investor, as well as the largest foreign trader, of the Comecon countries.[40] Historically, direct investment has offered to the Soviet Union the means to gain a foothold in some international markets (oil), or access to needed services abroad (banking and insurance, for example). Soviet foreign subsidiaries and banks abroad tend to be larger, on average, than those of other Comecon countries. In most cases this is a reflection of the scale of foreign operations of their Soviet parents, but in some cases it is because they have been longer established.

While some large Soviet marketing subsidiaries remain concentrated in traditional export activities (in oil, timber and diamonds, for example), the newer ones are directed to the marketing of industrial machinery, agricultural and transport equipment and consumer manufactures. Apart from Soviet multinational state banks and shipping lines, several foreign trade organisations are the most active Soviet multinational investors:

Soyuznefteexport (petroleum and petroleum products), Exportle (wood and paper), Avtoexport (automobiles) and Tractorexpor (agricultural machinery equipment). These have tended to push a higher share of investments beyond the simple import-marketing stage into direct retailing and various technical-support operations Historical and political considerations, as well as the nature and size of its investments, have dictated a marked Soviet preference for sole or majority ownership (see Table 3.1).

By contrast to its active investment role in the West, the Soviet Union has adopted a more conservative approach in the South where its direct investments have not been commensurate with the scale of its other economic activities. Political and ideological considerations have no doubt played a role here, with the Soviet Union, as the leader of the 'socialist camp', more conscious than most of its East European allies of the need to cast an image in the Third World which contrasts with that of the West. Moreover, the requirement for raw materials has been less important for the Soviet Union than for the East European countries, so that Soviet equity investments in the sphere of natural-resource exploitation in the Third World have been limited to off-shore fishing. The Soviet lag in Third World investments may also stem from reluctance to have recourse to the required joint-venture format.[41]

Poland and Hungary have been the most active and innovative among the East European Comecon countries in their approaches to the foreign investment option.[42] They have engaged in investment on a broad front, both functionally and geographically. They have extensively employed foreign marketing subsidiaries to support both traditional, agricultural exports and exports of their growing manufacturing sectors. Poland's investments have been concentrated in its major Western export markets: the Federal Republic of Germany, the United Kingdom and the United States (where it was long the only Comecon country to enjoy most-favoured-nation [MFN] tariff access). For Hungary, the German market has, besides the Austrian, been the major target of investment activity. Hungary has shown particular readiness to use investments in manufacturing facilities abroad as a means of exploiting technological advantages on foreign markets. With its maritime interests, Poland has been second only to the Soviet Union in its investments in shipping and fishing operations abroad.

Hungary has been more ready to grant enterprises autonomous export-import privileges and the right to engage in foreign investment activity, without the intermediary of specialised foreign-trade organisations. Nevertheless, aside from the large electronics manufacturer, Tungsram, several foreign-trade enterprises remain the most active Hungarian multinational investors: Hungarotex (textiles), Medimpex (medical equipment) and Monimpex (wines and foodstuffs). Poland has charged the specialised state foreign trade enterprise, DAL International Trading Co. Ltd, to act on behalf of other Polish state enterprises in the sphere of foreign investment, and accordingly DAL now accounts for a significant share of Polish investments in foreign marketing subsidiaries.

Romania's investment strategy has concentrated on the developing countries, where its investments are far more numerous than those of any other Comecon country. This is not surprising, in view of the strong emphasis Romania's foreign policy places on links with the Third World and its relatively high share of trade with the developing countries.[43] Romania's desire to limit its dependence on imports of Comecon (especially Soviet) raw materials has led it actively to seek extra-regional sources of supply to supplement domestic resources. A larger share of its foreign investments has accordingly been in the extractive industries, especially in the Third World. Given its extensive investment activity in the developing countries, Romania has had to be more constrained in its investments in the West, which have remained modest. Most of these have been in small importing agencies and in joint-venture banking operations.

As revealed by the functional and geographic pattern of its foreign investments, Bulgaria's approach has been broadly similar to that of Poland and Hungary, but on a smaller scale. In view of its size, as the smallest East European economy, and the dominance of its bilateral economic relationship with the Soviet Union, Bulgaria has, in fact, pursued a comparatively active and diversified foreign-investment strategy. Its investments have by no means been limited to the marketing of Bulgarian fresh and processed fruits and vegetables. They have also been in support of exports of machinery and equipment, where Balkancar, Bulgaria's giant manufacturer of industrial handling equipment, through its foreign trade arm, Balkancarimpex, has established a network of foreign subsidiaries. Bulgaria has also, after Hungary, established the largest number of production facilities in the West.

On the other hand, the two most industrially advanced of the Comecon countries, Czechoslovakia and the German Democratic Republic, have been comparatively conservative in their foreign investment strategies. This may primarily be ascribed to political factors, and the conscious primacy placed by both countries on the development of relations within the CMEA.

Czechoslovakia's foreign investments are, nevertheless, substantial. A number are long-established and, among the Comecon countries, Czechoslovakia is second to the Soviet Union in the way it has built up the most important technical facilities abroad in support of its machinery exports. The foreign trade enterprise, Strojimport, has been an especially active investor in this regard. Czechoslovakia has also invested in manufacturing operations in the developing countries, particularly in Latin America. A general-purpose foreign trade enterprise, Transakta, which took over the activities in this area of the former Czechoslovak enterprise, Fincom, has been the vehicle for a number of investment activities in the West and the South.

The German Democratic Republic, however, lags well behind its Comecon partners in investment activity, having undertaken few direct investments in either the West or the South. It has proved itself especially reluctant to engage in direct investment activity in the developing countries, where instances of East German equity participation are extremely rare (see Table 3.4). A sizeable share of the Democratic Republic's limited foreign investments are represented by the subsidiaries of its large optical equipment manufacturer, Carl Zeiss Jena, which inherited some of the assets from its capitalist predecessor after the war.[44] The German Democratic Republic has sought instead to supplement its official trade representation abroad through the creation in key foreign locations of special 'technical-commercial bureaux'. These have provided commercial representation and technical support for the foreign operations of the more externally active enterprises. It has sometimes proved expedient, however, to establish such representation under local laws. The resulting 'companies' remain in a number of cases little more than desks within the local East German trade mission.

Several factors account for the conservative investment strategy of the German Democratic Republic which, as indicated in Chapter 3, has followed a pattern unique among the Comecon countries, in terms of its limited geographic and functional spread and its revealed preference for sole ownership. While its diplomatic isolation has long made foreign investments risky, if not inappropriate, the normalisation of diplomatic relations since the early 1970s has seen the gradual growth of foreign investment activity by the Democratic Republic. Ideology, however, has remained a more significant impediment to foreign investment for the Republic than for other Comecon countries. Conscious of the need to differentiate itself from its capitalist rival, the German Federal Republic, the Democratic Republic has adhered to a more orthodox position than its allies in this as in other areas.[45]

NATIONAL STRATEGIES FOR FOREIGN DIRECT INVESTMENT

It is evident that the multinational 'actors' among the Comecon countries are all state-owned enterprises, subject to a considerable degree of central control by the state. In foreign investment, as in foreign trade, the state thus plays a much more direct role in the Comecon countries than is usually found elsewhere. They are 'state-investment' as well as 'state-trading' economies in the international arena.

In terms of the involvement of the state in foreign investment activity, however, the difference between the Comecon countries and other actors on the multinational stage – especially such relative newcomers as Japan, and some of the newly industrialised, developing countries – is of degree not kind. In these, and other Western countries, the state has sought to influence the multinational behaviour of national firms, either through direct involvement in state-owned enterprises or through indirect regulation of private firms. State-owned enterprises in the West have increasingly joined the ranks of the multinational enterprises.[46]

Still, in the case of the Comecon countries the role of the state is far more dominant, and it is especially meaningful here to speak of national foreign-investment strategies. It is the Comecon state that has consciously sought to capture the benefits perceived as accruing to Western, capitalist multinational enterprises from foreign-investment operations. It is the state that has identified the economic rationale for foreign direct investment and has established both the legal conditions and the institutional mechanism to implement it. To an extent unparalleled elsewhere, considerations of macroeconomic policy have been directly incorporated into investment decision-making. These include the balance of external versus internal investments, the regional distribution of external investments, the implications of foreign direct investment for the balance of payments, the relationship of investment activities to other foreign-policy goals and the consonance of foreign investment with the image of the state at home and abroad.[47] The growth of outflows of foreign direct investment are as much the result of a conscious determination of the state as are the legal conditions and regulatory restrictions which inhibit inflows.

At the same time, the direct role of central state authorities in socialist multinational enterprises, even in the more traditionally organised East European economies, should not be exaggerated. While these authorities ensure that objectives of macroeconomic policy determine the broad nature, and set the overall direction, of foreign-investment activity, they leave to the decision-making level of the enterprise the initiation, formulation and implementation of specific investment projects, albeit subject to supervision and approval, especially in the area of financing. There is no evidence of detailed co-ordination on a national basis. The day-to-day operations of foreign branches and subsidiaries, once they are established, appear to be determined significantly by the market forces in which they operate. State control of operations is exercised indirectly, through the targets imposed at home by the central plan on parent enterprises and supervisory ministries. The possibility even exists that the specific foreign investment behaviour of state-owned enterprises in the Comecon countries may not always conform to state interests.[48]

State involvement has, in any event, not prevented (and possibly contributed to) important errors of judgement and even the failure of investment strategies. Discussion, therefore, turns in the following chapters to a more detailed analysis of the multinational experience of Comecon state enterprises.

NOTES AND REFERENCES

1. All, however, possess 'second economies' where these characteristics apply, but which lie outside the officially-sanctioned, planned economies. In Hungary, even the official economy is geared more to market principles, and permits greater scope for private enterprise.
2. For details of the basic Soviet organisation of foreign trade, see G. Smith, *Soviet Foreign Trade: Organization, Operations and Policy, 1913–1917* (New York: Praeger, 1973) and, for its East European variants, H. Matejka, 'Foreign Trade Systems', in H. Höhmann *et al.* (eds), *The New Economic Systems of Eastern Europe, op. cit.*, pp. 443–78.
3. In the East European countries, but not in the Soviet Union, foreign trade enterprises may be directly subordinate to industrial (branch) ministries or to production enterprises and associations.

4. The Polish enterprise DAL and the Czechoslovak enterprise Transakta are examples.
5. Prominent examples of production enterprises which have long enjoyed these rights are Bulgaria's Balkancar (materials handling equipment), the German Democratic Republic's Carl Zeiss Jena (optical equipment) and Hungary's Tungsram (electronics). In East Europe, increasing numbers of production enterprises and associations have more recently been granted rights to engage directly in external transactions. (See H. Lapackova, 'Development of the Forms of Relationships between Foreign Trade and Industry', *Soviet and East European Foreign Trade*, Summer 1983.)
6. The shares range from highs of about two-thirds for Poland and the Soviet Union to lows of less than one-fifth for Czechoslovakia and the German Democratic Republic. All figures refer to the end of 1981, and to investments in the West; the available data on Comecon investments in the developing countries are insufficiently comprehensive to permit such calculations.
7. The enterprise in question, DAL, acts as an intermediary for other Polish enterprises and has, therefore, made investments in a wide range of foreign operations. More typical 'parent' enterprises in the Western, multinational sense, would be the Soviet freight transport enterprise, Sovfracht, with twenty-three foreign subsidiaries and affiliates, or the Hungarian enterprise Tungsram, with eight (see Table 4.2). All figures refer to the end of 1983 and to investments in the West. These enterprises and their activities in the multinational arena will be discussed in more detail in the following chapters.
8. The company, Globinvest AG, registered in Luxembourg in 1978 by the Hungarian foreign trade enterprise Interag Ltd, failed in its first major investment (majority interest in an ailing Danish radio and television manufacturer which proved beyond rescue), but it remains as a legal framework for future attempts.
9. State enterprises with investments in at least five foreign branches or subsidiaries in the West; see Table 4.2.
10. The required foreign-exchange allocations are made through the National Bank of Hungary while the Ministry of Finance approves the investment allocation.
11. See T. Ozawa, 'Japan's Multinational Enterprise: The Political Economy of Outward Dependency', *World Politics*, July 1978.
12. See the discussion in Wilczynski, *The Economics and Politics of East–West Trade* (London: Macmillan, 1969) and Pisar, *Coexistence and Commerce, op. cit.*
13. Inattention to quality and neglect of marketing generally have been characteristic of the Comecon domestic economies, where 'taut' plans have fostered a 'sellers' market' mentality. The chronic problem of shortages of spare parts in the planned economies is an important manifestation.
14. See P. Ericson, 'Soviet Efforts to Increase Exports of Manufactured Products to the West', *Soviet Economy in a New Perspective* (Washington, DC: US Government Printing Office for the Joint

Economic Committee, US Congress, 1976) pp. 709–26, and M. Bornstein, 'Systemic Aspects of the Responses of East European Economies to Disturbances in the International Economy', in E. Neuberger and L. L. Tyson (eds), *The Impact of International Economic Disturbances on the Soviet Union and Eastern Europe* (New York: Pergamon Press, 1980) pp. 308–20.

15. Barriers to entry on international commodity markets had nevertheless prompted the creation of some foreign subsidiaries to market primary products. To gain access to international oil markets, for example, the Soviet Union's Soyuznefteexport had established oil marketing companies in the United Kingdom (1959) and Belgium (1967).

16. Pursuing their own profits, local agents are said often to neglect Comecon manufactures in favour of the more readily marketable products of other clients, sometimes the direct competitors of Comecon export enterprises. On these points, see, for example, Engibarov, *Smeshannye Obshchestva na Mirovom Rynke*, *op. cit.*

17. *Ibid.*

18. The Soviet-owned Slava watch-assembly plant in Besançon, the French watch capital, was reportedly established in early 1976 to improve market access to the EEC area for Soviet watches. See *Soviet Business and Trade*, 26 May 1976, p. 4.

19. See Chapter 6. The multinational Hungarian electronics enterprise Tungsram established a plant in Ireland which benefited from special incentives and tax advantages available to foreign firms setting up in Ireland. The Soviet Union's Avtoexport has discussed the establishment of a plant in the Canadian Maritime region, to assemble Soviet Lada cars for the Canadian market, which would take advantage of incentives for regional development.

20. See Chapter 6 for examples.

21. Discussion will return to this question in more detail in Chapter 9.

22. See Lowenthal, *Model or Ally*, *op. cit.*, p. 366. Resource investments have been made in the Middle East (minerals) and Africa (metals) and to a smaller extent in Latin America. As will be seen in Chapter 6, Romania has been by far the most active Comecon investor in this sphere of activity, working primarily through its enterprise Geomin.

23. Discussion will return to these points, with examples, in Chapter 6.

24. The advantages of foreign direct investment analysed in Western theory under the categories of 'ownership-specific', 'internalisation-incentive', and 'location-specific' all come into play here. See J. Dunning, *International Production and the Multinational Enterprise* (London: George Allen and Unwin, 1981).

25. The Budapest-based foreign trade enterprise Medimpex, for example, has been the vehicle for Hungarian investment in pharmaceutical plants, producing on the basis of materials imported from Hungary. See Chapter 6.

26. Countries typically experience net outflows of direct investment at advanced stages of industrialisation. See Dunning, 'Explaining Outward Direct Investment of Developing Countries: in Support of the Eclectic Theory of International Production', in Kumar and McLeod, *Multinationals from Developing Countries*, *op. cit.*, pp. 1–22.

27. On the conditions for foreign equity investment in the Comecon economies, see McMillan and St Charles, *Joint Ventures in Eastern Europe, a Three-Country Comparison* (Montreal: C. D. Howe Research Institute, 1974) and the references cited in Chapter 2, note 31.

28. In a decree made in 1922 which still pertains today, the Soviet government provided for the establishment of joint stock companies with the participation of foreign capital. Among the stated objectives was the marketing of Soviet exports abroad. See *Resheniia partii i pravitel'stva po khoziaistvennym voprosam, tom 1, 1917–1928 godu* (Moscow: Izdat. Politicheskoi literatury, 1967) pp. 293–5.

29. The Soviet petroleum multinational enterprise Soyuznefteexport, for example, has an equity holding in a Soviet diamond-marketing company in Belgium, while its Belgian petroleum-marketing subsidiary (Nafta-B NV) has invested in a Soviet firm in Belgium which markets and services Soviet electronic equipment.

30. See, for example, the article by J. Szydlowski in *Rynki Zagraniczne*, 31 May 1983.

31. The discussion will return to this subject in more detail in Chapter 8.

32. For a recent example of this emphasis in the Soviet literature, see L. A. Rodina, *Sotsialisticheskaia integratsiia i novye formy sotrudinichestva Vostok-Zapad* (Moscow: Izdat. Nauka, 1983), pp. 72–89.

33. Much of the Soviet literature still reflects the official condemnation of the multinational activities of Western firms. Some Soviet authors nevertheless take note of their more positive features and the practical lessons to be derived from them. Compare V. V. Scherbakov and Iu. I. Iudanov, *Eksport kapitala v usloviiakh dal'neishego obostreniia obshchego krizisa kapitalizma* (Moscow: Vysshaiia shkola, 1981) and M. Maksimova, *SSSR i mezhdunarodnoe ekonomicheskoe sotrudnichestvo* (Moscow: Mysl', 1977). The East European literature often adopts a still more open view (see the discussion in Lauter and Dickie, *Multinational Corporations, op. cit.*, or Zurawicki, *Multinational Enterprises in East and West* (Leiden: Sijthoff, 1979)).

34. See Valkenier, *The Soviet Union and the Third World, op. cit.*, for discussion of the dilemma the Comecon countries have more generally faced on these issues.

35. L. Zevin, *Novye tendenstii v ekonomicheskom sotrudnichestve sotasialisticheskikh i razvivaiushchikhsia stran* (Moscow: Izdat. Nauka, 1970) pp. 160–70.

36. *Ibid.* See also A. Jung, 'Polish Production Partnerships in Developing Countries', *Soviet and East European Foreign Trade*, Spring 1982.

37. Hungarian enterprises, for example, liquidated their direct investments in Iran in the aftermath of the Revolution (in at least one case because the Iranian partner had fled the country), but there are conflicting reports about the fate of Soviet assets. See Chapters 5 and 6 for further details.

38. Compare the contributions to the volume edited by Radu, *Eastern Europe and the Third World, op. cit.*, whose common theme is that the East European states, despite a broad policy similarity, pursue particular interests in their relations with the developing countries.

39. See A. I. Bel'chuk, (ed.), *Novyi Etap Ekonomicheskogo Sotrudnichestva SSSR s Razvitymi Kapitalisticheskimi Stranami* (Moscow: Izdat. Nauka, 1978); N. Shmelev, *Sotializm i Mezhdunarodnye Ekonomicheskie Otnosheniia.* (Moscow; Mezhdunarodny Otnosheniia, 1979); and Rodina, *op. cit.* Also A. Vlasov, 'New forms of Economic Relations of CMEA Member-Countries with Developing Nations', *Foreign Trade*, No. 12, 1983.

40. The Soviet approach and experience has been treated in some detail in the author's 'Soviet Investment in the Industrialised Western Economies and in the Developing Economies of the Third World', in *Soviet Economy in a Time of Change* (Washington, DC: US Government Printing Office, for the Joint Economic Committee, US Congress, 1979) Vol. 2, pp. 625–47. See also J. Harrison, 'Commercial–Financial Dealings between the USSR and Market-Type Economies, with Special Reference to Soviet Banking, Maritime and Trading Operations in the West' (unpublished PhD dissertation, University of Glasgow, 1978).

41. American firms are also reputed to dislike joint ventures with foreign partners. Perhaps this is a shared trait of continent-sized megapowers.

42. Recent examples of discussion of the subject in the Polish and Hungarian literature and available in English translation are, Pulawski, 'A Method for Evaluating Polish Joint Ventures Operating Abroad', *Soviet and East ·European Foreign Trade*, Fall 1979; Jung, 'Polish Production Partnerships', *op. cit.*; 'Our Joint Ventures in the Developing World' (interview with the Deputy Minister of Foreign Trade), *Hungarian Foreign Trade*, No. 2, 1979; and S. Demcsak, 'Hungarian Entrepreneurs – Foreign Partners', *Marketing in Hungary*, No. 1, 1982.

43. See R. R. King, 'Romania and the Third World', *Orbis*, Winter 1978 and C. Lawson 'National Independence and Reciprocal Advantages: The Political Economy of Romanian–South Relations', *Soviet Studies*, July 1983.

44. Some of the personnel of the original company fled to the Federal Republic of Germany at the end of World War II and established a rival company, but the headquarters and principal assets of the company remained in East Germany.

45. The policy of differentiation (Abgrenzung) has been pursued with special urgency by the German Democratic Republic to counter the Federal Republic's Ostpolitik in the late 1960s and 1970s. See M. Croan, *East Germany: The Soviet Connection* (Beverly Hills: Sage Publications, 1976). For discussion of this rivalry with the Federal Republic as a function of East German policy towards the Third World, see M. Sodaro, 'The GDR and the Third World: Supplicant and Advocate', in Radu, *Eastern Europe and the Third World*, pp. 106–41.

46. Discussion will return to these points in Chapter 8.

47. In the more traditionally organised East European economies, the absorption by the state budget of profits and losses from external transactions permits the state in principle to take a broad view of the

return from foreign investments. In need not insist on the profitability of every foreign subsidiary, and may transfer funds among them as it

48. The growing domestic problem of the divergence of interest between enterprises and the state, under the traditional system, has been a major theme in discussions of systemic reform in the planned economies.

CHAPTER 5

Investments in the Service Sector: Nature and Experience

Multinational enterprises generally have directed an increasing share of their investments to the tertiary, services sector and, as latecomers, the Comecon countries have mirrored this global trend in the structure of their own foreign investments. Direct engagement in a variety of services abroad, especially in the OECD economies, has been a major Comecon objective for multinational enterprise. This chapter will look more closely at these investments, attempting in particular to assess to what extent the multinational operations of Comecon state enterprises have in practice approached the policy objectives set for them in this area.

FOREIGN COMMERCIAL OPERATIONS

Foreign direct investments have been increasingly regarded by the Comecon countries as important instruments of their extra-regional trade policy.[1] Significant shares of these investments have been in direct support of exports. It will be recalled from Chapter 3 that nearly 70 per cent of the wholly-owned or mixed Comecon companies in the West were principally engaged in the import of products from the home country and their marketing and distribution in the host country. In the South this share was about 25 per cent.

Not surprisingly, therefore, the pattern of investments in foreign commercial operations tends to reflect the structure of exports to a given market area. In particular, investments in commercial activities have been concentrated in those product categories in which individual Comecon countries have already demonstrated their export strength.

The product-distribution of commercially orientated investments by the seven Comecon countries is presented in Table 5.1, which reveals the emphasis on manufactured exports in their foreign-investment strategies. The table shows the investments of the largest investor-country, the Soviet Union, to be concentrated in machinery and equipment (machine tools, transport equipment and agricultural

Table 5.1 Distribution by export product category of marketing companies abroad, end-1983 (percentages)[a]

Category	Comecon country							
	Bulgaria	Czecho-slovakia	East Germany	Hungary	Poland	Romania	Soviet Union	Total
Machinery and equipment	48.7	55.2	65.4	18.9	26.1	18.4	41.8	35.4
Raw and semi-processed materials	2.6	1.7	3.8	3.8	6.8	0	13.4	5.3
Petroleum and its products	0	0	0	3.8	0	10.5	8.9	3.3
Pharmaceuticals	5.1	3.5	3.8	12.7	4.5	21.1	4.5	7.6
Textiles	2.6	0	0	10.1	3.4	0	0	3.0
Agricultural goods and food products	15.4	1.7	0	16.5	11.4	10.5	4.5	9.4
Other consumer goods	7.7	27.6	19.2	30.4	20.5	7.9	19.4	21.0
Technology, know-how, licences	0	0	0	1.3	0	2.6	1.5	0.8
Miscellaneous	17.9	10.3	7.7	2.5	27.3	29.0	6.0	14.2
Totals	100.0	100.0	100.0	100.0	100.0	100.0	100.0	100.0

[a] Distribution by principal product marketed of 395 companies, in both West and South.

Source: Comecon Foreign Investment Data Bank, East–West Project, Carleton University, Ottawa.

machinery), with some emphasis also on raw and semi-processe‹ materials (lumber, petroleum and chemicals). By contrast, far mor‹ important shares of Hungarian, and to a smaller degree Polish an‹ Romanian, companies are engaged in the marketing of consume‹ goods.[2] In addition to food products, Hungarian investments hav‹ been heavily in support of consumer manufactures, such as electrica‹ products, medical equipment, pharmaceuticals and textiles. Th‹ relatively high share of Bulgarian companies in the machinery an‹ equipment category is due to its investments in support of exports o‹ construction (materials-handling) equipment, especially forklif‹ trucks and related products. The investments of the more industrially advanced East European countries, Czechoslovakia and the Germa‹ Democratic Republic, reflect their levels of industrial development‹ Czechoslovak investments have been undertaken in a wide range o‹ industrial machinery exports and consumer manufactures. Th‹ German Democratic Republic's less extensive foreign investment‹ have been heavily in support of exports of optical equipment an‹ scientific instruments.

Far less numerous than those in the West, Comecon commercia‹ investments in the South have been directed principally in suppor‹ of capital goods exports, often associated with major developmen‹ projects. There is accordingly less variation among the seve‹ Comecon countries in the pattern of their product-distribution o‹ export-orientated investments in the South than in the West.

The pattern is further reflected in the multinational paren‹ enterprises involved. As seen in the preceding chapter, th‹ commercial orientation of investments has dictated that state foreig‹ trade organisations play a prominent role in implementing th‹ external investment strategies of the Comecon countries. The mos‹ active of these, in terms of multinational commercial operations, ar‹ those responsible for the principal extra-regional exports of th‹ home countries, especially on Western markets. At the same time‹ some producing enterprises, or associations, in the home countries‹ have also either directly or through domestic subsidiaries for foreig‹ trade, developed a network of marketing companies abroad‹ Examination of the foreign commercial investments of several of th‹ most active Comecon multinational enterprises will serve to convey‹ the range of operations and the variety of experience in thi‹ important area.

DAL International Trading Company Ltd., the Polish stat‹ foreign trading enterprise, has already been cited as having engage‹

n especially extensive multinational commercial operations. Unlike those of most other Polish (and East European) trading companies, DAL's activities are not limited to a specific product line.[3] Its function is rather to serve as the intermediary, on behalf of other Polish enterprises, when a wide range of products (and hence more than one Polish enterprise) are involved, or when special financial arrangements are required. DAL participates in a variety of external commercial transactions not involving foreign direct investment. It has, however, established or taken equity in a set of highly diversified (functionally and geographically) commercial companies in foreign market areas. It has direct equity in twenty-five companies in the West and fourteen in the South, as well as an indirect holding (through its foreign subsidiaries and affiliates) in another twelve companies. In these cases, DAL's role in these ventures is to represent other Polish enterprises which deal through it and its network of foreign companies in the performance of their export–import functions. DAL rarely is the sole shareholder in foreign commercial operations; nearly all of its investments are in mixed companies, but in several of these its equity is 90 per cent or more.

Broadly analogous to DAL in its functions is the Czechoslovak multi-purpose foreign trade organisation Transakta.[4] Through a number of wholly-owned or majority-owned, companies abroad – some long established – Transakta markets, distributes and services the products of other Czechoslovak enterprises. Its subsidiary in the United Kingdom, Exico Ltd, with sales in 1980 of nearly $20 million and fifty employees, markets a wide range of industrial products from its impressive headquarters building in central London (Exico House in Gray's Inn Road). An even larger subsidiary in Canada – Omnitrade Ltd. (Montreal) with sales in 1980 of over $36 million and 140 employees – also markets, distributes and services a variety of Czechoslovak industrial and consumer manufactures. Omnitrade itself has subsidiaries in Chile and Japan, as well as in Canada, and (through the last) operating divisions in the United States. Several of Transakta's commercial subsidiaries in the West are more specialised, marketing and servicing textile machinery on behalf of the Czechoslovak foreign trade organisation Investa (later Strojimport).

Many East European trading companies operate through their own networks of foreign subsidiaries and affiliates, rather than through intermediaries such as DAL and Transakta. The Czechoslovak foreign trade organisation already mentioned,

Strojimport, is an example of this.[5] Through a network of sixteen subsidiary companies in the West and South, most of them wholly owned, Strojimport markets and services machine tools and other equipment. In the South, Strojimport has concentrated many of its investments in Latin America, with subsidiaries or affiliates in Mexico, Guatemala, Venezuela and Peru, for the marketing and servicing of machine tools and agricultural equipment.

Hungary's Hungarotex Foreign Trading Company is an example of a large socialist multinational enterprise operating in the area of consumer manufactures and related products. Hungarotex has traditionally held the monopoly for Hungarian exports of textiles and clothing, and has established or invested in mixed commercial companies in its most important export markets.[6] Given the nature of its exports, these are concentrated in the developed economies, that is, six West European countries, as well as Canada and the United States. Exports to the developing countries have not yet justified investment on a similar scale, although a mixed company in Kuwait (Hungaro–Kuwait Trading Co.) services several Middle Eastern markets. In the West and South, the Hungarotex companies are typically owned jointly with local partners on a 50–50 basis.

The Soviet Union has long employed direct investments in local commercial operations as a means both of breaking into, and maintaining its share in, local oil markets. Before World War II Soviet-owned oil companies operated in Germany, the United Kingdom and Sweden. In the post-war period, Soyuznefteexport, the Soviet oil-export monopoly, has built a more extensive network of companies serving the West European market.[7] With subsidiaries located in eight different West European countries, Soyuznefteexport's most important investments have been concentrated in Belgium, Finland and the United Kingdom. In Finland, through two companies in which it has majority holding (Suomen Petrooli Oy and Oy Teboil AB) the Soviet parent has at its disposal an extensive network of retail outlets, fuel depots, oil tankers and other distribution facilities, through which it serves a large share of the Finnish market for oil and oil products. (The Soviet Union is the source of well over half of Finland's oil imports.) In Belgium, Soyuznefteexport, together with several other Soviet foreign trade organisations, has the majority holding in Nafta B NV, with 180 employees, major storage facilities (the largest in Belgium) in the port of Antwerp and an international distribution network through which it serves markets in Western Europe and

America. The wholly Soviet-owned subsidiary of Soyuznefteexport in the United Kingdom, Nafta (GB) Ltd, also has extensive retail outlets located throughout the country. With ninety employees, its sales turnover in 1980 was well over one billion dollars.

Examples of several production enterprises with significant direct investments in commercial operations abroad will serve to round out this sketch of the activities of Comecon multinational enterprises in direct support of exports. Hungary's Tungsram (United Incandescent Lamp and Electrical Co. Ltd), one of the world's leading producers and exporters of lighting equipment, has investments in commercial operations in seven different national markets in the West and three developing economies.[8] Some of these investments, as will be seen in Chapter 6, extend as well to production operations. Several of Tungsram's foreign subsidiaries have long histories; its Austrian company was established in 1891, and those in Denmark, Sweden and Switzerland date from the inter-war period. Its most recent investment is a company established in Ireland in 1980. These companies, in which Tungsram's holdings range from 100 per cent to a minority share, are engaged in the marketing of light bulbs, for both consumer and industrial use, and sometimes other electrical products as well.

Carl Zeiss Jena in the German Democratic Republic is another East European producer (optical equipment and scientific instruments) with an historic, pre-war, multinational role and long-established rights to operate directly abroad under the system of state-trading established after World War II.[9] Its nine, wholly-owned marketing companies, located in five West European countries, and the United States, account for an important share of the direct foreign investments of East German enterprises. Some of the companies are successors to pre-war investments; others are of more recent origin. The American subsidiary, Jena Scientific Instruments, Inc., of New York, was established in 1981.

Other well-known East European producing firms with significant foreign investments operate through independent or subsidiary home-based trading companies. Czechoslovakia's automotive producer, Skoda, has marketing companies in Belgium, the United Kingdom and Singapore which are operated through the foreign trade organisation responsible for the export of motor vehicles and parts, Motokov.[10] Bulgaria's Balkancar, the world's largest manufacturer of fork-lift trucks and other materials-handling equipment sells abroad through a network of nine marketing companies located in

five West European countries, Japan and Nigeria. These ar
operated by its own trading subsidiary, Balkancarimpex.[11] Lik
other Comecon companies established within foreign markets fo
the import and distribution of machinery and equipment produce
by their parent enterprises, the Balkancar subsidiaries maintai
technical facilities for pre- and after-sales servicing of the products.

It will be recalled that marketing subsidiaries are frequentl
established in partnership with nationals of the host country. If th
local partner is a firm, it may bring to the venture not only financi
capital but also useful, and perhaps scarce, tangible assets (wel
located offices, warehouse facilities and communications equipmen
for example) as well as intangible assets (established name, goo
will, trained staff and so on). Individual partners contribute not on
their local business and marketing expertise but also their familiarit
with the language, traditions, political and social institutions of th
country. They bring to the venture their personal reputations an
contacts. These factors can be important in helping the enterprise t
adjust to the variety of local regulations and requirements whic
often pose serious non-tariff barriers to imports on markets in th
host country.

These considerations, which are familiar arguments for join
ventures in general, have particular force in the case of East–Wes
marketing ventures. Comecon products face special barriers o
Western markets. At best they are unfamiliar to potential buyers
and local partnerships help them to become established more rapidl
in new markets. At worst they face discriminatory official trad
barriers and buyer aversion to communist products stemming no
only from political and emotional bias, but also from ingrained lac
of confidence in their quality. Distribution through a locally
identified company, sometimes under a local brand name or trad
mark, helps to overcome these prejudices. Such considerations als
dictate extensive local staffing and require that more visible sale
and managerial personnel (even in the case of wholly-owne
subsidiaries) be nationals of the host country, while East Europea
personnel remain in the background, usually in administrative o
technical positions.

The commercial operations of Soviet and East Europea
subsidiaries and affiliates abroad have been too diverse to permi
easy generalisations about their performance. The companies hav
dealt in a wide range of exports and in a highly varied set o
conditions in the host countries. In many cases, moreover, th

:cord is too short, or hard data on performance too incomplete, to
ermit systematic assessment.

There have been notable failures and significant successes.
listakes have been made both in the initial investment decision and
i the subsequent management of subsidiaries. There are also
xamples, especially in some of the West European countries where
omecon investments have a longer history, of well-established
)mpanies which have a record of impressive expansion and enjoy
substantial share of the local market.

In seeking to develop foreign markets, particularly for
lanufactured exports, Comecon parent enterprises have had to face
:rious difficulties. They have not only had to contend with the
nfamiliarity of the buyer with, and even their prejudice against,
omecon products, but no less importantly have had to surmount
)ecial tariff and non-tariff barriers. While the barriers faced have
aried in nature and intensity from country to country, they have
icluded quantitative restrictions (in Western Europe), the with-
olding of MFN tariff treatment (in the United States) and the
dministration generally of anti-dumping rules and other restrictive
:gulations. In the South, Comecon investors have often faced highly
ncertain and variable regulatory regimes. (These points will be
lustrated in terms of selected host countries in Chapter 7.)

Comecon commercial companies abroad have had further to
)ntend with adverse economic conditions. The timing of the push
)r the establishment of foreign investments by the Comecon
)untries in the late 1960s and early 1970s meant that many were
ist getting started when the markets for their products in the West
egan to collapse. In most cases, they have continued to face highly
nstable demand conditions in host countries. Moreover, as
ewcomers to markets, they have frequently had to work, at least
iitially, through weak retail systems, until stronger dealer networks
ould be developed. These factors, together with the high rates of
iterest that have accompanied recession in the West, have resulted
i many subsidiaries accumulating bad debts, which indirectly affect
ie general position of their parents and suppliers in the home
ountry.[12]

Comecon marketing subsidiaries and affiliates abroad have also
ad to cope with serious back-up problems. The establishment of
)reign subsidiaries has not resolved chronic problems of poor quality
nd insufficient and erratic supply from producers at home. These
ave often prevented subsidiaries from serving foreign markets in the

more flexible manner intended for them. In the case of exports of machinery and equipment, for example, the effective servicing of products requires more than qualified staff and well-equipped local facilities. It demands a continuous supply of spare parts, in adequate volume and assortment. The equity participation in a number of Soviet companies abroad of the foreign trade organisation Zapchastexport (which exports spare parts for several important categories of Soviet machinery and equipment) has been designed to alleviate the problem of the supply of parts.

These circumstances have meant that subsidiary companies have often been forced to operate at a loss for substantial periods before beginning to show a profit, and that even then their profitability may be low by Western standards. In a detailed study of Soviet and East European multinational enterprises in the United Kingdom, a British specialist in international marketing found that when the average profit margins (profit/turnover) of Comecon companies in the United Kingdom were compared to those of British firms, they appeared to operate at relatively low levels of profitability.[13]

It is questionable, however, whether their individual profitability is the principal criterion by which the performance of the marketing subsidiaries of Comecon countries are assessed at home. The preceding chapter indicated that their creation was intended primarily to serve national economic goals with regard to the promotion and diversification of exports. Parent state enterprises, especially under the more traditional Comecon economic regimes, are made to be interested first and foremost in fulfilling export targets set by the foreign trade component of the national economic plan.

In these circumstances, foreign currency revenues from export sales are the prime indication of performance from the perspective of the home country. This is clearly demonstrated by a Soviet author, himself the former director of one of the largest Soviet equipment-marketing companies in Finland. First admitting that capital investments in marketing companies in the West may not be amortised for a number of years, he then argues that, more importantly, such investments in a typical case represent less than 1 per cent of the revenues from sales through such companies in the first five years of operation.[14] Thus it is the return on investment measured in terms of gross sales revenue that is of primary consideration. A more recent Polish article on evaluating the performance of marketing ventures abroad is even more explicit. I ranks the 'value of exports' as the principal criterion of performance, and profits are accorded a distinctly secondary position.[15]

The divergence of interests which potentially exists in any relationship between a parent and its subsidiary is thus compounded in the socialist case. While the subsidiary operates in a market context, the parent works under the strictures of a central economic plan, and thus the objectives of parent and subsidiary have not always been in harmony. Subsidiaries tend to be more concerned with profits, for profitability is the basis of their survival and expansion in the market. At the same time, they have been required to meet sales targets imposed on them by the parent organisations at home, themselves under pressure to fulfil export plans. Sometimes subsidiaries have been forced to take on excess inventories to help the parent organisation meet export targets.

Any such divergence of interests is wider, or at least more apparent, when management is shared with a foreign partner. This is no doubt an important reason why the more traditional Comecon countries, where the profitability of the multinational enterprise still plays a decidedly secondary role, have shown a preference for wholly-owned or majority-owned companies (see Table 3.1) and why parent enterprises have often bought out their foreign partners after several years of operation.[16]

Operational difficulties are also created by basic differences between the partners in most mixed companies. Not only is the Soviet and East European partner typically much larger, but it tends to be highly bureaucratised with regard to organisation and method. The inevitable efforts of the parent to extend bureaucratic forms and procedures to the subsidiary are not infrequently the source of dissension among the partners. Their imposition may even seriously jeopardise the continued success of an existing enterprise which the Eastern partner has taken over, if its past performance was closely dependent upon operational informality and flexibility.

Probably the most important general conclusion to be drawn from the experience available is that marketing companies abroad, even when combined with their own retail networks and service facilities, may facilitate the sale of Comecon products, but they cannot by themselves solve the problems which have most fundamentally limited the marketability of Comecon manufacturers: deficiencies in quality and uncertainties of supply rooted in the behavioural characteristics of Soviet and East European producing enterprises.

In this, as in other areas, attempts to improve the foreign trade mechanism without attendant changes in the domestic back-up system are necessarily doomed to limited success.

There is nevertheless some aggregate evidence that foreign investment in marketing operations has contributed to the growth of hard-currency revenues from exports. The estimated value of sales turnover through subsidiaries and affiliates in the OECD economies for the seven Comecon countries in 1980–81 is presented in Table 5.2. These figures are, in turn, related to exports to these economies in this period. The share of annual exports apparently conducted through the multinational systems of parent state-enterprises in the Comecon countries is estimated at 35 per cent. In Chapter 2, it was seen that if the expansion of Comecon manufactured exports has not been as rapid as hoped (or required to finance desired imports) it has none the less been significant. It is especially interesting to note that those Comecon countries (Romania, the Soviet Union, Hungary and Poland) which experienced the most rapid real growth in manufactured exports to the West during the 1970s (see Table 2.2) were for the most part those which had established the most extensive marketing infrastructure in the West through foreign direct investments (see Table 3.5).

Table 5.2   Estimated annual value of sales by Comecon marketing companies in the West, 1980–82 ($US million)[a]

Product category	Value of sales
Machinery and equipment	1,097.1
Raw and semi-processed materials	7,275.6
Petroleum and products	1,293.9
Pharmaceuticals	822.0
Textiles	81.1
Food products	1,391.8
Other consumer goods	1,023.7
Miscellaneous goods	488.6
Total annual sales of marketing companies	13,473.8
Total average annual exports to the West	38,840.0

[a] Estimates derived from turnover figures reported by companies in period indicated. See Appendix for methodology employed.

Source: Comecon Foreign Investment Data Bank, East–West Project, Carleton University, and OECD trade statistics.

FOREIGN BANKING AND INSURANCE

Investment in services has extended well beyond commerce. It has been directed to a number of other areas of the service sector, although for the most part these have been closely related to trade. The principal areas of activity which will be examined in this section are banking and insurance. While their function in support of the extra-regional trade of the Comecon countries remains fundamental, it is important to note that the foreign operations of state financial organisations in the Comecon countries have extended to other, unrelated areas.

Banks in the Comecon countries have employed three principal forms of organisation to expand their direct operations abroad. They have opened branches, they have established subsidiary banks and they have entered into joint banking ventures with foreign banking partners. The Soviet Union, which has by far the most important investments in foreign banking of the Comecon countries, has clearly favoured the establishment of wholly-owned subsidiary banks; the East European countries have tended to employ the other two forms as well.

Soviet banks have operated abroad since soon after the 1917 Revolution. With the expansion after World War II of the older banks and the addition of new banks and branches in the course of the 1960s and 1970s, there is by now a well-established Soviet presence in international banking, especially in Western Europe. The phenomenon of wholly-owned Soviet banks operating extensively, and on the whole successfully, within the capitalist banking sector has attracted a considerable amount of attention in the West, academic as well as popular.[17]

In 1983, there were six Soviet-owned banks operating abroad which, together with their branches, were located in nine different countries. The status of a seventh bank, in Iran, remained uncertain (see below). Most were concentrated in major West European financial centres: London, Paris, Zurich, Frankfurt and Vienna, but there were also branch banks operating in financial centres of the Third World, such as Beirut and Singapore.

Table 5.3 lists the seven banks and their branches, and provides basic information on their age, ownership and size. While the oldest banks have been operating for more than half a century, the majority have been founded in the last decade and a half, in a wave of expansion which began with the establishment in 1963 of a Beirut

Table 5.3 Soviet-owned banks abroad, 1983

Name	Year Est.	Ownership[a]	Capital[b]	Assets[b]
Moscow Narodny Bank Ltd, London (branch banks in Beirut and Singapore)	1919	Gosbank, Vneshtorgbank, other Soviet interests 100%	78.0 (1982)	3,042.0 (1981)
Banque Commerciale pour l'Europe du Nord (Eurobank) SA, Paris	1921	Gosbank 48%; Vneshtorgbank 21%, other Soviet interests 30%	88.3 (1982)	4,845.4 (1982)
Russo-Iranian Bank, Teheran	1923	Gosbank 16%; Vneshtorgbank 84%	4.0 (1968)	171.0 (1978)
Wozchod Handelsbank AG, Zurich	1966	Gosbank, Vneshtorgbank, State Savings Bank (USSR), Soviet FTOs, Eurobank 80%; Moscow Narodny Bank 16%; Ost–West Handelsbank, 4%	37.7 (1982)	466.4 (1982)
Ost–West Handelsbank AG, Frankfurt	1971	Gosbank 15%; Vneshtorgbank 13%; other Soviet interests 72%	26.7 (1982)	756.0 (1982)
Donau-Bank AG, Vienna	1974	Gosbank 60%; Vneshtorgbank 40%	19.4 (1980)	333.0 (1980)
East–West United Bank SA, Luxembourg	1974	Gosbank 33%; Vneshtorgbank 28%; State Savings Bank (USSR), Moscow Narodny Bank, Wozchod Handelsbank, Eurobank, Ost–West Handelsbank 39%	16.0 (1980)	825.6 (1980)

[a] All Soviet banks abroad are 100% owned by Soviet interests.
[b] All figures expressed in millions of current US dollars.
Years to which figures refer shown in brackets – (end-year figures).

branch by the Moscow Narodny Bank Ltd of London. All seven are wholly owned by Soviet banks and other Soviet economic organisations, at home and abroad. The Soviet state bank (Gosbank) is a partner in all, and the Soviet foreign trade bank (Vneshtorgbank) in all but one. Their combined assets exceeded $10 billion by the early 1980s. Three-quarters of these assets, however, were held by the two oldest and largest Soviet banks abroad, Moscow Narodny and the Banque Commerciale pour l'Europe du Nord, SA, of Paris (known as 'Eurobank').

Soviet banks abroad serve a variety of useful purposes for their owners. They provide a channel to Western national and international money markets for the financing of Soviet trade. They facilitate the investment of the Soviet Union's hard-currency funds in the West. They also help to ensure the privacy of Soviet foreign financial transactions; and this last function has been especially important with regard to maintaining the secrecy of Soviet gold sales on international markets. They provide useful financial data and analysis of international monetary developments, to which direct operations within the Western banking sector give them special access. They also allow Soviet banking officials to gain experience and expertise in international finance. Over most of the period after World War II, Soviet banks abroad have conducted many of these functions on behalf of other Comecon countries as well. With the more recent assumption of multinational functions by several East European national banks, however, this intermediary Soviet role has declined in importance.

Individual banks were either established to perform, or have subsequently developed, particular functions within a broader range of banking operations.[18] Thus Moscow Narodny, which calls itself 'The Bank for East–West Trade', has sought to attract Western funds for the financing of East–West commerce. Eurobank, on the other hand, has functioned primarily as an intermediary in operations between banks, allowing the hard-currency funds of Soviet and other banks in the East to be placed profitably in Western banking institutions. Wozchod Handelsbank AG is principally engaged in gold sales on the Zurich market. The Ost–West Handelsbank AG of Frankfurt finances trade between the Soviet Union and the Federal Republic of Germany, in particular the sale on the Frankfurt exchange of Soviet diamonds and other precious stones.[19] The small Donau-Bank in Vienna concentrates on financing trade between Austria and the CMEA countries. The East–West United Bank SA, the most recent Soviet bank to be established in the West, has taken advantage of the legislative conditions for international banking in Luxembourg to engage in Euromarket operations and to finance Soviet trade with the Benelux countries. It is interesting to note that all of the Soviet banks in Europe took an equity share in East–West United Bank, which suggests that they too may have wished to make use of it as a flexible instrument for their own operations on Eurocurrency markets.

The activities of Soviet banks have increasingly been directed to the generation of long-term funds to finance Soviet imports of hard currency. For this purpose, Soviet banks have been especially active in Eurocurrency financing. The activities of both Moscow Narodny and Eurobank, in fact, involved them in a significant way in the formation of the Eurocurrency markets in the late 1950s and early 1960s.[20]

By no means all of the Soviet banks' participation in international financing had been on behalf of Soviet and East European clients, or in support of Soviet and East European foreign trade. Moscow Narodny, in particular, has engaged in international financial operations not directly related to East–West trade. It has also been active in domestic financing in the United Kingdom.

Through the operations of its banks in Europe, as well as those located in the developing countries, the Soviet Union has sought to extend its financial and commercial presence in the Third World. Moscow Narodny has long served as the London correspondent for client banks in the developing countries and has participated in the financing of trade and capital projects in the South. The establishment of a branch in Beirut in 1963 was clearly intended to boost Soviet exports, especially of manufactures, to the entire Middle East.[21] After slow initial growth, the branch bank prospered in the late 1960s and early 1970s, and despite the disruptions of the Lebanese civil war, was reportedly still operative in the early 1980s, although limited primarily to 'off-shore' banking. The opening of a Moscow Narodny branch in Singapore in 1971 further extended Soviet banking operations in the Third World. The bank was intended primarily to assist the development of Soviet trade with South East Asia and Australasia, but it also provided a channel through which Moscow Narodny could conveniently operate on the Asian-dollar market.

Pressures to extend banking operations into new geographical and functional areas also gave rise to new problems. The move away from the less risky, traditional area of trade-financing into other forms of lending combined with the recession in the West to result in losses from bad loans for several Soviet banks abroad.[22] The Donau-Bank reportedly suffered significant losses of this nature during 1974, its initial year of operation. Ost–West Handelsbank was forced into loan write-offs and received bad publicity in the Western financial press in 1976, when two German diamond importers which it had financed were charged with fraudulent bankruptcy and tax evasion.

The Singapore branch of Moscow Narodny grew rapidly until 1976, when it ran into serious difficulties. At that time, a number of highly risky ventures which it had financed (reportedly including a Bangkok gambling casino and speculative land-development schemes throughout South East Asia and Australia) proved unsound. By the end of 1976, the branch was faced with bad or doubtful debts amounting to an estimated $100 million.[23]

These various incidents prompted personnel changes, tighter parental control and more conservative loan policies. In addition to the losses involved, they served to damage the considerable prestige of Soviet banks abroad which had been based on a hitherto sound and successful record of operations.

The apparent fate of a Soviet bank in Iran suggests that Comecon investments are also not immune to the political risks endemic to multinational enterprises established in less stable areas of the world. The Russo–Iranian Bank, with headquarters in Teheran, was established in 1923 and was the only one of several joint Soviet–Persian ventures formed in the early 1920s to survive into the period after World War II. Wholly-owned after 1954, it remained small, its primary function being to promote bilateral trade. Its fortunes followed the course of Soviet–Iranian relations (a branch was opened in Isfahan in 1974) to 1979, when it was reportedly nationalised with other foreign banks by Iran's new Islamic government.[24]

Hungary and Poland are the only East European countries to have followed the Soviet course of conducting foreign banking operations through subsidiary banks established in the West. (Czechoslovakia's Zivnostenska Banka, based in Prague, retains a branch in London, a carry-over from pre-World War II days, as does Poland's Bank Handlowy w Warszawie.) Of the two Hungarian banks, the Zentral Wechsel-und-Creditbank AG, in Vienna, and the Hungarian International Bank Ltd, in London – both majority-owned by the National Bank of Hungary – the London bank, established in 1973, is the more important. Its specialisation in the trading of short-term paper in the *à forfait* market has proved highly profitable, yielding a reported 96 per cent return on capital and reserves in 1982–83.[25] Like the Hungarian banks, the Mitteleuropäische Handelsbank AG, of Frankfurt, in which the Polish foreign trade bank holds 70 per cent of the equity, engages in a range of international banking operations and participates in small syndications.

The East European countries' banking operations in the Third World are concentrated in the Middle East. The Bulgarian Foreign Trade Bank is the major shareholder in Litex Bank in Beirut, which offers a broad range of banking services and has representative offices in Sofia and London. Litex, together with Venezuelan and Dutch partners, is a minority shareholder in one of Lebanon's leading banks, Byblos Bank. Located in Beirut as well is Bank Handlowy for the Middle East, a subsidiary of Poland's Bank Handlowy w Warszawie. Bank Handlowy is also reported to be a minority shareholder in a Cairo bank.

In the course of the 1970s, the Romanian Bank for Foreign Trade established a series of joint venture banks in important West European locations – Paris, London, Frankfurt and Milan. These ventures, in which the Romanian bank typically maintains 50 per cent of the equity, with the rest held by major local banks, are intended to promote and finance Romania's trade and co-operation with the host countries. Romanian banks have also established a joint venture bank in Cairo in partnership with an Egyptian state-controlled bank, the Misr Bank.

Other East European countries have shown an interest in joint venture banking operations. Bulgaria and Hungary were reported in 1981 to have reached agreement with Kuwait banking institutions for the establishment of a joint bank (in which Austrian interests would also participate) to finance the planning and execution of various projects in third countries.[26] In Vienna, the Centro Internationale Handelsbank AG (Centrobank) is a joint venture bank in which Poland's Bank Handlowy w Warszawie shares equity with Austrian, French, Italian and British banks. While offering a full range of commercial banking services, Centrobank has been especially active in more specialised international financial transactions, such as countertrade.

Hungary and Poland (in London) and Romania (in Geneva) maintain financial companies which also provide specialised services in international trade and project-financing. The Hungarian company, Hibtrade Ltd, established in 1981, is the wholly-owned subsidiary of the Hungarian International Bank of London, in which the National Bank of Hungary is the major shareholder.[27]

It is also interesting to note that the Polish bank for foreign currency operations, Polska Kasa Opieki SA, has subsidiaries in Toronto and New York (the latter with a branch in Chicago) through which Polish consumer goods may be purchased for relatives and friends in Poland. These companies thus serve as a mechanism for tapping the dollar wealth of the large Polish communities in North America.

The two principal Soviet banks abroad, Moscow Narodny and Eurobank, extended their activities into other new areas through the establishment in 1973 with Western banking partners of two joint ventures for lease financing. In both cases, the partners selected were prominent capitalist banks. Moscow Narodny's venture with Morgan Grenfell is located within the latter's headquarters in London and operates under the name East–West Leasing. Its French counterpart is Promolease, in which Credit Lyonnais has a majority holding in partnership with Eurobank. The activities of these companies are not limited to the lease of Western capital equipment to Soviet and East European enterprises; they also rent to Western clients equipment purchased from Comecon sources.

Five of the seven Comecon countries have also invested in insurance operations abroad.[28] Bulgaria's Bulstrad (Bulgarian Foreign Insurance and Reinsurance Co. Ltd) holds 51 per cent of the equity in European Reinsurance Brokers Ltd of London, an insurance brokerage firm. Hungarian, Polish and Romanian state insurance companies are equal partners with American International Underwriters Overseas Ltd (AIUO) of the United States in European American Underwriters Agency GmbH of Vienna. The agency company is the European underwriter for three joint insurance companies which have been incorporated in Bermuda by AIUO together with each of the three East European state insurance companies.

It is the Soviet Union, however, which, in insurance, as in banking, has the most extensive multinational operations. Soviet insurance companies abroad have a similarly long history and are wholly owned by the Soviet state insurance company, Ingosstrakh. Two of the three Ingosstrakh foreign subsidiaries date from the period between the wars. The oldest, Black Sea and Baltic General

Insurance Co. Ltd of London, was established in 1925, while its German counterpart, Schwarzmeer und Ostee Transport-versicherungs AG, was first founded in Hamburg in 1927, and re-established after the war. The third, Garant Versicherungs AG, based in Vienna, has been in operation since 1958. All three under-write Western export and import transactions with the Soviet Union and other East European countries, and thus, like the Soviet banks and leasing companies, are primarily intended to serve the needs of East–West trade. Their operations now extend beyond transport insurance to a full set of insurance services related to East–West trade and industrial co-operation: non-payment insurance, manufacturing-risk insurance and insurance designed tc cover risks incurred over the installation and run-in periods of capital projects. Their diversification has also extended to profitable insurance services unrelated to East–West trade, such as accident, fire and life insurance. Garant provides transit insurance for goods shipped overland from Western Europe to Asia through Eastern Europe and the USSR. Black Sea and Baltic is even reported to have participated in the underwriting of US direct investments in the developing countries, under the expropriation insurance programme of the official US Overseas Private Investment Corporation (OPIC).[29]

TRANSPORT AND OTHER SERVICES

The Comecon countries have also undertaken investments in significant land, sea and air transport operations abroad. Some foreign subsidiaries and affiliates serve as brokers and chandlers for parent enterprises. Others engage directly in chartering or in operating their own equipment to transport cargoes between Comecon and foreign markets and in cross-trade transactions.

Here again the Soviet Union is the salient actor, as the source of nearly half of all Comecon investments in transport services in the West and over a quarter in the South (Tables 3.5 and 3.6). The Soviet principals engaged in multinational maritime transport operations are two state enterprises, Sovfracht and Sovinflot, subordinate to the Ministry of the Merchant Marine. The former holds the state monopoly for maritime freight and forwarding operations, and controls a family of twenty-three companies (in eleven Western countries) which perform brokerage functions in the chartering of both Soviet and foreign vessels.

Sovinflot is the general agent for the international operations of the various Soviet state shipping lines. Its affiliated companies abroad (thirteen in the West and two in the South) secure cargoes, co-ordinate liner activities and generally provide agency services for the Soviet lines. They also organise stevedoring and other services for Soviet vessels in foreign ports. They form part of Sovinflot's extensive foreign network, which includes as well representative offices and local agents employed on commission.

The establishment of Soviet companies in major world maritime centres reflects the rapid development of the Soviet merchant fleet and its operations on a global scale.[30] In order to establish direct foreign bases for their activities, Sovfracht and Sovinflot have bought into, or taken over, foreign agencies, and more occasionally founded new firms. These investments have been designed to ensure that local agency and support operations are managed in accordance with the Soviet Union's increasing international maritime interests and to reduce its hard currency outlays in agency commissions and fees. By establishing their own agencies and facilities in key foreign locations, the two Soviet parent companies are following an institutional path well trodden by their major Western competitors in the maritime shipping industry.

Soviet shipping companies abroad also engage more directly in sea transport. For example, Saimaa Line OY, a Finnish–Soviet shipping company, transports container and bulk cargoes between Western Europe and the Soviet Union. It thereby serves to relieve pressure on Soviet Baltic ports.

Poland and Bulgaria are, after the Soviet Union, the principal Comecon countries with foreign direct investments in maritime transport. The Polish Steamship Co. and Polfracht have subsidiaries in Australia, Belgium and Sweden. The Belgian subsidiary, PSAL, which is an agent for the Polish truck transport firm Pekaes, as well as a ship broker and charterer, has a subsidiary (Baltic Stevedoring and Tallying Co. NV) also located in the port of Antwerp, which provides in-port services for Polish vessels. Polish Ocean Lines has subsidiaries in New York and London, the latter with a branch in Piraeus. The Balkan and Black Sea Shipping Co. Ltd of London, wholly owned by Voden Transport of Sofia, provides marine insurance as well as a variety of maritime transport services, and itself has subsidiaries in Antwerp and Piraeus. Poland, Bulgaria, Romania and Hungary have all invested in maritime transport operations in locations in the Third World.[31]

Overland transport has also been an area of growing multinational activity by Comecon enterprises. These investments have been undertaken not only in support of the home countries' foreign trade, but also for the trans-shipment of goods overland between Europe and Asia, a route which has gained increasing importance. Transport subsidiaries have customarily provided technical support as well as agency services. The Soviet foreign trade organisation, Soyuzvneshtrans, has established subsidiary companies in Cologne, Vienna, Teheran and Kabul to provide storage, transport and forwarding services and to co-ordinate the activities of foreign agents employed for the transportation of goods in transit.[32] Bulgaria's International Road Transport Co. (SOMAT) has subsidiaries in Austria, the Federal Republic of Germany, Egypt and Togo. Hungary's Hungarocamion International Road Transport Co. has formed a network of forwarding agents through Eastern and Western Europe and the Middle East, and has its own representatives in major commercial centres. It also has set up subsidiary companies in Vienna, Trieste and Kuwait. Its company in Beirut, Lebanon Gulf Europa, became inoperative in 1979, while its Teheran subsidiary, Iran–Magyaristan Transport Ltd, with offices in Munich and Budapest, was liquidated following the Iranian Revolution.

The Comecon state airlines typically maintain representative offices in major commercial centres and work through local agents. The former have at times been locally incorporated as legally independent firms, while the latter have on occasion been converted to subsidiary operations. Foreign investment in this aspect of transport services is comparatively rare, however, and the sums involved are small.

Depending upon their location, foreign subsidiaries may be active in land, sea and air transport services. Hartwig, the Polish international forwarding firm, has subsidiaries in France, Germany, the United States and the United Kingdom, which arrange various modes of transport. The German Democratic Republic and Czechoslovakia have a joint venture company in London, Intrasped (a rare example of joint equity by state enterprises of more than one Comecon country), which acts as a general freight and transport broker as well as a chartering agent.

The scope of Soviet and East European foreign investment in the service sector extends well beyond the areas of marketing, financing and transport. These further service activities, whose frequency, as indicated by Tables 3.5 and 3.6 (see pages 38–9 and 40–1), is relatively ow, but somewhat greater in the South than in the West, can only very summarily be described in conclusion.

Engineering consulting firms which provide technical services to clients in a wide range of industries account for an important share. They function, in the developing countries, in support of capital projects with inputs of equipment, technology and credits from Comecon countries. Several mixed companies have also been established in the West to encourage, and furnish services to, joint East–West development projects in partner or third countries. The Soviet–Italian company Tecnicon in Genoa, the Polish–Austrian firm Technoprojekt in Vienna and the Bulgarian–Japanese company Atlas Engineering in Tokyo, are examples, as is the Romanian–West German company Rodeco in Bad Homburg, which has branches in Bogota, Khartoum and Bujumbura.

Construction firms have also been set up in the developing countries to play a role in carrying out capital projects usually in conjunction with other, East European, material, technical or financial contributions. Romania has been especially active in this regard, with construction companies established in Kenya, Libya and Morocco. Czechoslovakia's Skoda Engineering (Pilsen) has a construction subsidiary in India. Almost all of the Comecon countries have established construction firms in Nigeria (see Chapter 7).

The Soviet Union has several companies established in the West based on its own computer technology. The Soviet foreign trade organisation for electronic equipment, Electronorgtechnica, has invested in subsidiaries in Belgium, Finland and The Netherlands which not only market Soviet computer hardware but also rent computer time and provide software services on a contractual basis to local customers. These services earn revenue but, more importantly, are intended to promote sales of equipment by familiarising local firms with the capabilities of Soviet-built computers.

They are also a useful link to developments and trends in the Western computer industry. This information-gathering function was on one occasion pushed too far. In April 1976, the Soviet director of the Dutch subsidiary, Elorg BV, V. T. Khlystov, was expelled from The Netherlands following official allegations that he had used the company's resources to obtain confidential information about the aircraft production of the North Atlantic Treaty Organisation (NATO).[33]

Finally, wholly-owned and mixed companies have also been organised in the area of consumer services, such as travel, hotel and restaurant services. The latter are typically based on national cuisines, wines and beers. Since East European know-how in such cases is not easily transferable, it can most effectively be exploited commercially through direct investment in restaurant and catering facilities. The well-known Budapest restaurant, Matyaspince (Matthew's Cellar) has well-established branches in Vienna and Munich. During the 1970s, the Zlata Praha, a Czechoslovak-owned restaurant in the business area of Vienna, was staffed by employees who commuted daily from nearby border towns in Slovakia.

NOTES AND REFERENCES

1. The Hungarian perspective in this regard is clearly reflected in an interview in 1979 with the Deputy Minister of Foreign Trade (see Ch. 4 n. 42, p. 76). For a shared Soviet view, see Engibarov, *Smeshannye Obshchestva na Mirovom Rynke, op. cit.*

2. The product profile of Polish marketing companies is obscured by the activities of the numerous DAL companies, which cover a wide range of goods and·hence fall under the 'miscellaneous' goods category. A relatively high share of Romanian companies are also engaged in non-specialised marketing.

3. On the organisation and general international operations of DAL, see *Polish Foreign Trade*, No. 5, 1977 and No. 4, 1979.

4. Transakta merged with its compatriot foreign trade organisation Fincom in the late 1970s thus extending its foreign investments, especially in the Third World, to production as well as commercial operations. See also Chapter 6.

5. Strojimport's international operations are described in *Czechoslovak Foreign Trade*, No. 4, 1983. It absorbed the functions of the foreign trade organisation Investa in July 1983, extending its sphere of activities to a broader range of machinery exports.

6. A good account of the activities of Hungarotex may be found in *Marketing in Hungary*, No. 1, 1977.

7. For the development of Soyuznefteexport's operations, see the article occasioned by its fiftieth anniversary, in *Foreign Trade*, No. 5, 1981.

8. On Tungsram's history, organisation and international operations, see *Hungarian Foreign Trade*, No. 3, 1977 and *New Hungarian Exporter*, June 1983.

9. See also Chapter 4 for information on the origins of the company.

10. The Skoda Engineering Works at Pilsen are represented abroad by Skodaexport. It has several subsidiaries in locations in the Third World through which it carries out industrial development projects.

11. On Balkancar's international operations, see *Economic News of Bulgaria*. No. 6, 1977 and No. 10, 1978 and *Sofia News*, 8 February 1984.

12. *Rynki Zagraniczne*, 31 May 1983.

13. M. Hill, 'Soviet and East European Multinational Activity in the United Kingdom and the Republic of Ireland', Paper put out by the Department of Management Studies, University of Technology, Loughborough, March 1983, p. 39. Hill found some evidence to indicate that companies selling services (especially transport services) were more profitable than those selling products.

14. Engibarov, *Smeshannye Obschestva na Mirorom Rynke*, *op. cit.*, p. 10. The example refers to exports of automotive products.

15. Pulawski, 'A Method for Evaluating Polish Joint Ventures Operating Abroad', *Soviet and East European Foreign Trade*, Fall 1979 (translated from *Handel Zagraniczny*, No. 12, 1977).

16. Differences over business strategy and tactics between Comecon and local managerial personnel have occasionally surfaced in the Press. The French founder of the Soviet–French Slava watch company was ousted in 1983 in a publicised dispute. See *Les Echos*, 17 August 1983, p. 6.

17. Lenin stressed the role of banks, including their direct operations through branches abroad, as important instruments of capitalist imperialism. (Lenin, *Imperialism*, *op. cit.*, Chs. III and IV.) For further discussion of Soviet and East European banking operations abroad, see A. Zwass, *Monetary Cooperation between East and West* (White Plains, New York: International Arts and Sciences Press, 1976), p. 215 *et seq.*; Wilczynski, *The Multinationals and East–West Relations*, *op. cit.*, p. 144 *et seq.*; S. Tyrka, 'Multinationalisation des activités bancaires des pays de l'Est', *Banque*, October 1976; Rabin, 'Soviet-Owned Banks in Europe: their Development and Contribution to Trade with the West', unpublished Ph.D dissertation, The Johns Hopkins University, 1977; Wilczynski, *Comparative Monetary Economics* (London: Macmillan, 1978) pp. 42–9; and Danylyk and Rabin, 'Soviet-Owned Banks in the West', in *Soviet Economy in a Time of Change*, Vol. 2 (Washington, DC: US Government Printing Office, for the Joint Economic Commission, US Congress, 1979) pp. 482–505.

18. For detail on the operations of individual Soviet banks abroad, see Danylyk and Rabin, *ibid.* and Harrison, *op. cit.*

19. In this regard, it may be noted that the Soviet foreign trade organisation, Almazjuviler-export, established a subsidiary (Russalmaz AG) in Frankfurt in 1974 to trade in gems, precious metals and jewellery.

20. K. Robbie traces this involvement in 'Socialist Banks and the Origins of the Euro-currency Markets', *Moscow Narodny Bank Quarterly Review*, Winter 1975/76.

21. Rabin, 'Soviet-Owned Banks in Europe', *op. cit.*, pp. 128–9.

22. See N. McInnes, 'Ivan the Capitalist', *Barron's*, 13 December 1976.

23. Wilczynski, 'East–West Banking and Finance and their Relevance to Australian and Canadian Interests' (East–West Commercial Relations Series, No. 9, Institute of Soviet and East European Studies, Carleton University, Ottawa, February 1978) p. 35. As a result of defaults on its loans, the bank has acquired control of properties in Singapore and Hong Kong. Some observers have seen the entire incident as a ploy to

acquire important assets which would purportedly otherwise not have been allowed into Soviet hands. (See *Soviet Analyst*, 11 October 1978, pp. 5–6 and Times–Post News Service dispatch from Hong Kong in *The Citizen*, 19 October 1978, p. 49.) Monab Nominees Pte. Ltd another Singapore subsidiary of the London bank, may be the vehicle through which Soviet equity in these properties is held.

24. *The Arab Economist*, July 1979, p. 28. On the other hand, an article by an Iranian specialist cites (without further details or documentation) the bank's exemption from nationalisation as an example of 'numerous cases of Iranian indulgence of the USSR'. (See S. Chubin, 'The Soviet Union and Iran', *Foreign Affairs*, Spring 1983, p. 933.) Whether or not the Soviet bank was nationalised at the same time or under the same conditions as other foreign banking assets in Iran, its operations have apparently ceased. (The author is grateful for help from Charles Drace-Francis on this point.)

25. *Financial Times*, 7 December 1983, p. 18.

26. *Bulgarian Foreign Trade*, No. 2, 1983, p. 10.

27. Similarly engaged in specialised international financing, but based in Budapest, is Hungary's first 'off-shore' bank, the *Central European International Bank Ltd*, a joint venture combining Hungarian, Austrian, French, German, Italian and Japanese partner-banks, founded in 1979.

28. All of these are located in the West, although their operations may cover activities in the South.

29. *The Times*, 24 April 1972, as reported and discussed in *Radio Liberty Dispatch*, 27 April 1972. While this may have been simply a co-operative gesture at the height of *détente*, it could also have been intended to encourage Western firms to subcontract portions of Third World projects to Comecon suppliers.

30. See C. Haymen, 'Soviet Shipping', *Seatrade*, February 1976; *Soviet Oceans Development* (Washington, DC: US Government Printing Office, for the Committee on Commerce, US Congress, 1976) and The Atlantic Council of the United States, *The Soviet Merchant Marine* (Boulder, Colorado: Westview Press for the Council, 1979).

31. Singapore and Beirut are favoured locations.

32. In some cases, Soyuzvneshtrans operates through companies abroad jointly owned with Sovfracht. Its company in Iran, IRSOTR, apparently continues to operate, with increased Iranian participation.

33. According to Press reports, the authorities' decision did not affect Elorg's operating status and Khylstov was replaced by a new Soviet director.

CHAPTER 6

Dynamics of Investment in Production Facilities Abroad

Ideological principles, political considerations and financial constraints have all served to impede foreign investment in what, in socialist parlance, is called the 'sphere of material production'. None the less, the capital of Comecon multinational enterprises has by no means been limited to the service sector. All of the Comecon countries except the German Democratic Republic have increasingly invested in production facilities abroad, in both the West and the South.

This chapter will examine more closely the nature and scope of this activity. Because of the importance of the subject for any evaluation of the potential significance of direct investment from Comecon sources in the evolution of multinational enterprises worldwide, special attention will be paid to the dynamics of investment in this sphere. It will be convenient for the purposes of analysis to treat production abroad for foreign markets separately from foreign production for the home market.

FROM EXPORT MARKETING TO FOREIGN PRODUCTION

There is a generally observed tendency for foreign investments undertaken initially in support of the marketing abroad of home-country products to extend to forms of production abroad for the foreign market.[1] This evolution from marketing to production may occur within an existing subsidiary. It may also take place through the acquisition or establishment by the parent enterprise of foreign production facilities which assume the form of a separately organised company.

When the foreign market for the home product develops to a certain point, it often becomes apparent that it can no longer be served exclusively from production facilities in the home country. Under a variety of conditions which have been analysed in the Western literature, arms-length supply of the market is found to be inferior to on-site production.[2] In the case of the Soviet Union and East

Europe, investment in foreign production is further stimulated by systemic obstacles to flexible supply from the home base of goods suited for foreign consumption. A Comecon product which is otherwise competitive often cannot be sold because of poor or inappropriate styling or finishing. It is in this area of product adaptation and finishing that foreign manufacturing facilities are perceived as particularly useful.

The beginnings of the evolution occur in the marketing sphere, with the extension of subsidiary activities beyond agency functions to import-export operations and related warehousing and distribution. The next step is into retailing, through direct outlets or dealer franchises. Manufactured goods usually require pre-sale or after-sale testing and servicing, and hence the availability of technical support. It is the technical service centres established to perform these functions which often form the nucleus of future production facilities. This occurs as the demands of the user and the regulations of the host government (technical stipulations, local content rules, so on) push the progression further, into more elaborate pre-sale adaptation of the product to local requirements. Product adaptation may then entail the addition of foreign components and technology. In this way, what begins as a marketing venture becomes increasingly an extensive, if low-grade, form of manufacturing, carrying out such tasks as the modification of the imported product and the assembly of imported components. These operations in turn can evolve into more intensive forms of production.

The growth of an Avtoexport (USSR) subsidiary in Finland, established in 1947, illustrates this evolution.[3] The exclusive agent in Finland of the parent enterprise, the subsidiary Konela Oy, markets Soviet automobiles, motor cycles and trucks through some fifty shops and eighty-six service stations across Finland, organised into eight branches, each with its own showroom and technical service centre. In addition, Konela has organised a programme to train Finnish garage mechanics in the care and maintenance of Soviet cars and trucks. It sold nearly 150,000 vehicles between its inception and 1975, with more recent annual sales estimated to be in the range of 10,000–12,000 vehicles, representing approximately 10 per cent of the automotive market in Finland.[4]

Konela also has a large import-preparation centre at Raippo, which can handle up to fifty vehicles a day. Because of the difficulties involved in getting Soviet manufacturers to prepare vehicles suited to the Finnish market, Konela has become heavily involved in the preparation, and in some cases the extensive alteration, of imported vehicles. The company inspects, and paints some parts of, all cars before they go on sale. It has also undertaken to remodel some vehicles prior to marketing. For example, Konela extended the wheelbase of one truck model, and installed a Perkins diesel engine and a Western transmission system, to better suit it to Finnish conditions. Konela has also installed small, foreign-made diesel engines in many of the taxis it sells, finding demand for these to have strengthened following the 1973 oil crisis.

Another Avtoexport subsidiary, Scaldia-Volga, SA, founded in 1964 and located in Brussels, has carried the progression further. It maintains over 300 service stations and sales outlets through which it annually markets about 20,000 vehicles (a range of Soviet models) in the Benelux countries. Scaldia-Volga engages in assembly operations, as well as modification of imported vehicles, and fits a significant share of its output with Western components (engines, tyres, seats and other equipment).[5]

The extension of Soviet foreign investment into production is not limited to automobiles, nor even to machinery and equipment. A Finnish marketing subsidiary of Sojuznefteexport (USSR), OY Teboil AB, has established its own plant for the production of oil-based lubricants.[6] Nafta-B NV, the Belgian subsidiary of Soyuznefteexport, was variously reported in the 1970s to be considering the extension of its large-scale petroleum marketing operations and facilities to oil refining, through the construction of a refinery in Antwerp to process crude oil, primarily from the Soviet Union. The project was never carried out, but could be revived if market conditions were favourable.

As Tables 6.1 and 6.2 show, Hungary has been the most enterprising Comecon country in serving external markets through foreign manufacturing operations. These have tended to be concentrated in several areas in which Hungarian firms have demonstrated export strength on these markets: medical equipment, pharmaceuticals and electrical lighting products.

Hungary's Medicor, one of the world's largest manufacturers and exporters of medical equipment, has invested in companies in West Germany and in the United States to assemble, market and service Hungarian X-ray and other medical equipment.[7] In 1971, Medicor established a company in the United Kingdom, in partnership with a British firm, to produce and market miniature batteries. The

Table 6.1   Major Comecon investments in manufacturing in the West,[a]
end-1983

Company name and country of location	Product
Bulgaria	
Cetef (France)	truck tyres; foundary equipment
Contech C. Conradty-Technika Coating (FRG)	protective graphite coating
Rheinische Maschinenfabrik und Eisengiesserei A. Röper (FRG)	foundry equipment, machine tools
Gaelpirin Teoranta (Ireland)[b]	leather materials
Czechoslovakia	
Omnitrade (Canada)[c]	mining equipment
Semex (FRG)[c]	specialised truck and other transport equipment
Poland	
Tasmanian Alkaloids (Australia)[b]	pharmaceuticals
Mecobel (Belgium)	automatic measuring devices
Unidal (Canada)[b]	bicycles
Soviet Union	
Scaldia-Volga (Belgium)	automobiles
Fexima (Finland)	refrigerators
Teboil (Finland)	lubricants
Actif-Auto (France)	machinery and equipment
Rusbois (France)	wood products
Slava (France)	watches, clocks
Hungary	
Aurora-Honig (Austria)	foodstuffs
Metex (Austria)	steel products
Tungsram (Austria)	lighting materials
3-F (Denmark)[b]	radio and television sets
Optifaro (FRG)	pharmaceuticals
Romed (FRG)	medical equipment
Tuttlinger (FRG)	medical equipment
Hellenic Alloyed Steels (Greece)[b]	metallurgical products
Tungsram Manufacturers (Ireland)[b]	lighting materials
Byggin-Ungern (Sweden)	construction equipment
Labatec Pharma (Switzerland)	pharmaceuticals
Medicharge (UK)[b]	miniature batteries
Action Tungsram (US)	lighting materials
Medicor USA (US)	medical equipment

[a] Cumulative list, as of the end of 1983; includes assembly operations but not modification of imported product.
[b] No longer operative, or Comecon equity is liquidated.
[c] Companies engaged secondarily in manufacturing; hence not so classified in Table 3.5.

Source: Comecon Foreign Investment Data Bank, East–West Project, Carleton University, Ottawa; for details of companies see *The East–West Business Directory*.

Table 6.2 Distribution of Comecon investments in manufacturing in the West and South by category of product, end-1983 (number of investments)[a]

Product category	Bulgaria	Czecho-slovakia	East Germany	Hungary	Poland	Romania	Soviet Union	Total
Machinery and equipment	6	8	1	11	3	2	2	33
Petroleum products	0	0	0	0	0	1	1	2
Pharmaceuticals	1	0	0	8	3	2	0	14
Raw and semi-processed materials	1	1	0	2	1	3	1	9
Textiles	0	0	0	0	2	0	0	2
Food products	0	0	0	2	2	0	0	4
Other consumer goods	2	4	0	8	4	1	2	21
Total	10	13	1	31	15	9	6	85

[a] All but one (Czechoslovak) case of investments in manufacturing could be classified by product category.

Source: Comecon Foreign Investment Data Bank, East–West Project, Carleton University, Ottawa.

arrangement was based on technology furnished by the Hungarian enterprise. Medicor's 30 per cent equity in the joint venture company was later liquidated.[8]

Medicor has also invested in production facilities in the developing countries. It has plants in Jamaica, Bolivia, Uruguay, Peru and Brazil which serve the Central and South American markets. It also has a production venture in Nigeria. Its plant in Iran, set up in 1977, fell victim to the disruptions which accompanied the Islamic Revolution.

Hungarian technology contributes to the operations of a German company in which Hungary's Medimpex has 50 per cent holding. The company, Optifaro Pharmazeutische Produkte GmbH, located in Dörtmund, manufactures and markets pharmaceuticals based on Hungarian licences and know-how. It also makes use of the laboratory facilities of the Western partner to develop new pharmaceutical products for the West European market.[9] A Hungarian–Swiss company with 40 employees, located in Geneva, is also engaged in the production as well as marketing of pharmaceutical products.

Medimpex has been even more active in the South. It has pharmaceutical plants in India, Nigeria and Bangladesh, and has been negotiating for the establishment of additional plants in Thailand and Sri Lanka. These facilities typically produce pharmaceuticals for the local market on the basis of semi-finished products from Hungary.

In the third area of export strength, electrical and lighting products, Hungary's multinational enterprise, Tungsram, has added substantial foreign production facilities to its network of foreign marketing subsidiaries described in Chapter 5. Its long-established Austrian subsidiary, with 360 employees, manufactures a range of incandescent lamp bulbs and fittings. The output is marketed in Europe and the Near East, and sales in 1980 exceeded $25 million. Tungsram has set up additional plants in the United States and Ireland.

The Irish subsidiary, Tungsram Manufacturers (Ireland) Ltd, located in County Cork, was cited earlier as an instance of a Comecon response to investment assistance programmes put out by the host country.[10] Ireland was chosen both because of the generous tax incentives and subsidies offered by the Irish Development Authority as well as its location inside the European Common Market.[11] Production at the Irish facility was to be based on Hungarian technology (light-bulb assembly machines) and components imported from Hungary. The initial rate of production was set at twenty million bulbs per year, with eighty-five persons employed. There were plans – and plant capacity – for subsequent expansion.

After little more than two full years of operation, Tungsram's experience in Ireland ended in costly failure. The outlays incurred in the Irish and American ventures, as well as low overall profitability of operations, had by mid-1983 forced the parent into serious financial difficulties. In these circumstances, it announced in February 1984 that it was shutting down the Irish subsidiary, which had proved too ambitious for market conditions in the recession and had been plagued by labour difficulties.[12]

As part of the expansion of its overseas production facilities, Tungsram opened a plant (Aslo Electric Company) near Karachi in 1980. Tungsram has also taken equity in plants in other Third World locations, notably Nigeria and Sri Lanka, and elsewhere it has equipped a number of factories on a turn-key basis, without formal equity participation.

Bulgarian state enterprises have recently emerged as important Comecon sources of investment in production facilities in the West. Most of this activity has, in fact, occurred in the 1980s. Manufacturing subsidiaries, employing Bulgarian technology under licence, have been established through Bulgarian equity participation in the Federal Republic of Germany (1974) and in France (1981). Bulgarian enterprises have also been involved in attempted take-overs of well-established Western manufacturing firms. One of these was successful, the other not. Because they represent a new direction in Comecon foreign-invesment policy, these cases are worth examining individually.

The successful attempt occurred in late 1981, when Bulgarian interests, headed by Machinoexport, acquired full ownership of Rheinische Maschinenfabrik und Eisengiesserei Anton Röper, a medium-sized, family-owned firm established in 1916. Röper produces foundry machinery and machine tools, including fully automated machine drills. The West German firm, with 420 employees, had sales in 1981 of nearly $20 million, of which exports accounted for 60 per cent (in Europe, as well as to Africa and the Americas).[13] The take-over gave the Bulgarian partners access to Röper's technology and its long-standing links to other German and European manufacturers. It also provided a springboard to already established international markets.

The second, unsuccessful, attempt attracted considerable attention in 1983, when Balkancar bid for a stake in France's leading fork-lift truck manufacturer, Fenwick-Manutention.[14] The French government originally gave a green light to the Bulgarian bid, which was attractive both in terms of Balkancar's strength as the leading world producer, and the impact on jobs in the French industry relative to competitive offers. In the face of public outcry over the Bulgarian acquisition of what would probably be a controlling (if minority) interest in so large a national firm (nearly 2,000 employees), the French government later abandoned its support, and approval was ultimately given to an arrangement combining a leading West German manufacturer with a subsidiary of the French IDI, the partly state-owned vehicle for the promotion of industrial development in France.

Both Röper and Fenwick-Manutention were ailing companies, suffering from acute shortages of funds for investment. Bulgaria, having enjoyed positive trade balances with the West in recent years, was in a stronger position than other East European countries to take advantage of the possibilities which the Western recession afforded for attractive acquisitions. The companies in question offered Bulgarian state enterprises the potential benefits of established facilities and already developed markets in the West which they could integrate into their existing systems of production for the world market. This was especially true of Fenwick-Manutention, to which Balkancar reportedly intended to shift important lines of production.

The particular significance of these two cases, therefore, is that they represent the first important instances of a shift of East European foreign-investment activity to what is generally regarded as a more advanced stage of multinational enterprise. Most examples of Comecon investment in foreign manufacturing facilities fall under the heading of what a leading French specialist on multinational enterprises, Charles-Albert Michalet, has called the *filiale relais* (relay subsidiary). These are subsidiaries which produce for the particular foreign market in which they are located. The two recent Bulgarian investments bids belong to a category which Michalet classifies as the *filiale-atelier* (workshop subsidiary). These are production subsidiaries which play a specialised role in the integrated, international production systems of the parent multinational enterprises.[15]

To turn again to the Third World, if Hungarian state enterprises here, as in the West, have been the leading Comecon investors in manufacturing facilities, then Bulgarian, Czechoslovak, Polish and Romanian enterprises have also been active. The author is unaware, however, of any Soviet investments in the manufacturing industries of the Third World, and investment activity by the German Democratic Republic has been negligible. East European investments have been principally in machinery-assembly plants (motor vehicles – cars, motor cycles and scooters, trucks, buses – machine tools, tractors and other agricultural equipment) as well as in various light-industry operations (pharmaceutical and clothing manufacture and food-processing, for example). Table 6.2 summarises the distribution, by category of product, of Comecon investments in manufacturing in both the West and the South.

An example is the Bibiani Metal Complex in Ghana, in which Poland's Metalexport and DAL have a combined 50 per cent holding, with the remaining share held by the Ghana Cocoa Marketing Board, the State Mining Corporation and the Ghana Investment Bank. In the early 1970s, the Ghanaian government wished to make use of the industrial facilities remaining from a former gold-mining operation. Metalexport won the bid for a plant to manufacture agricultural implements on the basis of imported Polish machine tools and technology. The plant, with assets valued at 1.3 million cedis ($1.1 million) began operations in 1975, employing over 100 former miners trained by Polish technicians.[16]

FOREIGN SOURCING FOR HOME INDUSTRY

Comecon foreign investment has also been directed to foreign sourcing of raw materials, intermediate goods and, more occasionally, final products, which are primarily but not solely for home use.[17] The bulk of these investments have been in the primary sector, but they have also involved the manufacturing industries. In the case of the investment activity reviewed in the preceding section, considerations of market proximity have generally been the major, if by no means the only, determinants. In the cases to which the discussion now turns, cost factors, having to do with the relative availability of labour and material inputs, have provided the primary impetus.

Manufacturing

A share of the investments in foreign manufacturing analysed i
Table 6.2 are directed at serving home demand, exclusively o
while also serving the requirements of the foreign markets. Th
increasing scarcity of labour in the Comecon countries has dictated
search for convenient, low-cost foreign-production locations
especially for more labour-intensive operations.

Foreign-based textile operations have, for these reasons, been a
object of interest for Comecon enterprises, as they have fo
multinational enterprises in the West. Three Polish enterprises
DAL, Textilimpex and Varimex, joined with local partners in 197.
to establish the Western Textile Company in Iran. In addition to 4
per cent of the equity, the Poles supplied most of the equipment an
technical know-how for the company's first plant, near Kermanshah
Equipped with 25,000 spindles, the plant had an annual capacity o
more than 2,000 tons of cotton yarn. Under the arrangement
Textilimpex was to purchase 80 per cent of the output. Plans fo
expansion of the facilities to double this capacity and rais
employment to 1,200 workers were brought to a halt by the Irania
revolution. Textilimpex maintains a similar sourcing arrangemen
(Poltex) in Brazil, importing textiles fabrics from the Brazilia
subsidiary.

In the late 1970s, the Hungarians negotiated for the establishmen
of cotton-spinning mills in Iran, Egypt and Greece. All were t
produce primarily for export to Hungary. None of these efforts t
shift textile production to foreign locations came to fruition, and th
failure of the project in Greece, which had been carried the furthes
but had encountered a variety of obstacles which made the projec
unworkable, was a particular disappointment.[18]

The leather-processing industry provides further examples. A no
defunct Czechoslovak venture in Iran (International Leather
produced primarily for the Iranian shoe industry, but surplu
production was exported to Czechoslovakia. In 1981, a Bulgarian
Irish mixed company was set up in County Galway (Gaelpirir
Teoranta) to process sheepskins for the Bulgarian leather-garmen
industry using machinery and know-how supplied by the Bulgarians
The company was also to supply various kinds of leather for use i
the Bulgarian shoe industry.[19]

In these cases, the choice of the foreign location is determined no
just by direct wage costs. The welfare programmes in the Comeco

ountries mean that the total labour payments by the state can be
wo to three times higher than the direct wage cost. Relative
roductivity levels also weigh into the calculation. Wage costs were
stimated to be higher in Greece than in Hungary, for example,
ut not total labour costs.

Calculations of relative costs of production evidently incorporate
ther costs as well, notably the cost of material inputs. Textile and
eather manufacturing operations abroad were designed to process
oreign raw materials, to which they would provide easier access.

Czechoslovakia, which faces a more severe labour-force constraint
han do Hungary and Poland, has also pushed this strategy into
nore sophisticated industries. A subsidiary in Brazil, Centrimpex,
nanufactures tyres, all of which are exported to Czechoslovakia.
'hrough the agency of Fincom (later Transakta), Czechoslovak
nterprises have also shifted several specialised manufacturing
perations to Malta. Fincom took a 40 per cent equity in two mixed
ompanies in Malta, both formed in 1977. One manufactures
iydraulic components on the basis of Czechoslovak specifications
nd parts and these are then brought back to Czechoslovakia for
inal assembly. The other company uses Czechoslovak-made
omponents to assemble precision instruments, which are then
hipped back to the home country. As a result of these operations,
he turnover of bilateral trade more than quadrupled in value
etween 1976 and 1979.[20]

Another interesting and illustrative case is the acquisition in 1978
y Hungary's Interag, in partnership with Tungsram, through a
vholly-owned holding company in Luxembourg, of the controlling
iterest in a Danish manufacturer of radios, television sets and
tereo equipment. The interest acquired in the Danish company (3-F
'abrikken of Horsens) had formerly been held by Rank Xerox
UK). In 1978 the company had a work force of 140 and produced
oods valued at $13.2 million. A fire in the plant, combined with a
lack market, prompted Rank Xerox to close it. The Danish
iunicipal authorities then sought another investor, to protect local
mployment, and approached the Hungarians. Interag hoped to
iake the ailing Danish operation profitable by adding the Hungarian
iarket to 3-F's traditional markets, in Denmark and elsewhere in
Vestern Europe. The Hungarian initiative proved a major and
ostly mistake, however, and by 1981 the Danish operation was
nder liquidation. The problems encountered included the difficulty
f adapting to two television technologies: Secam, the French system

used by the Comecon countries, and PAL, the German system used in Denmark. Also, Hungarian components had proved both costly and unreliable.[21]

Extraction and Processing of Raw Materials

Comecon investments in primary industries abroad have a somewhat longer history than those in manufacturing. Most have been directed to the developing economies. Of the fifty-six cases of investments in primary production activities reported in Tables 3.5 and 3.6, only seven were located in the OECD economies.

Fisheries constitute the activity which have attracted the most direct investments in the primary sector (representing nearly all such investments in the West). Here the Soviet Union has been the most active Comecon country, followed by Poland. Sovrybflot, a state enterprise subordinate to the Soviet Ministry of Fisheries, is engaged in multinational fishing operations and related activities on a world-wide scale.[22] These are performed through mixed companies, with Sovrybflot (and occasionally other Soviet enterprises) typically holding at least 50 per cent of the equity.[23] In the West, Sovrybflot has invested directly in fishing operations in France, New Zealand, Spain, Sweden and the United States. These companies provide port and service facilities to the Soviet fishing fleet and its factory ships, serve a liaison between the fleet, shore authorities and local fishermen, and market part of the processed catch locally. The remainder stays in Soviet hands for home consumption or re-export. Sovrybflot also has other companies – in Italy, New Zealand, Spain and Sweden – which are engaged exclusively in marketing the Soviet catch or in providing technical services to the Soviet fishing fleet. In the South Sovrybflot has established similar sets of operations. Almost all the Soviet fishing companies in the Third World are located in coastal states of Africa.[24]

As suggested earlier, the establishment of mixed companies of this nature has in large part been in response to the creation of exclusive, off-shore economic zones by coastal states. These regulated zones threatened, in the mid-1970s, to disrupt the operations of the Soviet fishing fleet, in which the Soviet Union had invested heavily over the previous decade. As a result, the following years, especially 1974–6, saw the rapid proliferation of Soviet investments in foreign fisheries.[25] The establishment of mixed companies permits Sovrybflot to share in the partner's national privileges with regard to catch quotas.

Two examples will serve to illustrate this impetus. In 1976, Sovrybflot entered into partnership with Bellingham Cold Storage Co., of Bellingham, Washington, USA to create Marine Resources Co. Under the set of contracts which outline the arrangement, American fishing boats deliver hake to Soviet floating factory ships. After processing, a part of the catch is shipped on American refrigerator vessels to the American partner, which is responsible for marketing the joint product in the United States.[26] In France, in the same year, Sovrybflot established a mixed company, Fransov (based in Cannes), with a French firm, Casacrus, and several minor French partners.[27] The joint venture was formed to secure licences from the French authorities, particularly for French overseas territories, and to gain access to the coastal waters of African nations with which France has maintained special ties. Fransov has also been used as a channel for investment in mixed companies in Africa with Soviet equity involvement.[28]

It has occasionally been alleged that Soviet investments in joint fishing operations, especially in the Third World, have been motivated by military and strategic considerations, since they have coincided with the growth of Soviet naval power. By helping to ensure access to coastal waters and to support facilities on shore, joint companies may in some areas have potential strategic significance. For the most part, however, the activity of multinational enterprises in the fishing industry appears to be dictated primarily by the straightforward economic objective of ensuring the Soviet fishing fleet an adequate catch.

Poland has been the only other Comecon country with widespread multinational investments in fisheries, having formed joint ventures in New Zealand and Sweden in the West, and Peru, Morocco, Senegal, Nigeria, the Phillippines and India in the South. In these instances, the principal Polish enterprise involved is Rybex. The nature of these joint companies and the motivation for their creation are similar to the cases in the Soviet Union.

The other major area of primary production activity in which Comecon state enterprises are found to be involved on the scale of a multinational enterprise is that of metal ores and minerals extraction and processing. Here Romania comes to the fore, with its more marked strategy of developing extra-regional sources of raw materials as alternatives to Comecon, especially Soviet, supplies. It is Romania's investments in this area that give it pre-eminence as the most active Comecon country in terms of the number of direct investments in the Third World (see Table 3.6).

The Romanian state enterprise principally involved in these investments is Geomin. Officially designated as an 'enterprise fo co-operation in the mining industry and in geology', Geomin i charged with executing a variety of tasks abroad, including prospecting, research, technical assistance, construction and the organisation of production activities through equity participation.[2] Most of Geomin's exploration and mining ventures (in which it equity shares vary from 25 to 49 per cent) are in Africa, with other in South America and the Middle East. Copper mining is an industr of particular investment interest. In these cases, the host country' contribution, on which its majority holding is based, is the minera rights, with the Romanian partner undertaking to finance the cost of bringing the mine into operation.

Another Romanian enterprise, Mineralimportexport, has minorit shares in joint ventures directed to the development of iron or deposits in Guinea and Gabon. It is interesting to note that, unlik most Comecon mixed companies in the Third World, these venture also involve Western firms as equity partners.[30]

Romania's only mining interest in the West is in the Unite States, and is not strictly a direct investment. Apparently for ta reasons, Mineralimportexport chose not to take an equity interest i Garden Creek Coal Co., in Virginia, owned by Island Creek Coa Co., a wholly-owned subsidiary of Occidental Petroleum Corp. Th Romanian Bank for Foreign Trade did, however, provide $5 million in funds for the development of one of the Garden Cree coal mines, under a 1975 agreement, and in return Romania is t receive one third of the million-ton annual output, with an option t purchase another third.[31] The arrangement thus falls within th compensation format, described in Chapter 2.

Hungary invested directly in the American coal industry, in partner ship with Island Creek Coal, with the formation in 1981 of a join company, Tata-Island Creek Coal Recovery Co., in which eac partner has an equal equity share. The objective of the venture is t set up a processing plant to recycle coal slag, using a patente Hungarian coal recovery process and the related equipment an know-how. The partners hope to construct other similar plants i the United States and to market the technology internationally.[32]

In final areas of primary production activity – agriculture an forestry – again, Romania is found to be the predominant acto These investments, too, are for the most part located in Africa Romania's Romagrimex has invested in farms and nurseries, poultr ınd livestock-breeding facilities and various agro-industrial activities. These are usually of an experimental or innovative nature and perform a technical-assistance as well as a business function. Romania's Forexim has established companies for the exploitation, ındustrialisation and marketing of wood and wood products in a ıumber of countries in Africa and the Middle East. In several of these cases, Forexim's equity represents a majority holding.

Given the strong interest of the Comecon countries, especially the East European states, in Middle Eastern and Libyan oil, it is ınteresting to note that the instances of their direct investment in Third World petroleum production have been relatively rare. Bulgaria, in Iran and Libya, and Hungary, also in Libya, have entered into joint equity ventures with local partners for exploration ınd development of petroleum resources. Romania's Petroexport ıas a 50 per cent equity in a company (Merol) established in Beirut n 1971 which, while primarily engaged in marketing petroleum products in the Middle East and Africa, reportedly also engages in some oil-processing operations. Otherwise, Comecon countries have tended to employ the compensation format to gain access to new sources of energy in the developing countries.[33]

It is also somewhat surprising that the most developed members of the Comecon countries have been the least active in terms of Comecon foreign investments in the extractive industries. Certainly this is not due to any lack of requirement for additional sources of ındustrial raw materials. The German Democratic Republic's inaction may be laid at the doorstep of the political and ideological factors discussed in Chapter 4. While these apply to some extent to Czechoslovakia as well, its apparent inertia is more difficult to explain, and may simply reflect inadequate data. There were certainly indications in the early 1970s that Czechoslovakia was searching for investment possibilities in this area.[34] A specialised enterprise, Fincom, was organised in 1970 (formally established in 1972) specifically to ferret out opportunities whereby Czechoslovak capital and technology could be used to develop raw materials for Czechoslovak industry. Subsequently, Fincom reportedly invested in mining companies in Argentina, Nigeria and Tanzania, but as it has been impossible to substantiate these investments, they have not been included in the cases reported in Table 3.6.[35]

CONCLUSIONS

This chapter has reviewed the activities of Comecon multinationa
enterprises in a wide range of production activities across a broa
geographic spectrum. Although a greater proportion of Comeco
production investments are in the South, they are none the less o
some significance in the West also. The evidence presented clearl
demonstrates that Comecon foreign investment has extended, we
beyond commercial functions and related support activities. Th
difference between East European and capitalist multinationa
enterprises in terms of their production operations abroad appear
to be primarily a question of magnitudes.

A certain country specialisation was discernible. The Sovie
Union has developed a number of its marketing companie
especially those selling machinery and equipment, into large-scal
concerns engaged in a number of related activities, including form
of production. The Soviet Union and Poland have been active i
investments in fishing operations on a world-wide scale, particularl
since the establishment of 200-mile national economic zones i
coastal waters. Hungary was seen to be in the forefront o
investments in manufacturing facilities abroad, followed by Polan
and Czechoslovakia. These have been orientated primarily to foreig
markets, although production for the home market was als
undertaken in a number of instances. Bulgaria has emerged mor
recently as an important actor in this area, seeking opportunities fo
the establishment of new manufacturing capacity abroad, especiall
in the West. These included cases where the foreign productio
facilities were to be integrated into the parent's multinational syste
of production and trade rather than merely to serve the host-countr
or home-country market. Romania was found to be engaged mor
actively than others in agriculture, forestry and mining, with thes
operations concentrated in the African countries. The activities o
the German Democratic Republic in all forms of productio
investments abroad were negligible.

With some exceptions, notably the progression of several long
established Soviet companies from marketing to production, th
experience in this sphere of most of the Comecon countries has bee
too recent to permit valid assessment. Intentions, however, hav
often clearly exceeded the ability to implement them. Moreove
mistakes have been made in the initial investment decision whic
have come quickly to light. The Bulgarian investment in Ireland a

vell as Hungarian investments in Ireland, Nigeria and Denmark are
examples of initiatives in the production sphere which reportedly
ave not worked out and have either been liquidated or allowed to
emain legally in existence, but inoperative.

NOTES AND REFERENCES

1. The process elsewhere has been analysed especially in terms of Swedish experience. See S. Carlson, 'Company Policies for International Expansion: the Swedish Experience', in T. Agmon and C. Kindleberger (eds), *Multinationals from Small Countries* (Cambridge, Mass.: MIT Press, 1977) pp. 50–7 and B. Swedenborg, *The Multinational Operations of Swedish Firms: an Analysis of Determinants and Effects* (Stockholm: Industrial Institute for Economic and Social Research, 1979). For more general discussion, see C. Michalet, *Le Capitalisme Mondial* (Paris: Presses Universitaires de France, 1976) pp. 131 and 167 *et seq.*

2. The Western literature has recently been surveyed by R. E. Caves, *Multinational Enterprise and Economic Analysis* (Cambridge University Press, 1982). On these points, see especially his Chapters 2 and 3. For a different perspective, see Michalet, *Le Capitalisme Mondial, ibid.*

3. Avtoexport has 95 per cent of the equity in the Finnish company. For a more detailed case study of Konela, see McMillan, *Direct Soviet and East European Investment in the Industrialized Western Economies* (Ottawa: Institute of Soviet and East European Studies, Carleton University East–West Commercial Relations Series, No. 7, February 1977, pp. 59–60.

4. *Soviet Export*, No. 1, 1982, p. 16.

5. Standard components for various Soviet models are imported from the Soviet Union and assembled at Scaldia-Volga's technical and commercial centre at Diegem, on the outskirts of Brussels. For further details of the company's activities, see *Foreign Trade*, No. 7, 1974, pp. 18–20.

6. X. Linnaimaa and K. Mettelia, 'Ekonomicheskoe sotrudnichestvo Finlandii co stranami-chlenami SEV', *Voprosy Ekonomiki*, No. 2, 1978, p. 86.

7. On the technological basis for Medicor's international operations, see *New Hungarian Exporter*, June 1978 and November 1982.

8. This case has been analysed in some detail in McMillan, *Changing Perspectives in East–West Commerce, op. cit.*, pp. 63–5. Medicor sold its shares to the British partner in 1978.

9. Author interview with Medimpex officials. The Western partner is a pharmaceutical group based in Holland.

10. See Chapter 4, footnote 19.

11. Author interview with responsible Hungarian officials. Malcolm Hill also cites the availability of natural gas as a factor in the locational decision. See M. Hill (Ch. 5, n. 13, p. 101), pp. 87–91, for a case study of the company.

12. *East European Markets*, 19 August 1983, p. 9; *Quarterly Economi* *review*, No. 4 *The Economist* Intelligence Unit, 1983, p. 9; *Financi* *Times*, 2 February 1984, p. 2.
13. Information supplied by company.
14. Details were reported in *The Economist*, 8 January 1983, pp. 62–3; *Le* *Echos*, 1 April 1983, pp. 1 and 6; 17 June 1983, p. 6 and 1 July 1983 p. 5.
15. Michalet, *Le Capitalisme Mondial*, *op. cit.*, p. 149 *et seq.*
16. *African Development*, March 1975, p. 43 and *Polish Foreign Trade* No. 5, 1980, pp. 29–30.
17. A Hungarian economist was among the first to call attention to thi general trend in multinational enterprise. See Gy. Adam, 'New Trend in International Business: Worldwide Sourcing and Dedomiciling', *Act* *Oeconomica*, No. 3–4, 1971, pp. 349–67.
18. Author interview with responsible Hungarian officials.
19. Information supplied by company. Bulgarian officials report, howeve that the Irish venture has not proved successful, and remains legally i existence but inoperative.
20. *Czechoslovak Foreign Trade*, No. 4, 1980, p. 4.
21. Author interview with company officials.
22. On Soviet international fishing operations, see *Soviet Ocean* *Development*, pp. 377–463.
23. In the Third World, in particular, Soviet equity is occasionally les than 50 per cent in these ventures.
24. The others are situated in Iran and Singapore.
25. See J. Martens, 'Likelihood of Communist Joint Ventures Inside th US Fishery Conservation Zone', (US Department of Commerce Bureau of East–West Trade, May 19, 1978) (mimeograph).
26. The mixed company also provides support services to the Soviet ships
27. Casacrus was later replaced by another firm, Interagra, which belong to the Doumeng group in France.
28. It has a 20 per cent interest in a joint venture in Sierra Leone: Sierra Leon Trading Co. Ltd.
29. *Vos Partenaires d'Affaires en Roumanie* (Bucharest: Publicom, 1982) See also M. Ericsson, 'Geomin', *Raw Materials Report*, Vol. 2, No. 2 1983.
30. UN Economic Commission for Europe, 'Promotion of Trade Throug Industrial Cooperation: Tripartite Industrial Cooperation Contracts Results of an Inquiry', note by the Secretariat, TRADE/R.373 Ad 1, October 12 1978.
31. The Romanian bank raised the funds for this purpose through syndicated loan on the Euromarket. *Moscow Narodny Bank Pres* *Bulletin* 15 February 1978, p. 17.
32. Information supplied by company. See also *Hungaropress*, No. 4 1982, p. 30.
33. See Hannigan and McMillan, 'CMEA Trade and Cooperation with th Third World in the Energy Sector', *op. cit.*
34. *Latin America*, 6 March 1970, p. 95, reported Czechoslovak investment i a tannery in Uruguay, while the same source, 29 January 1971, p. 3

indicated interest in the establishment of mixed companies for tin and tungsten mining in Bolivia.

35. When interviewed, Czechoslovak officials have been unable or unwilling to discuss these activities. It will be recalled that Fincom has since merged with Transakta, which has assumed its functions and responsibilities in this area.

CHAPTER 7

Investment Conditions and Experience in Four Host Countries

Comecon investments have encountered varying conditions abroad which have served as major determinants of the geographical pattern observed in Chapter 3 (Tables 3.3. and 3.4). It was seen that these conditions went well beyond considerations of demand and cost alone, to include such factors as intergovernmental relations, the local regulatory environment and popular attitudes in the host countries.

The purpose of this chapter is to make these conditions more explicit through an examination of the Comecon investment experience in selected countries. It is hoped that this shift in perspective will serve to deepen understanding of the phenomenon of Soviet and East European multinational enterprise. In terms of the OECD countries, this essay has focused on Canada and the United States, since research in progress elsewhere is designed to produce country studies of several important West European examples.[1] When completed, these will then serve to complement the analysis here. In the South, Nigeria and India have been selected for study. It will be recalled that a large proportion (43 per cent) of identified Comecon investments in the Third World have been in Africa, and that Nigeria accounts for nearly a third of these. India has been chosen as a major Asian country with which the Soviet Union and Eastern Europe have had a long history of active political and economic relations.

In these country studies, the emphasis will be on the conditions influencing flows of investment from the Comecon countries, including the climate of intergovernmental relations which affects and can be affected by, Comecon investment activities. Details of individual Comecon investments in these countries will be presented only to the extent necessary to understand the general investment experience in the case of the host country in question.

DEVELOPED COUNTRIES

These countries for the most part do not regulate inflows of foreign direct investment or restrict the activities of foreign multinational enterprises. Their approach is based on an economic philosophy favouring free international movement of capital and equality of treatment under law of both national firms and those established by foreign investors.[2] The multinational enterprises of the Comecon countries thus face a generally hospitable climate in the West in which to develop their operations.[3] This has been explicitly recognised in the East.[4] In these circumstances, the geographical pattern of Comecon investments in the developed economies has, as already pointed out, been determined primarily by economic considerations, first and foremost among these being the relative importance of the host country as an export market.

There are, nevertheless, exceptions to the general, *laissez-faire* posture of the developed countries, and these have inevitably affected Comecon enterprises, as they have other foreign investors.[5] The comparatively few Comecon investments in Japan, for example, are a reflection of restrictive Japanese policy in this area. Japan's Foreign Investment Law, dating from 1950, was liberalised only in 1967 and 'a multiplicity of regulations and a variety of restrictions are still in force'.[6] The Japanese Cabinet approved in 1977 the decision of the Foreign Investment Council to reject an application for the formation of a joint Soviet–Japanese company, Nippon Soviet Transport Co. Ltd (Nisotra), to handle cargo shipments between Japan and the Soviet Far East.

Other countries have also imposed various controls on foreign investment. Sweden regulates the establishment of new companies by foreign investors, but leaves investment in existing firms unrestricted. It does, however, control the acquisition of real property by such firms and appointment of foreign nationals to senior executive positions.[7] In Switzerland, the majority of a company's directors are required to be Swiss nationals, or if there is only director, he must be Swiss. Australia's Foreign Takeovers Act (1972) controls foreign acquisition of existing Australian companies, but does not cover new foreign investment. Canada's Foreign Investment Review Act (1974) establishes procedures to screen new foreign investment as well as take-overs. In both cases, however, foreign investment which does not exceed a specific amount is unrestricted.[8] There are also foreign-exchange controls and sectoral restrictions which in some countries affect the direct investment activities of foreign firms.[9]

Western residency restrictions *vis-à-vis* Soviet and East European nationals attached to subsidiary companies probably serve as more general impediments to the activities of Comecon multinational enterprises in the West than do foreign investment controls. In major Western countries, the application of visa regulations effectively limits the entry, residence and sometimes internal travel of Soviet and East European nationals. Since these restrictions are often a matter of administrative discretion in implementing general regulations, they are difficult to document and to assess systematically. Nevertheless, by all accounts, they constitute an impediment not only to the establishment of foreign subsidiaries but also to their successful performance and growth. They also tend to encourage the joint equity relationships and extensive local staffing seen earlier to be characteristic of Soviet and East European companies in the West.

Canada

Soviet and East European investments in Canada are in most respects a microcosm of their overall investments in the developed countries.[10] The essential details are presented in Table 7.1. All seven of the European Comecon countries, except the German Democratic Republic, are represented, with the share of Czechoslovakia higher, and that of Hungary lower, than in the OECD countries as a whole. The absence in Canada of East German investments is representative, as has been seen, of a more general East German lag in foreign investment activities behind the other Comecon countries. The growth of diplomatic relations between Canada and the German Democratic Republic has been slower than in the case of most West European countries, and a trade agreement between the two was concluded only in 1983.

Although the earliest investment, Omnitrade Ltd (Czechoslovakia) predates the establishment of a state-socialist economy in the home country, the overwhelming majority of the companies in Canada date from 1965.[11] There was a particularly noticeable surge in Soviet investment activity in the first half of the 1970s.

It does not appear that Soviet and East European investment activity was much affected after 1974 by the new Canadian foreign investment controls. While the Foreign Investment Review Agency has had to rule on several new Comecon investments since it began

Table 7.1 Soviet and East European companies in Canada

Company name	Head office	Year established*	Comecon partner	Comecon equity	Authorised capital (Canadian $)	Principal activity
Omnitrade Ltd	Montreal	1947	Transakta (CSSR)	100	1,000,000	Markets and services wide range of Czechoslovak manufactured goods
Pekao Trading Co. Canada Ltd	Toronto	1956	Bank Polska Kasa Opieki (Poland)	99	32,000	Markets Polish consumer and manufactured products
Cebecom Ltd[a]	Toronto	1965	Industrialimport (Bulgaria)	100	42,600	Markets Bulgarian food products
Dalimpex Ltd	Montreal	1965	DAL (Poland)	95	500,000	Markets and services wide range of Polish consumer and industrial products
Motokov Canada Inc.[b]	Montreal	1966	Motokov (CSSR)	100	750,000	Markets and services Czech motorcycles, bicycles and mopeds
Superflux Canada	Montreal	1967	Glassexport (CSSR)	100	100,000	Markets Bohemian and East German glass products
Omnitrade Industrial Co. Ltd	Montreal	1969	Transakta (CSSR)	100	50,000	Markets and services Czechoslovak textile machinery and other products
Morflot Freightliners Ltd	Vancouver	1971	Sovinflot (USSR)	95	50,000	Agent for Soviet shipping to Canadian West Coast

Company name	Head office	Year established*	Comecon partner	Comecon equity	Authorised capital (Canadian $)	Principal activity
Belarus Equipment Ltd	Toronto	1972	Traktorexport, Zapchastexport (USSR)	100	2,950,236	Markets and services Soviet agricultural equipment in Canada
Stan-Canada Machinery Ltd	Toronto	1972	Stankoimport (USSR)	100	1,380,000	Markets and services Soviet machine tools in Canada and the United States
EMEC Trading Ltd	Vancouver	1973	Energomachexport (USSR)	95	414,000	Markets and services Soviet electricial generators and turbines
Hungarotex Canada Ltd	Montreal	1974	Hungarotex (Hungary)	50	50,000	Markets Hungarian clothing and textile products in Canada
Terra Power Tractor Co. Ltd	Saskatoon	1974	Universal Tractor (Romania)	100	100,000	Markets and services Romanian agricultural equipment in Western Canada
Socan Aircraft Ltd[c]	Calgary	1975	Aviaexport (USSR)	67	50,000	Markets and services Soviet aircraft
Belfor and Co. Ltd	Ottawa	1978	Glassexport (CSSR)	40	n.a.	Markets Czech glassware
Unidal Cycle Inc.[c]	Montreal	1979	DAL (Poland)	49.95	200,000	Imports bicycle parts from Poland for assembly and distribution in Canada

Company name	Head office	Year established*	Comecon partner	Comecon equity	Authorised capital (Canadian $)	Principal activity
The Bowcutter Corp.[c]	Montreal	1980	DAL (Poland)	49	100,000	Exports fish and fish products to Poland
Bultex Co. Ltd	Montreal	1980	Industrialimport (Bulgaria)	100	42,000	Markets Bulgarian textiles
Aro-Dacia	Montreal	1980	Universal Tractor (Romania)	100	n.a.	Markets Romanian automobiles

[a] Later restructured as Bultex.

[b] Motokov originally established under the name Skoda & Jawa Motors Canada Ltd; then changed to CZ & Jawa Motors Canada Ltd, in 1972; present name since 1978.

[c] Inoperative, although Socan remains legally in existence.

* In this and other tables in this chapter, when year of establishment unknown, the year of fist report of investment (as for example, Pre-1977) is given. Comecon partner listed is state enterprise or group in Comecon country holding principal share of Eastern equity, although its ownership may be indirect, through another foreign subsidiary.

Source: Comecon Foreign Investment Data Bank, East–West Project, Carleton University, Ottawa.

operations, there is no record of its having turned down an application from this source. Recent Comecon efforts in Canada have, nevertheless, concentrated more on the development of existing companies, while the principal locus of new investment activities in North America has shifted to the nearby United States market (see below).

Most of the Comecon investments in Canada are in commercial operations. These show the trend towards increased product specialisation that is found in Comecon investment activity elsewhere. While the earliest subsidiaries, such as Omnitrade, Pekao Trading and Dalimpex, were charged with marketing a wide range of products, many of them consumer goods, the more recently established companies have engaged in the marketing of specific categories of industrial goods, such as agricultural machinery, electric turbines, machine tools and aircraft. The latter also typically undertake a broader range of operations, including warehousing, product modification, distribution and after-sales servicing. Their generally higher capitalisation reflects the importance of these auxiliary functions. For example, the Soviet machine-tool firm, Stan-Canada, has an impressive headquarters in Toronto with large showrooms and built-in warehouse and staging areas. It also has similar, though smaller, facilities in Montreal.

Soviet and East European investments in Canada have extended more directly into production operations. In 1970, Omnitrade established through acquisition a division for the manufacture of rock drilling equipment and other mining machinery to promote speciality steels imported from Czechoslovakia. Dalimpex, in partnership with a Canadian firm, established a joint company to assemble bicycle components imported from Poland.[12] While the Soviet Union's Avtoexport decided in 1976 to market Lada cars in Canada through a Canadian agent, rather than through a subsidiary company, there have been discussions of Soviet investment in a Lada assembly plant in Nova Scotia.[13] The primary industries are also an area of probable future investment activity. Polish–Canadian fishing ventures have been discussed. The Romanians have expressed interest in Canadian coal mining and in agriculture.

A major difference in the operational profile of Soviet and East European investments in Canada from those in Western Europe is the absence of banking and other financial operations. It is natural that state banks in the Comecon countries should have exploited opportunities for direct investment in European financial centres before moving overseas. Nevertheless, this is a case where legislation in the host country restricting foreign investments in certain sectors has no doubt also played a role. The Canadian Bank Act has only recently been amended to permit the operation in Canada of branches and affiliates of foreign banks, although their activities are still subject to limitations.[14] Under more positive economic and political conditions, the Comecon countries might take advantage of these new opportunities. The Soviet-owned Moscow Narodny Bank of London at one time considered the establishment of a branch in North America.[15]

In all but four of the nineteen cases of Comecon investment in the Canadian economy, East European capital participation represents a majority share and in fourteen cases is 95 per cent or more. There has been a notable tendency for East European equity in a given company to increase over time. Original partnerships with foreign firms or individuals are reduced or eliminated as the affiliate or subsidiary becomes established and as its development requires capital expansion. Between the middle and late 1970s, the share of investments with majority participation by Comecon enterprises increased from about two-thirds to four-fifths and those with 100 per cent East European equity from 40 per cent to 70 per cent.[16]

Because of their primarily commercial nature, the capital invested in these companies is not great, however, with the authorised capital in individual cases ranging from less than 50,000 to nearly 3,000,000[17] Canadian dollars. In terms of their balance-of-payments, the book value of the stock of direct investment in Canada by the seven Comecon countries rose from little over one million Canadian dollars in 1970 to an estimated $50 million in 1980, including long-term loans from parents to subsidiaries as well as invested capital.[18] The source of 70 per cent of this amount was the Soviet Union. While the growth over a short period is impressive, the total investment is a negligible share of the total foreign direct investment in Canada in 1979, estimated over $54 billion.[19]

This capital, supplemented by reinvested profits and local borrowings, financed the considerable development of some subsidiaries, as they diversified their activities and branched out into new market areas, both in Canada and in other parts of the Western hemisphere. Omnitrade, the oldest of the Comecon companies in Canada, with assets in 1980 of $28.8 million and 150 employees, markets a wide range of products, from sporting goods to machine tools in Canada, South America and Third World markets. It also exports Canadian industrial goods to Czechoslovakia. It has major facilities (for storage and technical servicing, for example) at its headquarters in Montreal and in Toronto, as well as offices in Vancouver. Through the acquisition of a Canadian mining machinery manufacturer, Pontiac Manufacturing, it extended its activities into production. It has marketing subsidiaries in Japan and Chile, and its wholly-owned Quebec subsidiary, Omnitrade Industrial, which sells a wide range of Czechoslovak consumer goods, and markets and services textile machinery, has two operating divisions in the United States.

Other Comecon subsidiaries have experienced similar growth. Poland's Dalimpex has greatly expanded its product lines and has opened branch offices in Toronto, Edmonton and Vancouver. Two Soviet companies, Belarus and Stan-Canada, whose headquarters are in Toronto, have branch offices in Eastern and Western Canada. The latter also has a subsidiary in Mexico and made an unsuccessful attempt to establish a presence in the United States through direct investment. Both companies have technical facilities, and engage in pre-sale product modification as well as after-sales servicing. Belarus has developed its own dealer network throughout the country.[20] Morflot Freightliners, based in Vancouver, opened offices in Seattle and Portland in 1971.

In the case of mixed equity companies, the Canadian partners are frequently individuals (company lawyers or former commercial agents) who are senior executives or directors. In other cases, the partners are usually small Canadian companies with prior association as representatives in Canada of the Comecon parent enterprise. Well-known Canadian companies are rarely found as partners in these ventures. The major exception was the case of Socan, a company established to market a small Soviet passenger jet aircraft (the YAK-40) in which the wholly-owned subsidiary of Allarco Developments Ltd of Calgary held a one-third share.

The staff of a Comecon subsidiary is a mixture of Canadians and nationals from the home country. The nationals usually occupy some of the principal management and most technical positions, while Canadians are typically in sales, public relations and clerical positions.

Canadian visa regulations do appear to have restricted the number of East European nationals assigned to these companies. In the mid-1950s, the Czechoslovak nationals employed by Omnitrade were counted as part of Czechoslovakia's official establishment in Canada and subject to the ceiling placed on it. Beginning with Dalimpex, in the 1960s, a new, less restrictive, approach was taken. A 'commercial quota' was established, separate from the one placed on the East European country's official establishment. Nationals of Comecon countries are usually given six-month visas with options for renewal. The only restriction placed on them is one of residence. This serves as a control on the opening of branch offices, if the company wishes to assign nationals to them.[21]

Despite these limitations, the number of Soviet and East European nationals employed in subsidiaries and affiliates in Canada has grown significantly. Their number increased from eleven in the mid-1960s to well over one hundred by the early 1980s. Over half are technical personnel, while another 30 per cent fall into the senior executive category.[22]

One of the more serious set of problems with which Comecon multinational enterprises have had to contend in the West, given their predominant commercial focus, are trade barriers. While all of the Comecon countries have long enjoyed MFN treatment of their exports to Canadian markets, a number of non-tariff barriers have impeded the growth of their operations. These include import quotas (especially relevant to those subsidiaries engaged in marketing textile products), valuation procedures, anti-dumping regulations and certification requirements.[23] A ruling against EMEC Trading by the Canadian Anti-Dumping Tribunal in 1976 effectively brought to a halt its sales of Soviet hydraulic turbines for electric power projects in Western and Eastern Canada. Another Soviet–Canadian company, Socan, has undergone protracted and unsuccessful certification procedures with the Canadian Ministry of Transport in its efforts to market a modified version of the YAK-40 in Canada.[24] In late 1983, the Canadian Press reported a court ruling against Belfor and Co., a Czechoslovak Glassexport affiliate, for under-valuation of imports. The settlement of the government's suit against Belfor for the evasion of customs duties exceeded $2 million.

Foreign investments have nevertheless played an important part in the growth of Comecon exports to Canada. As the major active investor, the experience of the Soviet Union in this regard is especially significant. Over the 1970s, since the formation of Soviet machinery-and-equipment-marketing companies in Canada, exports of this category (excluding cars, which are marketed through a Canadian agent) increased from a negligible 1.9 per cent in 1970 to 45.6 per cent of total Soviet exports to Canada in 1980.[25]

Nevertheless, the experience of newly established Comecon subsidiaries in Canada bears out the proposition that even under normal market conditions the initial period of operating losses due to start-up and market-entry costs can be prolonged.[26] Here host-country regulations are no doubt joined by a number of other marketing problems discussed earlier, including the relative inexperience of Comecon parent enterprises in managing foreign-marketing subsidiaries. The Soviet and Romanian companies set up in Canada to market and service tractors and other agricultural equipment began operations at a time when the Canadian market was especially strong.[27] Their operating losses continued, however, into the late 1970s.

In the early 1980s, these problems have been compounded by slack equipment markets, under conditions of high rates of interest. Belarus, which in the period 1973–82 had marked 9,360 tractors in Canada and over 1,500 pieces of other agricultural machinery, sold only 530 tractors in 1982, compared to the 1,000 sold in 1981. Continuing unprofitability could force it to discontinue operations.[28] Similar problems appear to have plagued Czechoslovak and Polish attempts to extend investment activity into the Canadian manufacturing sector.

In sum, despite Canada's regulation of foreign investment, which is greater than that of most OECD countries, the activities of Comecon multinational enterprises in Canada have developed significantly in size and scope since the mid-1960s. They have become an important and permanent part of the mechanism through which the Comecon countries conduct their economic relations with Canada. In the case of the Soviet Union, this was formally recognised by the Soviet Deputy Minister of Foreign Trade at a meeting of the Canada–USSR Mixed Commission in Moscow in June 1983, when he devoted the majority of his remarks on the Soviet export strategy on the Canadian market to a review of the activities of Soviet-owned companies in Canada.

United States

As noted, Comecon subsidiaries and affiliates in Canada also frequently served a broader purpose, that of providing a base for commercial operations in the rest of North America, and more occasionally in Latin America also. These have been conducted through their agents, branch offices and occasionally through operational divisions located in other parts of the hemisphere. A brief look at the conditions affecting Comecon investment in the United States will help to clarify the rationale for this strategy.

The United States has no legislation specifically regulating foreign investment, and laws and regulations which indirectly serve to restrict investment flows are minimal.[29] Its historic role as the foremost international source of multinational enterprise has given the United States a major stake in liberalisation rather than regulation. Nevertheless, the rapid growth of foreign-investment flows into the United States in the more recent period since World War II has aroused some concern and a cabinet-level committee was set up in 1975 to monitor the impact of foreign investment in the United States and to co-ordinate federal policies in this area.[30]

Among its responsibilities the Committee on Foreign Investment in the United States was directed to establish procedures for 'advance consultations with foreign governments on prospective major governmental investments in the United States'. Although the term 'governmental investment' is ambiguous, and such procedures would not be directed exclusively at investments from the Comecon countries, they would potentially affect them most comprehensively. This initiative does not appear to have been carried further, however, and no formal screening process has been established.[31] Nor, as of the end of 1983, had the Committee reviewed any investments from Comecon sources. The issues raised by Comecon investment in the United States were apparently undergoing study by the Reagan Administration. Here, however, the United States Government is faced with the dilemma that any intervention to regulate investments from Comecon sources would undermine the principle of open foreign-investment policies which in general it advocates.

Other government polices and regulations have, however, effectively constrained the activity of Comecon multinational enterprises in the United States. Before 1972, Poland was the only Comecon country to enjoy MFN tariff treatment for its products entering the American market.[32] The others faced tariff barriers, especially on their manufactures, which seriously limited their competitiveness. There was little commercial basis, then, on which to establish marketing subsidiaries directly in the United States.

While discriminatory tariffs, combined with liberal foreign investment regulations, would in themselves seem to create incentives for direct investment in production operations within the American market, other factors deterred such an approach by the Comecon countries. American visa restrictions on Soviet and East European personnel have been especially severe. The conditions attached by the United States government to normalisation of commercial relations with the East European countries and the unsettled bilateral issues with some of them acted as further deterrents. Most importantly, the failure to implement a trade agreement with the Soviet Union and the continuing climate of rivalry and tension between the two superpowers made direct investment in the United States a politically risky, if commercially attractive, possibility.

These circumstances go far to explain the nature and evolution of Comecon direct investments in the United States. Poland, the East European country which, until recently, enjoyed the best bilateral relations with the United States and had long benefited from MFN access to the American market, accounts for a large share (46 per cent) of Comecon investments undertaken in the United States. Hungary – whose relations with the United States was greatly improved after the settlement of important bilateral issues which had long plagued them, and the signing of an MFN tariff accord – is the source of another 26 per cent.[33] Thus Poland and Hungary together account for nearly two-thirds of all Comecon investments in the United States. Most of the thirty-five Comecon investments undertaken in the United States have been in the marketing of Comecon exports. There have been several investments in shipping and freight services, but few in production. No banking branches or affiliates have been established, so that with the exception of the Pekao companies, whose specialised operations in the United States and Canada were described in Chapter 5, no Comecon companies in North America engage in any form of financial services.

Because of the special interest they attract, Soviet direct investments in the United States merit some elaboration. There are five instances of this, and all but one are in wholly-owned companies. The oldest of these is Amtorg Trading Corp. of New York, which was founded in 1924, long before diplomatic relations had been established, and which continues to act as a general commercial intermediary between American firms and Soviet enterprises.[34]

The remaining four were all set up in the mid-1970s. Morflot America Shipping Inc., based in New Jersey, and Sovfracht (USA) Ltd in New York, have agency responsibility for American ports. (On the north-west coast, a sister company, Morflot Freightliners, based in Vancouver – see Table 7.1 – represents Soviet Far Eastern shipping lines, which are heavily engaged in cross-hauling between Japanese and North American ports.) The Soviet–American fishing venture, Marine Resources of Seattle, has already been briefly described in Chapter 6. The most recent Soviet direct investment in the United States, Belarus Machinery Inc. of Milwaukee, set up in 1977 to market and service Soviet tractors, is the only example in the United States of the more ambitious form of marketing subsidiary which has been seen to play a major role in Soviet machinery and equipment exports in Europe and Canada.

Comecon investment activity in the United States mushroomed between 1975 and 1981. Nearly two-thirds of Comecon investments in the United States were made during these years. For the reasons outlined earlier, this attention to the investment possibilities of the American market occurred later than in the case of other, major Western host countries. The worsening of the political and economic climate in the early 1980s led to a tapering off of this activity and no new investments were made in 1982–3.

Five of the Comecon investments in the United States are known to have been liquidated or to be no longer operative. Three of these are Polish companies whose operations were affected by the worsening of relations between the two countries after 1980. The withdrawal in 1982 of MFN privileges for Polish imports is likely to lead to the winding down of other Polish companies in the United States in the next few years.[35]

In the circumstances, Comecon direct investments in the United States remain relatively limited. Most are in commercial companies engaged primarily in import–export operations. Their average size is, accordingly, small: an estimated $250,000 in authorised capital. While data on the book value of cumulative direct investment in the United States from the Soviet Union and Eastern Europe are not available, it can be reasonably assumed to be well under $100 million (at the end of 1983). Official American statistics placed the total stock of foreign direct investment in the United States at $102 billion in 1982.

DEVELOPING COUNTRIES

In the Third World, the Comecon countries have faced a variety of conditions for investment much wider than in the OECD countries.

Table 7.2 Soviet and East European companies in the United States

Company name	Head office	Year established	Comecon partner	Comecon equity (per cent)	Authorised capital (US$)	Principal activity
Amtorg Trading Corp.	New York	1924	Vneshtorgbank, Centrosoyuz (USSR)	100	n.a.	Agency services – acts as intermediary between US and Soviet firms
Gdynia America Line Inc.	New York	1926	Gdynia America Shipping Lines Ltd (Poland)	100	250,000	Ocean-going transport services
Pekao Trading Corp.	New York	1948	Bank Polska Kasa Opieki SA (Poland)	100	24,000	Marketing of Polish consumer goods; also arranges banking transactions
Cepelia Corp.	New York	1959	Coopexim-Cepelia (Poland)	100 owned by company officers	380,000	Marketing and distribution of Polish art, handicraft and folklore items
Linen Trading Inc.	New York	1961	Bank Polska Kasa Opieki SA (Poland)	100	n.a.	Marketing of Polish textiles
WATA Commercial Society Inc.	Texas	1970	Ibusz (Hungary)	2	n.a.	Consumer services
Romanda Co. Ltd[a]	New York	1971	Terra (Romania)	50	n.a.	Technical services and arranging large-scale trade financial deals, joint ventures, licensing, know-how and technology transfer

Company	Location	Year	Polish partner			Description
Melex USA Inc.	Raleigh, North Carolina	1973	Pezetal (Poland)	100	n.a.	Marketing and servicing of Polish golf carts, agricultural aircrafts, engines and distributors
Polish-American International Arts (ARTPOL) Inc.[a]	New York	Mid-1970s	Pagart (Poland)	n.a.	n.a.	Marketing Polish classical and popular records; promotion of Polish artists
Toolmex Corp.	Natick, Massachusetts	1973	Metalexport (Poland)	100	n.a.	Marketing of Polish machinery, precision instruments and small tools
Unitronex Corp.	Elk Grove Village, Illinois	1974	Metronex (Poland)	66	368,259	Marketing of electronic products, manufacturing equipment and consumer goods, laboratory and medical equipment; agency services for US firms doing business in Poland
Prominex Glass and Ceramics Corp.	New York	1974	Minex (Poland)	n.a.	n.a.	Marketing ceramics, artistic glass and construction materials
Amerpol International Inc.	New York	1974	C. Hartwig (Poland)	60	n.a.	Sea and air transport services
Polish-American Machinery Corp. (Polamco)[b]	Elk Grove Village, Illinois	1975	Metalexport (Poland)	100	640,000	Marketing and servicing of Polish machinery and equipment; provides agency services for export-import transactions of firms involved in Polish-US trade

Company name	Head office	Year established	Comecon partner	Comecon equity (per cent)	Authorised capital (US$)	Principal activity
Morflot America Shipping (MORAM) Inc.	Clark, New Jersey	1976	Sovfracht (USSR)	100	n.a.	Agency services for Soviet shipping lines operating in the US
Polfoods Corp.	New York	1976	Animex (Poland)	100	100,000	Marketing and distribution of Polish food and food products
Marine Resources Co.	Seattle	1976	Sovrybflot (USSR)	50	100,000	Harvesting and marketing of fish off the US Pacific coast
Polikee Inc.[a]	Chicago	1976	Polimex-Cekop (Poland)	50	100,000	Importing capital equipment for food, chemical, steel, metal and light industries; exports equipment to Poland; engineering services
Minibattery Corp.[a]	Los Angeles	Pre-1977	Medicor (Hungary)	30	n.a.	Marketing of mini-batteries produced by Medicharge of UK
Sovfracht (USA) Ltd	New York East Brunswick,	1976	Sovracht (USSR)	n.a.	n.a.	Ocean-going transport services
Action Tungsram Ltd	New Jersey	1977	Tungsram (Hungary)	49	2,750,000	Marketing and manufacturing of light bulbs, transistors and electrical accessories
Ampag Furniture and Wooden Products Corp.	High Point North Carolina	1977	Paged (Poland)	n.a.	n.a.	Marketing of Polish furniture and wood products in the US; exports wood products to Poland

Company	City	Year	Foreign partner	%	Capital	Description
Belarus Machinery Inc.	Milwaukee, Wisconsin	1977	Traktroexport (USSR)	100	n.a.	Marketing and servicing of Soviet tractors
Medicor USA Ltd[c]	Columbus, Ohio	1978	Medicor (Hungary)	100	100,000	Marketing, assembly and servicing of medical equipment
Medimpex North America Inc.	New York	1978	Medimpex (Hungary)	100	300,000	Marketing of Hungarian pharmaceuticals
Getex, Inc.[a]	New York	1978	Textilimpex (Poland)	100	n.a.	Marketing of finished textile products
Agropol Chicago Corp.[a]	Chicago	1978	Agros (Poland)	50	10,000 shares, no par value	Marketing of foodstuffs
American Jawa	Plainview, New York	Pre-1979	Motokov (CSSR)	100	n.a.	Marketing of Czechoslovak-made mopeds and motor cycles
Superlux Ltd	New York	Pre-1980	Glassexport (CSSR)	probably 100	n.a.	Marketing Bohemian and East German glass products
Hungarotex USA Inc.	New York	1980	Hungarotex (Hungary)	100	n.a.	Marketing of Hungarian clothing and textiles
Jena Scientific Instruments Inc.	New York	1980	Carl Zeiss Jena (GDR)	100	10,000 shares, no par value	Marketing of scientific instruments and electronic products

Company name	Head office	Year established	Comecon partner	Comecon equity (per cent)	Authorised capital (US$)	Principal activity
La Tanni Corp.	New York	1980	Tannimpex (Hungary)	50	n.a.	Marketing of Hungarian leather goods, including women's shoes
Amrochem Inc.	White Plains, New York	1980	ICE Danubiana (Romania)	50	200,000	Marketing Romanian chemicals and chemical products in the US; exports US minerals and chemicals to Romania
Taurus International	Wayne, New Jersey	1981	Taurus Hungarian Rubber Works (Hungary)	50	n.a.	Marketing of Hungarian rubber products
Tata-Island Creek Coal Recovery Co.	Dover, Delaware	1981	Tatabanya Coal Mines (Hungary)	50	n.a.	Recycling and marketing of US coal slag, based upon a Hungarian process

[a] Defunct, inoperative, or Comecon equity liquidated.

[b] As of the end of 1983, winding down operations.

[c] Company originally established in 1978 as a 50–50 US–Hungarian mixed company under name of Transmed X-Ray. US partner bought out by Hungarian side in 1980, when company was given present name.

See also general notes to Table 7.1.

Source: Comecon Foreign Investment Data Bank, East–West Project, Carleton University, Ottawa.

These include incentives for, as well as restrictions on, foreign investment, and volatile political and economic conditions. This complexity and uncertainty has rendered the investment decision more difficult and generally more risky, and in some cases has bred serious mistakes.

Many Third World countries have comprehensive laws governing foreign investment, in others legislation is fragmented or is partial in coverage. In nearly all, major foreign-investment proposals are subject to close scrutiny by governmental authorities. Given the centralised nature of Soviet and East European systems, this means that Comecon foreign investment in developing economies frequently becomes a matter of state-to-state negotiation and the specifics of major projected investments are incorporated in inter-governmental agreements.

The screening process in host developing countries is intended to ensure that minimum local participation is achieved and that foreign investment in certain sectors is prohibited or restricted. It also establishes eligibility for the investment incentive schemes which play a major role in the foreign investment policies of most developing countries. A variety of financial regulations, including rules on taxation and repatriation, also affect the process of foreign investment.

Most African countries are characterised by relatively liberal regulations governing foreign investment: fewer restrictions and a greater number of incentives.[36] These, combined with complementarities in the level and structure of development, account for the pattern which emerged in Chapter 3 (see Table 3.4), where Africa appeared as the most favoured location for placement of Comecon investments in the South. Ironically, however, the countries viewed as 'progressive' (socialist-orientated) by the Comecon countries, and with which they have more in common with regard to politics, ideology and organisation, are not those which are most open to foreign direct investment. Developing countries whose governments allow scope to market forces and initiatives outside the state sector, but follow principles of non-alignment in foreign policy, appear to offer the most fertile field for direct investment by Comecon countries.

Nigeria

Nigeria is a good illustrative example of these propositions. At the same time, given the number and variety of Comecon investments in Nigeria, it also provides a comparative wealth of examples with regard to the activity of Comecon multinational enterprises in a developing country.

The most populous African nation, Nigeria, is the largest black African economy and is rich in natural resources. No less important from the perspective of this book, Nigeria has chosen a development strategy based on the conditions of an open market economy and has attracted more investment from multinational enterprises than any other country in black Africa.[37] The Nigerian approach to economic development has been characterised by one authority as a 'process of industrialization, activated by the competition of foreign enterprises for the Nigerian market and accelerated by the industrial policy of the government'.[38]

For most of its independent history, moreover, Nigeria has pursued a non-aligned foreign policy which has provided scope for the development of economic relations with the Comecon countries. Following its independence in 1960, when an official delegation from the Soviet Union attended the ceremonies, cautious diplomatic contacts with the Soviet Union led to the establishment of permanent missions in Moscow and Lagos by 1963. In the years (1961–3) immediately following independence, trade agreements were concluded with Poland, other East European countries and the Soviet Union. Trade grew rapidly as a result.

The first independent government was reluctant, however, to allow economic relations to develop further. It rejected offers of economic aid from the Comecon countries, although it did accept educational assistance in the form of university scholarships for Nigerian students. Then the 1966 coup, which brought a new military government to power, led to the adoption of a non-aligned stance in foreign policy. During the civil war that followed, the military government turned to the Soviet Union, when the Western powers refused it military aid.[39] These events opened the way for an expansion of economic relations, and the improved climate awakened Soviet and East European interest in the possibilities of investment in Nigeria.

In the 1970s, relations developed primarily on pragmatic grounds.[40] Agreements were signed for Soviet assistance in the development of Nigeria's resources of coal and iron and, later, in the construction of an iron-and-steel complex. The increased importance of Nigeria's potential as an oil-producing country also attracted the interest of the Comecon countries. Soviet enterprises received contracts for the construction of two pipelines in Nigeria's planned, nationwide, oil-pipeline system. East European countries, especially Romania, have also participated in the development of Nigerian petroleum resources and related infrastructure.[41]

Nigeria's foreign investment laws were comparatively liberal. Under the 1971 Industrial Development Decree, Nigeria tried to attract foreign investment to industries where local investment was considered inadequate. Nigeria's five-year national development plans gave priority to the production of intermediate and capital goods with high value-added, to petrochemicals, textiles, iron and steel, automobile assembly, pharmaceuticals, agri-business and export-orientated manufacturing.[42] Under the 1972 Nigerian Enterprises Promotion Decree, however, certain sectors (notably services and light industry) were either reserved for Nigerians or foreign involvement in them was restricted.[43] The indigenisation policy was extended in 1977 (see below).

It is in these circumstances that the equity participation of Comecon state enterprises in Nigerian ventures has evolved. Although a few investments date from the 1960s, most of the thirty-three cases listed in Table 7.3 were undertaken in the 1970s. In number, Soviet and East European subsidiaries and affiliates probably comprised, at the end of 1983, around 10 per cent of the total number of companies in Nigeria with foreign capital participation. In terms of capital invested, they probably represented a smaller share of the total stock of foreign investment in Nigeria which the latest available official statistics valued at 2.5 billion naira ($1.7 billion) in 1977.

By contrast to the pattern observed in Canada and the United States, few Comecon investments in Nigeria are in purely commercial operations. Most, in fact, are in the manufacturing sector, with a number of others in related engineering services, such as design, construction and technical support. Only a handful are found in the primary sector – concentrated in the forest-based industries and fishing. Thus Comecon direct investment has eschewed the mining and other resource-extractive industries which have attracted the largest share of foreign investment in Nigeria. Some elaboration of examples in these basic categories will serve to illustrate the Comecon experience in Nigeria.

Table 7.3 Soviet and East European companies in Nigeria

Company name	Head office	Year established	Comecon partner	Comecon equity[a] (%)	Principal activity
Daltrade (Nigeria) Ltd	Kano	1962	DAL (Poland)	40	Marketing machinery, building materials, chemicals, household goods
Afro-Commerce/ W.A. Ltd.	Lagos	1966	Balcancarimpex (Bulgaria)	Max. 40	Marketing and servicing broad range of industrial machinery
WAATECO Ltd	Lagos	1967	Avtoexport (USSR)	60	Assembly, marketing and distribution of automobiles
Imarsel Chemical Co. Ltd	Ikeja (Lagos)	1968	Medimpex (Hungary)	40	Manufacture and marketing of pharmaceuticals
Nigeria Globe Fishing Ind. Ltd	Lagos	1968	Ribno Stopanstvo (Bulgaria)	Max 40	Fishing, fish processing, marketing
Nigerian Mapping Co. Ltd	Lagos	1970	Tesco (Hungary)	40	Geodesic and cartographic services
Tesco-Közti Consulting Ltd	Kano	1970	Tesco (Hungary)	40	Engineering contracting
Polfa (Nigeria) Ltd	Lagos	1970	Polfa (Poland)	10	Manufacture and marketing of pharmaceuticals
Fertesco Industries[b]	Lagos	1970	Hungarocoop, Tesco, Ferunion (Hungary)	50	Metal working; manufacture of ceramic and plastic products

Company	Year	Partner (country)	Nigerian equity (%)	Location	Activity
Polconsult Association (Nigeria)	1972	Polservice (Poland)	Max. 40	Lagos	Consulting in industrial construction, electrification, agriculture, geology
Seromwood Ltd	1972	Forexim (Romania)	40	Calabar	Exploitation, processing marketing of wood
Nirowi Ltd	1972	Forexim (Romania)	30	Ondo	Manufacture and marketing of wood products (plywood, veneers, furniture)
Ronitex Ltd	1973	Institute for Technological Studies of Light Industry (Romania)	40	Calabar	Construction of textile plants
Nigerian Commercial and Industrial Enterprise Ltd[b]	Pre-1975	Metalimpex (Hungary)	Max. 60	Lagos	Manufacture and marketing of steel products
Strojexport Development (Nigeria) Ltd	1975	Strojexport (Czech)	40	Kaduna	Construction, geological work, surveying
Nigpol Ltd	1975	Rybex (Poland)	49	Lagos	Fishing, fish processing, marketing
Tungsram Nigeria Ltd[c]	1977	Tungsram (Hungary)	Max. 60	Lagos	Manufacture of light bulbs

Company name	Head office	Year established	Comecon partner	Comecon equity[a] (%)	Principal activity
Videoton Nigeria Ltd[c]	n.a.	1977/78	Videoton (Hungary)	Max. 60	Television set assembly
Czechoslovak Nigerian Miners Development Co. Ltd	Jos	Pre-1978	Transakta (Czech)	Max. 40	Zinc mining
Motor Assembly Co.	n.a.	Pre-1978	Polimex-Cekop (Poland)	Max. 60	Automobile assembly
Budimex (Nigeria) Ltd	Lagos	1978	Budimex (Poland)	Max. 40	Construction services
Elektrim (Nigeria) Ltd	n.a.	1978	Elektrim (Poland)	60	Marketing of power generating and other electrical equipment
Nigerian Wood Industries Ltd	Ekole	1978	Polimex-Cekop (Poland)	Max. 40	Manufacture, marketing of sawn timber, veneer furniture, doors, chipboard
Czechoslovak Nigerian Export Import Co. Ltd (CNEICO)	Lagos	Pre-1978	Strojimport (Czech)	40	Marketing machinery, lathes, engineering goods
Oraria Metalomplex	Oraria	Pre-1978	Metalexport (Poland)	Max. 40	Manufacture of metal buckets and furniture
Arcom Ltd	Ibadan	Pre-1978	Arcom (Romania)	40	Technical services for construction projects
Medicor Nigeria Ltd	Lagos	1980	Medicor (Hungary)	40	Manufacture of medical instruments and equipment

Skoda Electrical Works Ltd	Yaba (Lagos)	Pre-1980	Skoda (Czech)	Max. 40	Marketing engineering equipment for complete industrial plants, farming machines
Pollamp Ltd.	n.a.	Pre-1981	Unitra (Poland)	Max. 40	Manufacture and marketing of light bulbs
Transproject Nigeria Ltd	n.a.	1982	Transkomplekt (Bulgaria)	Max. 40	Transport design services
Transkomplekt Nigeria Ltd	n.a.	1982	Transkomplekt (Bulgaria)	Max. 40	Transport construction services
Technoexportstroi Nigeria Ltd	n.a.	1982	Technoexport (Bulgaria)	Max. 40	Construction services
Jevora	Lagos	pre-1983	Water Transport Corp. (Bulgaria)	Max. 60	Transport services

[a] Where exact Comecon equity unknown, but Nigerian indigenisation laws set a limit on foreign capital participation, this has been indicated (for example, Max. 40 per cent).

[b] Defunct, inoperative or Comecon equity liquidated.

[c] It is not clear to what degree these two Hungarian investment projects, for joint manufacture of lighting equipment and television set assembly, were carried through. Hungarian officials reported the first venture to be defunct in 1979 and the second in 1981, but were unable to furnish details. They are at least indicative of investment intentions.

See also general notes to Table 7.1.

Source: Comecon Foreign Investment Data Bank, East–West Project, Carleton University, Ottawa.

The oldest company, established soon after independence, is Daltrade (Nigeria). A subsidiary of the Polish general-purpose foreign trade organisation DAL, the company is based in Lagos, with a branch office in Kano. Like other DAL companies abroad, it markets a wide range of Polish products. With the industrialisation of the Nigerian economy, however, its product line has tended to shift from primarily finished consumer goods to a larger share of intermediate and capital goods.[44] Before the establishment in 1975 of a specialised, Polish–Nigerian fishing company, Daltrade was also active in the fields of fishing and fish processing. Nigerian restrictions on foreign personnel have reportedly hindered the expansion of Daltrade's sales network.[45] Polish sources nevertheless consider Daltrade to have played an important part in the expansion of Polish exports to Nigeria, in which its share has grown to more than 80 per cent.

In 1967, the Soviet Union's Avtoexport established operations in Nigeria which are analogous to those it has undertaken in Finland (Konela) and Belgium (Scaldia-Volga) with which the reader is now familiar. WAATECO Ltd, its Nigerian subsidiary, is headquartered in Lagos and has branches in nine other Nigerian cities. Its primary mission is to market passenger cars (of a range of models) and other motor vehicles imported from the Soviet Union. In 1969 it opened one of the largest commercial and technical-service centres in Lagos; and in 1970 began assembling vehicles in a plant in Kaduna, in Northern Nigeria. WAATECO's sales grew rapidly in the early 1970s, with the Soviet Lada proving especially successful. Some 4,000 Ladas were sold in 1974.[46] The Soviet company then began to experience sharpened competition, as output from the Volkswagen and Peugeot assembly plants erected during Nigeria's second industrial development plan (1970–4), came on the market.[47] The long waiting lists for cars from the local vehicle assembly plants suddenly vanished.[48] Moreover, Nigerian import restrictions (duties, licences, advance deposits, and so on) were tightened in the second half of the 1970s. These factors slowed WAATECO's performance and induced it to diversify its product range to include industrial products for Nigeria's light industries.[49] At the same time, Avtoexport's original equity share of 80 per cent was reduced to 60 per cent under the pressure of Nigerian indigenisation laws.

In the manufacturing sector, Comecon investments have been concentrated in metal products, pharmaceuticals and wood processing. This emphasis accorded with the priorities of the

Nigerian development plans. Manufacturing operations which are less resource-intensive tend to be located in the Lagos industrial area, but some of the regional governments have also attracted Comecon investors to their jurisdictions.

Hungarian and Polish enterprises have been most active in the manufacture of metal products and pharmaceuticals. In terms of the latter, a Polish company, Polfa (Nigeria) Ltd, located in Lagos, employs a workforce of close to 150 in the production of a wide range of Polish pharmaceutical products. Imarsel Chemicals Co. Ltd, also in the Lagos area, produces various medicaments, with an emphasis on drugs for tropical diseases. Imarsel is jointly-owned by Hungary's Medimpex and a Medimpex affiliate based in Geneva.

The most advantageous locations for the wood-based industry are in the heavily forested southern parts of Nigeria. Romania's Forexim has set up operations in Calabar, in the south-east, and Ondo, in the south-west, in collaboration with the local state governments.[50] In both cases, Forexim's investments have been directed at the establishment of wood-based manufacturing complexes, including sawmills, plywood and particle-board plants and furniture factories. The final cost of the Ondo complex was placed at 24 million naira ($16.5 million).[51]

The third area in which Comecon enterprises have been active through direct investment in the Nigerian economy is engineering and construction services. Several mixed-capital companies formed in the early 1980s with Bulgarian equity participation will serve as examples here. Technoexportstroi (Nigeria) Ltd, was established in 1982 by the Bulgarian foreign trade organisation of that name, which engages internationally in the 'planning, study, design and construction of all types of public utility, industrial and infrastructural projects', including the supply of related machinery, equipment and materials, and has been active in Nigeria since 1972.[52] The Nigerian company has settled on the construction of a modern administrative complex in Kano as its first project. It has also been awarded the contract for a bank headquarters bulding in Bauchi.[53] Two other recently established companies, Transkomplekt (Nigeria) Ltd and Transproject (Nigeria) Ltd, owned by the Bulgarian enterprise Transkomplekt-Engineering, are to participate in the design and construction of roads and port facilities.

These examples, together with the data in Table 7.3, illustrate the range of investment activities in Nigeria by Comecon enterprises. They demonstrate that, in a growing number of cases, direct investment has been chosen as the most effective vehicle for Comecon involvement in the Nigerian economy. Although political circumstances provided the initial opportunity, the development of investment relations has been essentially pragmatic.

Nevertheless, the experience has not been an entirely happy one. Comecon enterprises have at times found it difficult to compete in an unfamiliar environment with longer-established, European companies; while Nigeria's regulatory system has increasingly put them at a disadvantage in competition with local firms. Nigerian content requirements have sometimes pushed Comecon companies prematurely into local manufacturing operations for which they were inadequately prepared.

Like other foreign-owned companies in Nigeria, Comecon subsidiaries and affiliates have faced mounting operational difficulties. Although Comecon investments tended to be concentrated in sectors which were not the primary target of Nigeria's successive indigenisation programme, tightened rules for foreign investment forced some disinvestment in cases where Soviet and East European equity in local companies exceeded newly prescribed limits.[54] Nigeria's balance-of-payments crisis, following the oil glut of the early 1980s, and related political instability, seriously worsened the business climate and reduced profitability.[55]

The experience of Fertesco, a mixed company engaged in the production and marketing of steel products, with Hungarian capital participation, illustrates several of these points. Direct marketing of imported products was hindered by high duties and other import controls. Local production proved unprofitable. As a consequence, the Hungarian investor ultimately decided to sell its stake in the venture.

Nigeria nevertheless continues to be regarded as a key country in Africa, and there is no sign of a loss of interest, much less a general withdrawal of Hungarian or other Comecon investments from the country. Problems encountered have tended to be viewed rather philosophically in the home countries as part of an inevitable learning experience. Comecon investment activity in Nigeria continued to develop, following the adoption in 1977 of Nigeria's second indigenisation decree, at a rate comparable to that set in the preceding decade, and showed signs of maintaining its momentum despite the economic and political instability of the early 1980s.

India

India has long held a central position in Soviet and East European theories of development and views of the Third World.[56] It has accordingly been a major object of Comecon policies to develop significant relationships with key Third World countries. Although in these circumstances, aid and trade have attained substantial magnitudes and assumed varied forms, Soviet and East European economic relations with India have not extended with any importance to the sphere of direct investment. The purpose of the following section will be to explore the reasons for this.

Its size and commanding geographic position in South Asia would alone have assured India a major place in Comecon relations with the Third World. Other factors have also been important, however. India's philosophy of economic development, with its emphasis on the role of the state, reliance on public sector development and national economic planning, have provided common ground for the expansion of relations with the Comecon countries. At the same time, India's foreign policy of non-alignment early created a favourable political climate for them. War with China and American military aid to Pakistan added impetus, as India sought a counterbalance in closer relations with the Soviet Union.[57] While Soviet–Indian relations have not been without their ups and downs, the special status they have generally been accorded by both sides was formally recognised in the bilateral Treaty of Peace, Friendship and Co-operation signed in 1971.

The less doctrinaire approaches, which have formed the basis for more recent Soviet policy towards Third World countries, have had a counterpart in a transition observed in India's foreign policy, away from the optimistic idealism and high principle of earlier years towards a more sober realism.[58] The greater pragmatism on both sides has been reflected in the course of their mutual relations.

India's trade with the Comecon countries grew especially rapidly after 1960, when payments for all transactions were shifted to a rupee basis, under the terms of bilateral trade and clearing agreements.[59] In 1981–2, transactions with these countries accounted for 15.5. per cent of India's foreign trade, owing primarily to the Soviet Union's position as India's principal trading partner.

The trade relationship was, however, an imbalanced one. In contrast to the 1960s, when India incurred consistent deficits in clearing trade, by the 1980s it had become a net exporter in trade with the Comecon countries, especially with the Soviet Union. Although the Soviet Union was the largest market for India's exports in 1981–2 (of, for example, wheat, other cereals and some capital goods), India's imports from the Soviet Union totalled only 77 per cent of exports. Moreover, the share of machinery and equipment in these imports had declined dramatically over the preceding decade, with Soviet oil now assuming a predominant role (80 per cent in 1981). India's emergence as an industrial power in its own right and its growing reluctance to accept second-best technology appear to be at the root of these trends.[60] Meanwhile, the United States had become the primary source of Indian imports, with its status as a supplier of industrial products especially pronounced.

These trends are also reflected in the altered aid relationship between India and the Comecon countries. In the 1960s, these countries, and most notably the Soviet Union, constituted a significant, though not dominant, source of aid to India. From the Indian perspective, they were particularly useful in their eagerness to channel assistance to public-sector development projects to which India gave high priority but found other aid donors, especially the United States, reluctant to support.[61] Soviet participation in the development of the Indian steel and oil industries was especially significant in this regard.[62]

More recently, Soviet aid to India, as to Third World countries in general, has been in decline.[63] Large-scale aid projects such as the Soviet-assisted Bhilai and Bokaro iron-and-steel plants are vestiges of an earlier, different period in Indo-Soviet economic relations. Although some concessionary terms may still be present in individual projects, there has been an effort to shift Soviet and East European involvement in Indian industrial development to a more commercial basis. Special importance has been attached to production co-operation on a compensation basis, with Comecon machinery and technology repaid in return flows of Indian raw materials or manufactures to Comecon markets. As the trends in trade cited above suggest, however, these efforts have met with limited success. The Indians have apparently been reluctant to incur the technological and commercial dependence which such arrangements seemed to entail.[64]

It is surprising in these circumstances that the Comecon countries have not sought to make more use of joint production enterprises and on-site trading and marketing companies as a vehicle to promote a new, more business-orientated presence in the Indian economy.

As has been noted, these ventures are also emphasised in East European literature as a 'new form of economic relations between CMEA member-countries and developing countries'.[65] As Table 7.4 shows, however, Comecon direct investments have been rather rare, especially in consideration of the extent of overall economic and political relations with India.

There is no known Soviet direct investment in the Indian economy. As for the handful of joint companies which East European enterprises are known to have established, these can scarcely be regarded as representing a significant contribution to the development of the economic ties of Comecon countries with India. None has been principally engaged in export marketing. The two best-known companies have been for the joint manufacture of pharmaceuticals. One of these, Themis Chemicals Ltd of Bombay, in which Hungary's Medimpex has a quarter of the equity, reportedly accounts for a sizeable share of the Indian market for vitamin products. A few joint fishing ventures were set up in the late 1970s in response to India's declaration of a 200-mile, offshore Exclusive Economic Zone.[66] Several joint companies have been created to process the products of India's agricultural sector. Only Czechoslovak enterprises have invested in the equipment sector (tractor assembly) or used a locally established company as a vehicle to participate in industrial projects in India.

Several factors may be advanced as possible reasons for this relatively unimpressive record, with the full explanation no doubt resting in a combination of all of them.[67] As noted, the Soviet Union is India's principal economic partner among the Comecon countries and even then has been seen generally to lag behind the East European countries in direct investment activity in the Third World. India's 'socialist-orientated' approach to industrial development may well have made the Soviet Union especially reluctant on political and ideological grounds to depart from more traditional forms in the Indian case; and this tendency has probably been reinforced by the Soviet preference for state-to-state arrangements, for which the Indian economic system appeared to provide ample scope. It should be recalled, on the other hand, that Soviet efforts since the late 1960s, at the inter-governmental level, to promote production specialisation and other forms of industrial co-operation between Soviet and Indian enterprises, without recourse to joint ownership, have not been notably successful.[68]

No doubt a major further inhibiting factor has been India's

Table 7.4 Soviet and East European companies in India

Company name	Head office	Year established	Comecon partner	Comecon equity %	Principal activity
Indopol Shipping Lines[a]	Bombay	1960	Polish Ocean Lines (Poland)	n.a.	Shipping services
Curewel (India) Ltd	Faridabad	1967	Technoexport (Bulgaria)	49	Manufacture of pharmaceuticals
Themis Chemicals Ltd	Bombay	1969	Medimpex (Hungary)	25.4	Manufacture and marketing of pharmaceuticals
International Leathers Ltd	Madras	1974	Production Association for Hides and Skins (Romania)	12.5	Processing and marketing of sheep and goat skins
Kelbex	n.a.	1977	Rybex (Poland)	n.a.	Fishing, processing and marketing of fish
(Unknown)	n.a.	1977	Agros (Poland)	n.a.	Processing of potatoes into alcohol and potato starch
Skoda India Pvt. Ltd	New Delhi	Pre-1977	Skodaexport (Czech)	n.a.	Construction and technical services for industrial projects
KS Diesels Pvt. Ltd	Bombay	1972	Motokov (Czech)	n.a.	Manufacture of multi-cylinder fuel injection equipment
Peejay Bulgarian Fisheries Ltd	New Delhi	1978	Ribno Stopanstvo (Bulgaria)	n.a.	Fishing, processing and marketing of fish products

[a] Similar functions appear to be performed by Polish Ocean Steamships Pvt. Ltd of Bombay.

Note: In addition to the above there have been reports of a German Democratic Republic company in India, established in 1977, but no further details are available. See also general notes to Table 7.1.

equivocal attitude towards foreign investment.[69] Most foreign investment in India occurred either during British rule or during the first twenty years of independence – well before the Comecon countries embarked on their own foreign-investment strategy. In the following two decades, foreign investors faced an increasingly complex set of restrictions administered by a large state bureaucracy according to the practices of an unfamiliar political culture. At the same time, the Indian government has sought to encourage foreign investment in some sectors – export-orientated and high-technology industries – through the creation of special incentives, including the establishment of free-trade zones.[70]

Foreign equity holdings in India have, since 1973, been limited to a maximum of 40 per cent of an enterprise, except in special circumstances. A Foreign Investment Board screens and approves proposals for new investment to ensure that they are in the national interest, bringing capital and technology to priority sectors where indigenous capabilities are regarded as insufficient. There has also been a system of state licensing of all new industrial undertakings in effect in India since 1951. Moreover, India's Industrial Policy Resolution of 1956, which established the mixed character of the economy, reserved certain sectors exclusively for state investment.

Most significantly, from the perspective of potential investment by Comecon countries in India, the government has, under the 1973 Foreign Exchange Regulation Act, specified a number of industries for which new foreign investment is no longer needed. These include many of the areas in which Comecon investments elsewhere have been concentrated: machine tools, agricultural machinery, transport equipment, medical and surgical appliances and electrical equipment, among others. Those sectors to which India is interested in attracting foreign investment are not those in which Comecon countries have gained sufficient strength to be competitive with other sources. Furthermore, Indian regulations prohibit the establishment of purely commercial companies under foreign ownership.

In sum, Comecon investment experience in Nigeria and India offers an interesting contrast. Nigeria's industrial planning and indigenisation programmes have nevertheless left considerable scope for direct investments by Soviet and East European enterprises, while India's earlier and more comprehensive policies in both these directions have not. Probably at the root of the difference in experience in the two countries is what can be observed as a shifting economic relationship between the Comecon countries and the more

advanced developing countries.[71] India's industrial development has
produced domestic capabilities in areas which are competitive with
those of most of the Comecon countries. The erosion of earlier
complementarities has not only created new problems in traditional
patterns of trade, but has impeded their replacement with forms of
industrial co-operation and joint investment.

NOTES AND REFERENCES

1. The Institute for Research on Multinationals in Geneva is sponsoring
   studies on Austria, the United Kingdom, Ireland, France, Sweden and
   the Federal Republic of Germany. A dissertation by Julien Brabants at
   the University of Leuwen examines the Belgian experience.
2. The Capital Movements Code of the OECD (1959) envisaged the
   progressive elimination of restrictions on capital movements among
   member countries.
3. *National Legislation Relating to Transnational Corporations*, ST/CTC/6
   (New York: United Nations, for the Centre on Transnational
   Corporations, 1978). These are in marked contrast to the severe
   restrictions which the Comecon countries impose on inflows of Western
   and other foreign investment.
4. A Polish author has recently affirmed that, 'the regulations in the
   developed countries offer considerable freedom in the establishment of
   firms with foreign capital. Most of those countries post in general no
   obstacles concerning the proportion between the foreign and local
   shares of capital' (H. Sawicki, 'Polish Firms Abroad', *Polish Foreign
   Trade*, No. 3, 1983, p. 10.)
5. Restrictive conditions encountered in the United States, which have
   taken a somewhat different form, are discussed later in this chapter.
6. *National Legislation Relating to Transnational Corporations*, ibid., p. 19.
7. *Sweden Your Market*, published by the state-owned PKBanken
   (Stockholm 1982).
8. Foreign Investment Review Agency, Government of Canada, 'A
   Comparison of Foreign Investment Controls in Canada and Australia'
   FIRA Papers No. 5, (Ottawa, April 1979).
9. *National Legislation Relating to Transnational Corporations*, ibid., pp.
   19–20.
10. For an earlier account, see McMillan, 'Soviet and East European Direct
    Investment in Canada', *Foreign Investment Review*, Spring 1979. All value
    data in this section are expressed in Canadian dollars.
    was revived and restructured in 1955.
12. Ultimately, neither of these ventures proved successful. The Omnitrade
    manufacturing operations were reportedly liquidated in the early 1980s.
    Established in 1979, just prior to the Polish crisis, the bicycle assembly
    project soon foundered as the result of a dispute over partner
    contributions to the venture.
13. See Chapter 4, note 19. A renewed effort (since 1983) to market

Czechoslovak Skoda cars in Canada has followed the Soviet example of selling through a Canadian agent company (rather than through the Motokov subsidiary in Canada, which only plays a liaison role in the operation).

4. The new Bank Act (1981) allows non-Canadian banks to incorporate Canadian banking subsidiaries and engage in the same banking activities as Canadian chartered banks, but restricts their share of total bank assets in Canada to 8 per cent. See, for example, W. Mitchell and D. Derr, 'Opportunities in Canadian Banking', *Foreign Investment Review*, Spring 1981.

5. Author interview with bank officials.

6. Sole ownership also allows profits to be taken at home, to avoid Canadian taxes.

7. Total assets were, of course, considerably greater, approaching Canadian $30 million in 1980, in the case of Belarus, the largest Comecon-owned company in Canada.

8. Statistics Canada, Ottawa. Long-term loans for a variety of purposes comprise much of the cumulative investment.

9. *Statistics Canada Daily*, 28 October 1983, p. 12.

20. A case study of Belarus was included as Appendix E in McMillan, *Direct Soviet and East European Investment in the Industrialized Western Economies*', *op. cit.*, pp. 56–8.

21. There are indications that the visa rules were tightened in the early 1980s. At a meeting of the Canada–USSR economic commission in June 1983, the Soviet side complained that the visa application procedure has become slower and more complicated, that visas are issued for only three months and that they had been requested to reduce the technical staff in the Belarus office in Regina.

22. This category includes directors, chief executive officers, vice-presidents and chief financial officers.

23. Canadian barriers of this sort are described in K. Stegemann, *Canadian Non-Tariff Barriers to Trade* (Montreal: Private Planning Association of Canada: 1973). The Comecon countries have long faced serious obstacles in terms of Western non-tariff barriers, especially with regard to valuation procedures and the related application of anti-dumping rules. See Wilczynski, *The Economics and Politics of East–West Trade*, *op. cit.*, Ch. 9.

4. The Soviet aircraft would have been in competition with the Canadian built Dash-7. Similar problems blocked Soviet efforts to market a modified YAK-40 in the United States. See Appendix G, on the Socan case, in McMillan, *Direct Soviet and East European Investment in the Industrialized Western Economies*, *op. cit.*

25. This indicator of the growth of exports over the decade neglects the sales through EMEC Trading of Soviet power machinery, which were temporarily significant in the mid-1970s.

6. As discussed in Chapter 4.

7. *Financial Post* (Toronto, 19 May 1973).

28. Statement of V. N. Sushkov, Soviet Deputy Minister of Foreign Trade, to Canada–USSR Mixed Economic Commission, 1 June 1983.

29. *National Legislation Relating to Transnational Corporations*, *op. cit.*, Appendix III. The few restrictions on foreign investment which the United States Government does impose in certain sectors are mostly on national security grounds, and apply equally to all foreign investment, regardless of source.

30. On the growth of foreign capital investment in the United States, see the survey article in *The Economist*, 25 October 1980. US Presidential Executive Order 11858 of 7 May 1975 directs the committee to review investments which 'might have major implications for United States national interests' and to 'consider proposals for new legislation or regulations relating to foreign investments as may appear necessary'.

31. President Reagan issued a major investment policy statement on 9 September 1983 reaffirming that the United States in general welcomes foreign direct investment. American officials stress that the Committee for Foreign Investment in the United States does not have the authority to establish entry requirements for foreign investments, nor does it have the power to require notification or to allow or disallow investment in the United States, but exists and operates entirely within the context of the basic open American policy on foreign investment.

32. Romania received MFN status in 1972 and Hungary in 1978. In both cases, MFN privileges are subject to periodic congressional review, under the provisions of the 1974 Trade Act.

33. These issues, which had contributed to the disruption of bilateral relations after 1956, were Cardinal Mindszenty's refuge in the American Legation in Budapest, settled in 1971, and the dispute over the Crown of St Stephen, returned in 1978.

34. Pisar, *Coexistence and Commerce*, *op. cit.*, discusses Amtorg's legal status and activities in the United States.

35. In one case, there have been other contributing factors. The official of one Polish company, Polamco, based in Chicago and engaged in the marketing and servicing of Polish machinery and equipment, was arrested on charges of espionage in 1981 (*New York Times*, 4 July 1981). While Polamco, a medium-sized firm with 95 employees, has continued in operation, the impact of the affair and the deterioration in overall business conditions have reportedly led to a decision to shut down its operations once its inventory has been liquidated. Agropol established in Chicago in 1978 to market Polish foodstuffs, was reported in 1983 to be inactive, but still legally in existence.

36. *National Legislation Relating to Transnational Corporations*, *op. cit.* p. 10.

37. T. Biersteker, *Distortion or Development? Contending Perspectives on the Multinational Corporation* (Cambridge Mass.: MIT Press, 1978) Ch 4.

38. L. Schaetzl, *Industrialization in Nigeria: a Spatial Analysis* (Munich Weltforum Verlag, 1973) p. 27.

39. E. Ajayi, 'Nigeria–Soviet Relations 1960–68', *Nigerian Bulletin on Foreign Affairs*, January 1972, p. 7.

40. See O. Ogunbadejo, 'Ideology and Pragmatism: the Soviet Role in Nigeria', *Orbis*, Winter 1978.

1. G. Wild, 'La Présence Economique Soviétique en Afrique Subsahrienne', *Le Courrier des Pays de l'Est*, December 1979; *African Development*, May 1971, p. 4.

2. See N. Berger, *Industrialization Policies in Nigeria* (Munich: Weltforum Verlag, 1975).

3. A. Hilton, 'The Changing Role of Private Foreign Investment in Nigeria', *Bulletin on Foreign Affairs*, May 1972.

4. *Polish Foreign Trade*, No. 5, Warsaw, 1977.

5. *Polish Economic Survey*, No. 12 1976.

6. *West Africa*, 7 October 1974, p. 1238.

7. Berger, *Industrialization Policies in Nigeria*, *op. cit.*, p. 98.

8. *The Economist*, 4 November 1978, pp. 78–81.

9. *Soviet Business and Trade*, 5 July 1979, p. 9.

10. *Romanian Foreign Trade*, No. 3, 1973; *African Development*, November 1974; *Bulletin on Foreign Affairs*, February 1977.

11. *West Africa*, London, 11 July 1977.

12. *Bulgarian Foreign Trade Organizations* (Sofia: Bulgarian Chamber of Commerce and Industry, 1981) p. 40; *Bulgaria Today*, No. 420, 1983, p. 14.

13. 'Technoexportstroi in Africa and the Middle East', *Economic Bulletin*, No. 5, 1983, p. 12.

14. The Nigerian Enterprises Promotion Act of 1977 reserved certain business activities exclusively for Nigerians and limited foreign ownership in the remainder to maxima of 40 per cent and 60 per cent, depending upon their nature.

15. An article in *The Economist*, 28 January 1984, p. 64 described importing in Nigeria as 'a nightmare of forms, fiddling and delays'. See also the survey 'Nigeria after the Coup' in *Financial Times*, 23 January 1984.

16. See, for example, S. Clarkson, *The Soviet Theory of Development: India and the Third World in Marxist–Leninist Scholarship* (University of Toronto Press, 1978).

17. S. Surindar, *Politics and Society in India* (Calcutta: Naya Prakash, 1974) and P. Chopra, *Before and After the Indo-Soviet Treaty* (New Delhi: S. Chand & Co., 1971).

18. S. Surindar, ibid. See also T. Bergmann, *The Development Models of India, the Soviet Union and China* (Amsterdam: Van Gorcum, 1977).

19. D. Nayyar, 'India's Trade with Socialist Countries' in Nayyar (ed.), *Economic Relations between Socialist Countries and the Third World*, *op. cit.*, pp. 105–42.

20. By 1980, manufactured goods comprised 62 per cent of India's exports, with machinery and transport equipment accounting for 10 per cent. On these points, see also Valkenier, *The Soviet Union and the Third World: an Economic Bind*, *op. cit.*, p. 141.

21. A. Datar, *India's Economic Relations with the USSR and Eastern Europe* (London: Cambridge University Press, 1972) and P. Chaudhuri, 'East European Aid to India' in Nayyar, *Economic Relations*, ibid., pp. 143–62.

22. Desai, *The Bokaro Steel Plant, a Study of Soviet Economic Assistance* (Amsterdam: North-Holland, 1972).

63. *The New York Times*, 2 January 1984.
64. Valkenier, *The Soviet Union*, *op. cit.*, p. 142 and sources cited therein.
65. Recall Vlasov, 'New Form of Economic Relations' (Ch. 4, n. 39, p. 76).
66. For a discussion of the impact of these zones, see J. Kurien, 'Entry of Big Business into Fishing', *Economic and Political Weekly*, 9 September 1978.
67. Even if the cases presented in Table 7.4, which have been checked against the Indian official registry, fail to include several instances of Comecon direct investment in the Indian economy, they would still comprise only a tiny share of the upwards of 800 foreign companies in India.
68. Valkenier, *The Soviet Union*, *op. cit.*, p. 18.
69. For a Western assessment of the business climate for multinational enterprise in India, see *The Economist*, 8 January 1983.
70. Details of Indian foreign investment regulations and incentives are based on *National Legislation Relating to Transnational Corporations*, and on information furnished by the Indian Investment Centre in New York.
71. Compare the discussion of this theme in Nayyar (ed.), *Economic Relations*, *op. cit.*

CHAPTER 8

Trends, Issues and Prospects

The rise of foreign direct investment from the Comecon countries has already begun to pose important questions of national and international policy. These have emerged both at the multilateral level and in bilateral relations. Before the discussion turns to these issues, however, it will be useful to review the major characteristics of the growth of multinational activity by Soviet and East European state enterprises. These should already have begun to take shape for the reader in the course of the preceding chapters, so that a restatement in summary form will be sufficient here.

TRENDS IN SOCIALIST MULTINATIONAL ENTERPRISE

Foreign direct investment from the Comecon countries is essentially a phenomenon of the period since the mid-1960s. The Soviet Union, it will be recalled, set up (or re-established) a handful of companies abroad in the 1920s, under the impetus of Lenin's New Economic Policy and with the opening of diplomatic and commercial links to the capitalist world. All but a few were either abandoned in the 1930s, when under Stalin the Soviet economy was reorganised and the country retreated into relative isolation, or they disappeared during World War II. In Eastern Europe after the war some of the newly nationalised enterprises inherited foreign business assets along with other property from their capitalist predecessors which they in most cases reactivated as external relations resumed. A few scattered new investments were undertaken in the early post-war years, notably by Poland and the Soviet Union. Less than 15 per cent of the total number of investments in the West which had been recorded by 1983, however, date from before 1965. In the South, the level of investments made before 1965 was even less significant – about five per cent of the cumulative total for 1983 (see Figures 8.1 and 8.2).

Foreign investment activity began to gain momentum in the second half of the 1960s. The major exception in this regard was the German Democratic Republic, whose limited investments have been

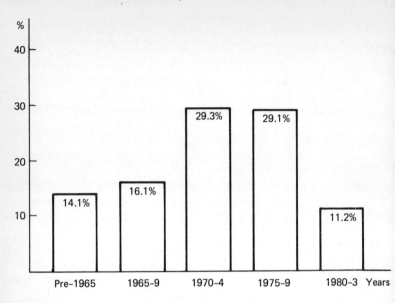

Figure 8.1   *Periods of growth of Comecon direct investment in the West*[a]

[a] Based on date of initial Comecon investment in a branch, subsidiary, or other affiliated company abroad. Percentage shares for various periods of cumulative total as of the end of 1983. Sample of 354 cases where date of initial investment established.

Source: Comecon Foreign Investment Data Bank, East–West Project, Carleton University, Ottawa.

undertaken sporadically, and do not reveal any significant upward trend over the period since World War II. The first Bulgarian investment was made in 1964, and the first Romanian investment in 1967. The activity of the other countries also began to pick up at this time, and an early surge of foreign investments placed by Czechoslovak enterprises in 1968–9 is especially noteworthy.[1]

The rate of investment really began to accelerate in the 1970s, especially from 1972. Fourteen new Hungarian companies were established abroad in that year and eleven Romanian companies were formed the following year. In 1974, fourteen Polish and nineteen Soviet companies were set up, while an additional seventeen Soviet companies were established in 1976. The remaining years of the decade saw significant, if smaller, rates of new investment by individual countries. Altogether, the Comecon countries' multinational network of foreign companies had grown by the end

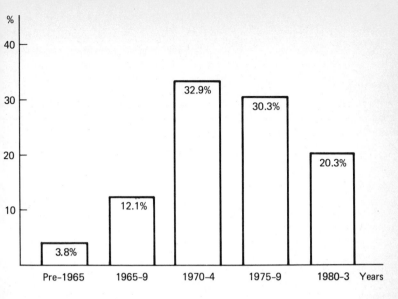

Figure 8.2 *Periods of growth of Comecon direct investment in the South*[a]

[a] Based on date of initial Comecon investment in a branch, subsidiary, or other affiliated company abroad. Percentage shares for various periods of cumulative total as of the end of 1983. Sample of 158 cases where date of initial investment established.

Source: Comecon Foreign Investment Data Bank, East–West Project, Carleton University, Ottawa.

of 1979 to nearly three-and-a-half times its size at the beginning of the decade.

Activity in the early 1980s presents a more mixed picture, though the analysis is far from final. In the developing countries, new Comecon investments continue to be recorded, Bulgaria and Hungary being especially active. In the West, however, the formation of subsidiaries, which had continued until 1980 at rates set in the 1970s, slowed in 1981 and declined dramatically in 1982–3.

These data all concern the rate at which decisions about new foreign investments have been taken. They do not tell much about trends in the volume of activity within the established multinational framework of Comecon state enterprises, or about the associated levels of investment in them. Significant growth in this regard can occur without any expansion by Comecon parent enterprises of their total number of foreign branches, subsidiaries and other affiliates.

The value data available on the foreign investment activity of Comecon state enterprises is not sufficiently comprehensive to enable broad trends to be quantified in this sense. A good deal of evidence has, however, been presented in the preceding chapters to indicate that this dimension, of intra-subsidiary growth, has also been significant. It will be recalled, for example, that the continued rapid increase of foreign direct investment in Canada from the Comecon countries over the latter half of the 1970s was primarily in terms of the expansion of existing companies. The three longest-established (that is, before 1965), East European marketing companies in Canada enjoyed a combined average annual growth of sales of nearly 16 per cent throughout the later years of the 1960s and through most of the 1970s.[2] Subsidiary growth has entailed not only the expansion of facilities (regional offices, retail networks, branch plants, and so on) in the host country where the subsidiary has its headquarters, but also the establishment of branch offices or affiliated companies in third countries.

The stock of Comecon foreign direct investment at any point in time – as measured by the number of foreign companies operative or by some index of their real value or volume of activity – is the net result of both additions and subtractions. It has been seen that there have been investment failures as well as successes. The level at which an enterprise may operate is a matter of degree, however, and activities may be wound down without ceasing completely. A foreign subsidiary may also cease operations, but continue in formal existence as a legal shell for possible future use. Cases of the sale of Comecon equity or the liquidation of all the assets of a foreign subsidiary are relatively rare. Such cases have been more thoroughly documented in the OECD countries than in the developing economies, but in both areas they appeared to constitute some ten per cent of the cumulative total of investments recorded by the end of 1983.

Comecon multinational enterprise has undergone significant changes in function over the last two decades of its major period of growth. There has been a diversification of primary activity from marketing to other functions, including production. In the sphere of production, there has been a tendency to integrate foreign operations into a broader system of production specialisation. In services generally, activities which were initially concentrated in support of the foreign trade of the home country have increasingly expanded to include other, unrelated functions. Finally, within the marketing sector, there has been a trend from simple trading operations, often involving a wide range of goods, to the more specialised marketing of industrial products and the addition of important auxiliary activities.

It is the broad, first trend which is easiest to quantify in terms of the statistical data available. Export marketing functions are no longer the overwhelming object of Comecon foreign direct investment that they were little more than a decade ago. Although investments in commercial operations have continued to grow, they constituted a substantially larger share of total Comecon investments in 1969 than they did in 1983. In the earlier year, marketing was the major activity of an estimated 73 per cent of the operations of Comecon multinational enterprises in the West and of 48 per cent in the South. It will be recalled from Tables 3.5 and 3.6, however, that by the end of 1983, these shares had fallen to 69 per cent and 26 per cent respectively. Moreover, in the later year, fewer of these investments were in purely commercial operations, while many incorporated as important secondary functions activities closely related to production, such as product modification and servicing.

As more economic activities take place within the tertiary sector, they are inevitably accompanied by an internationalisation of the production of services. The diversification of Comecon foreign investments to a broader range of service industries follows this general international trend. While some Soviet and East European banks abroad date from before World War II, much of the present level of investment in banking is due to a burst of investment activity that occurred in the period between 1971–7. The same period also saw a surge of investment in shipping and other transport services. The major growth of engineering and construction operations by Comecon enterprises, supported by direct investments, also occurred in the 1970s.

It is the internationalisation of material production by Comecon state enterprises that constitutes the most striking aspect of the diversification trend. The number of investments in the West in material production (especially manufacturing) increased more than five-fold between 1969 and 1983, with two-thirds of this growth concentrated in the years 1975–81. In the South, where they have a longer history, the second half of the 1970s and the early 1980s were also a period of signal expansion, witnessing nearly 45 per cent of all the investments in production undertaken to date in the developing economies by Comecon-based enterprises.

This extension of foreign investment to the creation of production capacity abroad is a response to many of the forces that have similarly motivated Western multinational enterprises. While specific motives were seen to vary widely in relative importance from case to case, they have had as their origin the same search for markets, for raw materials and for lower production costs. Occasionally the choice of investment was imposed by the regulations of the host country rather than being motivated by the needs of the home country or dictated by international commercial strategy.

Diversification of function has occurred within, as well as between, sectors. Apart from the case of a few (most Soviet and high-volume) companies engaged in trade in primary products, the traditional Comecon commercial enterprise established abroad has represented several home-based foreign trade enterprises and hence has imported and marketed a range of products from the home country. Newer companies tend to be more specialised (especially when dealing in technically more sophisticated, manufactured goods) and handle a narrower range. As already noted, this trend has been accompanied by increasing recourse to investment in auxiliary functions – the modification, distribution and servicing of the product – which the development of markets for such goods has required. Commercial subsidiaries abroad have also been placed at the service of home-country import requirements and charged with purchasing as well as selling goods. Some have undertaken to represent foreign firms on home markets and have established branch offices at home to carry out these more diversified trading objectives.

There has also been a marked trend towards diversification of commercial, banking, insurance, transport and other services to areas not directly related to the home country's foreign trade. This has increasingly occurred as companies abroad have gained experience which they could put to profitable use in serving a range of clients. Thus marketing companies have operated on behalf of other Comecon and Western firms on host markets, or have carried out trade transactions between host markets and third markets. Comecon banks abroad have financed other areas of international trade and have engaged in a variety of local banking operations. Insurance firms have followed a similar course of diversification. Transport companies have engaged in cross-shipping and hauling. Engineering and construction firms have placed their services at the disposal of a broader set of clients.

Such diversification suggests the increased autonomy of the

subsidiary and, in the case of marketing subsidiaries, an attenuation of the objective to fulfil export targets traditionally imposed on them by Comecon-based parents. Greater concern for profits means greater readiness to accept business orders from any sources. This in turn places greater competitive pressure on suppliers in the home country. It also renders more difficult the traditional practice of shifting excess inventories to subsidiary accounts. When soundly based, diversification thus serves to strengthen a subsidiary's operations, to enhance its reputation abroad and to provide a firmer foundation for expansion on the basis of its own, or locally raised funds.

Also noted in Chapter 6 was an important diversification within the relatively new sphere of material production abroad by Comecon enterprises. The 'classic' investment in foreign production has been undertaken to commercialise a technical advantage directly within a host economy, or otherwise to serve local demand more effectively from an on-site production base. What occurred, however, were the beginnings of investment in foreign production facilities intended to serve a broader international market and to form part of an integrated multinational system of production and distribution. This, in turn, entailed the search for convenient foreign locations from which home requirements could be served at lower cost. Both of these forms of multinational sourcing have been observed to be the object of increased investment interest by Western firms as well.

Noted, too, was that diversification of Comecon multinational enterprise has not always been a smooth process. There were the setbacks which several Soviet banks encountered in Western Europe and Asia when they sought to diversify their investment portfolios. There were unsuccessful bids to take over and revive ailing Western manufacturing operations, and several instances of investments in the establishment of new facilities which ended in failure. Nor have attempts to expatriate labour-intensive processing operations (especially textiles) through direct investment in the Eastern Mediterranean and the Middle East achieved notable results. Diversification of subsidiary activities outside the confines of East–West trade not only involves larger and more complex investment decisions, but also raises the visibility of Comecon investments and can expose them to the danger of becoming involved in local power struggles and political controversy. The failure of Balkancar's bid for Fenwick-Manutention shows that even a socialist government in power in the host country is no guarantee against such risks.

The functional diversification of Comecon multinational enterprise has contributed to shifts in the locational pattern of investments. These are no longer so concentrated in the traditional commodity markets and financial centres of Western Europe, such as London and Paris, or in neighbouring, politically neutral countries, such as Austria and Finland. They have increasingly moved into new parts of Europe (Ireland, Spain and Greece) and to North America and Australasia. In the South, investment activity remains more concentrated. Attempts to diversify geographically have been at least partially offset by political setbacks, such as the Iranian nationalisations. The fortunes of Comecon multinational enterprises have also been affected by political changes elsewhere in the Third World, for example, by the overthrow of the Allende regime in Chile and the termination of left-wing military rule in Peru. Diversification trends have also been blocked by indigenisation programmes and other restrictions on foreign investments by host governments.

The functional diversification of investments contributed to another notable trend, the concentration of Comecon ownership of foreign business assets through increases in equity holdings. This tendency, characteristic more of investment in the West than in the South, where it has faced legal limitations, has occurred both in the organisation of new companies abroad and through the re-organisation of existing ones. It was clear that the difference in preference among the Comecon countries for a particular structure of ownership was largely explicable in terms of the functions served by their investments. Significant local capital participation was far more typical of small, import–export firms than of large subsidiaries engaged in retailing, servicing and manufacturing. Banks and shipping companies were other areas in which a controlling interest was preferred. Hence, over time, the shift towards these activities has been accompanied by a rise in average Soviet and East European equity holdings.

There is evidence that other factors may have contributed to this trend in the structure of ownership. Divergence of objectives between East European parent enterprises and their local partners have led to resignations and buy-outs. National differences in temperament and outlook have also created friction. While these are problems common to the experience of all international partnerships, the differences in socio-economic system as well as national character present in the East–West case appear to have exacerbated them. Sole, or majority, ownership is seen as a way of reducing these problems, if it does not eliminate them entirely.[3]

The diversification of Comecon multinational enterprises to more specialised marketing and servicing functions, and to increased manufacturing abroad, has also served to raise the ratio of East European personnel to host-country nationals on the staffs of subsidiary companies. The higher ratio is due especially to the assignment of larger numbers of technical personnel from the home country. Both of these trends (increased East European equity and staffing) are, as was noted, limited in some host countries by foreign-investment regulations requiring local participation and by administrative restrictions on the residence of East European nationals.

QUESTIONS OF POLICY RAISED BY THE SPREAD OF SOCIALIST MULTINATIONAL ENTERPRISE

The growth of direct investment from the Comecon countries has raised controversial policy questions that affect relations at both the multilateral and bilateral levels. The purpose of this section is to set out and attempt to clarify these issues in light of the findings reported by the preceding chapters. The fundamental question to be addressed is whether or not direct investments from Comecon sources pose problems distinct from those to which the activities of multinational enterprises generally give rise, and hence whether they require special policy responses.

1. *Should the foreign direct investment activity of state enterprises based in the Comecon countries be subject to any agreed international code of conduct for multinational enterprise?*

In recognition of the broad concern over the economic and political issues arising from the growth world-wide of multinational enterprises, the Economic and Social Council of the United Nations created in 1974, the Commission on Transnational Corporations. At the same time, it established the Centre on Transnational Corporations, located in New York, to serve as the Commission's secretariat. This initiative had the stated aim of addressing collectively, at a broad, multilateral level, the task of developing regimes for international business appropriate to the interests of member states.

The centrepiece of the work of the Commission has been the preparation of a Code of Conduct on Transnational Corporations. In January 1977, an Intergovernmental Working Group was established for this purpose. By the end of 1982, its preparatory work had reached the point where it was felt that a special session of the Commission should be called for the Spring of 1983, 'with the objective of continuing and completing the formulation of the United Nations Code'.[4]

One of the most difficult issues in the preparation of the Code has been its scope and application and, in particular, whether it should apply to all state-owned enterprises, including those based in the Comecon countries. The 'Group of Eminent Persons', appointed by the United Nations in 1972 to launch its studies on the question, opted for broad coverage, asserting that 'multinational coporations are enterprises which own or control production or service facilities outside the country in which they are based. Such enterprises are not always incorporated or private; they can also be cooperatives or state-owned entities'.[5] In its 1973 report on *Multinationals in World Development*, the United Nations Secretariat was less explicit on the aspect of ownership, but otherwise no less comprehensive in its definition, stating that the term 'multinational corporation' applies to 'all enterprises which control assets – factories, mines, sales offices and the like – in two or more countries'.[6]

With the creation in 1974 of the Commission and the Centre, the United Nations shifted its terminology to 'transnational corporation'. This was possibly in the hope that, by adopting fresh terminology, without the contentious connotations attached to the older label, a broader consensus could be reached. The Commission continued, however, to define 'transnational corporation' in the same terms as the United Nations Secretariat has used 'multinational corporation' in its 1973 report.[7]

The representatives of the Comecon governments meanwhile argued that state entities in the Socialist countries and their affiliated companies abroad 'can in no way be regarded as, or be put on one level with, transnational corporations'.[8] They contended that the activities abroad of enterprises owned and managed by a socialist state are qualitatively distinct from those of capitalist firms orientated to the pursuit of private profits. It is the search for profits, they maintained, that causes multinational capitalist firms to cross the boundaries of law and decency. Socialist state enterprises, by contrast, are subject to discipline and control exercised by responsible authorities in their home countries.

The draft Code sought to resolve the issue through an integrated approach to the questions of definition and scope of application. In accordance with this approach, the following text was agreed at the working-group level:

> 1(a). The term 'transnational corporation' as used in this Code means an enterprise, comprising entities in two or more countries, regardless of the legal form and fields of activity of these entities, which operates under a system of decision-making, permitting coherent policies and a common strategy through one or more decision-making centres, in which the entities are so linked, by ownership or otherwise, that one or more of them may be able to exercise a significant influence over the activities of others, and, in particular, to share knowledge, resources and responsibilities with the others.
> 2. This Code applies to all enterprises having those characteristics mentioned in paragraph 1(a) above, regardless of their ownership.
> 3. The Code is universally applicable in and open for adoption by all States, regardless of their political and economic systems and their level of development.[9]

Nevertheless, the issue surfaced again in June 1983 when the Commission considered the draft of the third United Nations survey of transnational corporations in world development, prepared by the Centre. By contrast to its second survey, made in 1978, where the direct investment activities of Comecon state enterprises were cited as a notable new trend, the Centre's new survey sidestepped the question.[10] Even the section of the survey which treated state-owned enterprises made no mention of the activities of those based in the Comecon countries.[11] The only (passing) reference to the subject was contained in an annexe to the survey which dealt broadly with 'recent trends in international business arrangements' involving socialist state enterprises.[12] The annexe followed the approach seen to have been characteristic of East European literature, which treats the foreign investment activities of socialist state enterprises as a 'new form of international economic cooperation' rather than as a development in the evolution of multinational enterprise.

Objecting to this omission, several Western countries introduced a draft resolution requesting the Centre to prepare a study on the transnational operations of state-owned enterprises from both market-economy and centrally-planned economy countries, with respect in particular to their activities in developing countries.[13] While a motion was adopted which postponed consideration of the draft resolution to the next session of the Commission, the controversy made an important contribution to the failure to complete the Code in 1983.

If the Soviet and East European position were accepted, the foreign investment activity of Comecon state enterprises would be placed in a special category, exempt from any international code of conduct for multinational enterprises to which the enterprises of other countries, developed or developing, were subject. The Comecon countries are no doubt less concerned about the potential impact of the provisions of the Code, however, than about the ideological and political implications of accepting its applicability to their own enterprises.

The flexibility of the Soviet and East European countries on the issue is limited first of all by the terms of their traditional ideological position on the issue of multinational enterprises. Having long equated multinational enterprise with imperialist exploitation, they cannot easily accept application of the label to their own activities, especially in the Third World. To do so would not only be embarrassing, it would also involve a major ideological reversal, with potentially damaging domestic as well as international repurcussions, to regimes whose legitimacy is to a considerable degree based on ideology.

Acceptance of the applicability of the Code would counteract the long-standing efforts of the socialist countries to offer themselves to the Third World as an alternative model of development. The success of such efforts depends in part on dissociation of the foreign economic activities of Comecon enterprises from those of Western firms. The high-level official importance attached to the need for differentiation is illustrated by a statement in 1976 by the Romanian Minister of Foreign Trade on the nature of Romania's economic activities in the Third World. Their orientation, he concluded, 'fundamentally differentiates our country's policy with regard to the states of the "Third World" from the relations promoted by their former mother countries and by the multinational companies'.[14]

Acceptance would also serve to undermine the basic position of the Comecon countries on the claims of the developing countries advanced under the aegis of the New International Economic Order. This position rejects any responsibility for the economic problems of the Third World, which it attributes to the history of exploitation by the developed capitalist countries.[15] Here, in addition, the East European position hinges on clear differentiation of socialist relations with the developing economies from those of the capitalist countries.

The differentiation also helps to justify the restrictions which the Comecon countries impose on the foreign activities of multinational enterprises within their own economies. Moreover, these have been offered to the developing countries as an example of how the latter might similarly defend themselves against the 'imperialist' threat faced in common.

If the East European stand on the issue of applicability of the Code is thus understandable in ideological and political terms, it is not well grounded in fact. The Comecon countries have presented very little in the way of argumentation or evidence in extension and support of their position.[16] Meanwhile, their actions, in emulation of those of Western multinational enterprises, have served to develop the opposite case.

State-owned enterprises are by no means a phenomenon exclusive to Eastern Europe, and are now common in most developed and developing countries. Studies show that while their behavioural patterns vary, and although they may enjoy the advantages of special state policy support and financial backing, state-owned enterprises in most respects operate little differently from counterpart, private firms. In fact, they pride themselves on competing successfully with the latter within the rules of the market-place.[17] This also holds true for their foreign operations; and state-owned enterprises based outside the Comecon countries have increasingly joined the ranks of the multinational enterprises.[18] Moreover, for larger private firms, the profit motive is attenuated by other objectives of a more bureaucratic nature, such as desired rates of corporate growth, targeted market shares, and so on. An important determinant of the behaviour of private firms in the capitalist countries are the goals of the state including, in some cases, national foreign investment strategies.[19] The original distinction between private and state enterprises, based on ownership, has been blurred by the acquisition by capitalist states of discretionary powers to direct enterprise operations through a growing variety of regulations.[20] Hence the phenomenon of multinational enterprise can no longer be regarded as originating exclusively in the private sector and rooted in the profit-maximising initiatives of individual firms.

It is perhaps not very surprising, therefore, if it should often have been found that the behaviour of Comecon state enterprises operating in a similar economic environment abroad, bears many of the characteristics of Western multinational enterprises, both state and private. Their foreign direct investments were seen to be motivated by many of the same commercial considerations. Neither these companies, nor their parents, are indifferent to their profit position, although other goals are important for them also – gross (hard-currency) revenue, market penetration and so on – just as they are for capitalist firms. The foreign branches and subsidiaries of Comecon enterprises compete directly with capitalist counterparts; and in interviews their managers betray many of the same attitudes, also taking pride in the operation of their companies in a competitive, businesslike fashion within a market setting. In their behaviour abroad, Comecon state enterprises tend rather to conform to international commercial norms than to reflect the particular ideology of their home country.[21] Comecon subsidiaries are often indistinguishable from other firms in host countries and their origins generally go unrecognised.

The multinational operations of Comecon enterprises certainly lag far behind those of Western firms in magnitude and development. They reveal, however, many of the features of Western multinational enterprises at earlier stages and show signs of following a similar evolutionary course. The trends in Comecon multinational enterprise traced in the first section of this chapter are generally characteristic of the development of Western multinational investments.

Even at the present stage, to pass off the foreign investment activities of Comecon state enterprises simply as 'joint marketing ventures' is highly misleading.[22] Many are wholly-owned or majority-owned by Comecon-based parents, or are otherwise effectively controlled by them. A large share, even in the West but especially in the South, are engaged in production, or in services other than commercial. Moreover, there was evidence of increasing concentration of East European ownership, unless obstructed by the regulations of the host country, and of a functional diversification over time away from purely commercial activities.

It is, perhaps, more appropriate to compare the multinational activities of Comecon enterprises with those of firms in the developing countries, another emergent source of foreign direct investment. Comprehensive studies of the rise of foreign investment from the developing countries have only just begun to appear. They do, however, suggest a number of close parallels with the multinational enterprise of the Comecon countries.[23] These are found not only in terms of the form and function of investments, and in the economic forces motivating them, but also in the often more salient role played by the state than is true in the case of Western multinational activity.[24] A major difference is that the bulk of Third World direct investment flows are intraregional, whereas those of the Comecon countries – for reasons rooted in their ideologies and institutions – are entirely extraregional.

In sum, the motives for foreign investment and the behaviour of Comecon state enterprises are sufficiently analogous to those of firms based in the West and South, state or private in ownership, to warrant their inclusion in any comprehensive survey of multinational, or transnational, enterprise in the world economy. By extension, it would seem reasonable, therefore, to incorporate them in any international regulation of multinational behaviour.[25] All enterprises, regardless of their origins, nature or relative importance, should be covered by the international Code of Conduct. If their behaviour is proved benign, the Code should have no inhibiting effect on their activities. The question remains, however, whether in addition to foreign investment behaviour sufficiently characteristic to warrant coverage by the Code, Comecon-based multinational enterprises display attributes which require special attention on the part of host governments.

2. *Does foreign direct investment by Comecon state enterprises pose a special threat to the economic interests of host countries?*

The potential for such a threat may be delineated along two lines. The first is in the relative impact of Comecon investments on the host economy, in terms of their nature and scope. The second lies in the potential for manipulation, given the special relationship of control which exists between enterprise and state in the Comecon countries.

Comecon investments abroad are scattered across a wide range of countries and sectors. They seldom account for more than a negligible share of the total stock of foreign direct investment in a given host economy, nor do they play a major role in individual sectors. Often, the foreign investments in a given economy of a large Western multinational enterprise are economically more significant than those of any single Comecon country. Relative to the nature, magnitude and concentration of foreign investment from major Western sources, that of Comecon enterprises gives little cause for concern at present in terms of domination or control of the industries of the host country. (A possible exception that might be cited is international maritime transport, where the Soviet Union, as noted earlier, has become a major force. Here it is, the size of the Soviet merchant fleet which it helps to support rather than the extent of foreign direct investment in shipping itself which poses the competitive challenge.)

Because of the centralised decision-making structures of the Comecon countries, the foreign investments of a Comecon state enterprise nevertheless provide potential for the exercise of greater economic power than do the investments of an equal magnitude by a private, Western firm. Comecon investments are backed by the force – political and economic – of the state, and are linked through systems of centralised planning and management to the foreign investment operations of other national enterprises subject to the state's control. Thus the full set of investments in, say, the European Common Market by a given Comecon country are potentially subordinate to single direction.

In practice, however, whatever potential exists for such centralised state management and control does not appear to be exercised to any significant degree. Although Comecon investments are intended to advance broad, state goals of a macroeconomic nature, such as improvement of the external balances of trade and payments, there is no evidence that subsidiary operations are centrally-managed in any detail.[26] The newness of these investments may have contributed to the failure to have developed the mechanisms for more systematic co-ordination of subsidiary operations. Their still-limited extent in any foreign sector has, no doubt, reduced the incentive for central direction.

There is no evidence, in fact, of even broad co-ordination of foreign direct investment activities among Comecon-member countries.[27] Only one instance of joint foreign investment by enterprises based in different Comecon countries has been identified (a joint Czechoslovak–East German freight-forwarding company in London). There are, on the contrary, examples of sharp competition among Comecon enterprises abroad.[28] This situation is reflective of a more general failure of the Comecon countries to co-ordinate their extraregional economic relations in important areas, especially the acquisition of foreign technology. There has been some joint borrowing, through Comecon regional banks, but otherwise co-ordination has been limited to relatively minor matters, such as the standardisation of contracting procedures.

At this juncture, the multinational activities of Comecon state enterprises are more significant as an interesting new development, in terms of both global trends in foreign-investment and the evolution of Comecon systems of foreign trade, than as a major new economic force in the world economy. Moreover, and perhaps more importantly, their potential to develop into such a force is limited by the scarcity of investment resources and convertible currency funds which Comecon countries can allocate to the purposes of external investment at this stage in their development.

Comecon foreign investment can, in fact, be of mutual economic benefit to home countries and host countries. Comecon trade with the West has suffered from chronic imbalances, in volume and structure, which have limited its growth. Investments in support of Comecon exports and other foreign-currency earning activities are aimed at reducing these imbalances. They are particularly important for the development of stable West European markets for Comecon-manufactured goods. If successful, they would obviate the necessity for the elaborate counter-trade arrangements which currently encumber East–West trade.

The functional importance of Comecon foreign investments in support of exports to the West has increased dramatically in the conditions of the 1980s. West European credits are unlikely to continue to support the trade imbalances which they bridged in the 1970s. At the same time, substitutes must be developed for important traditional Comecon primary-product exports to the West, which are in decline. Meanwhile, more effective means must be found to gain and maintain access to Western markets characterised by rising domestic protection and sharpened foreign competition. The alternative, in the circumstances, is the stagnation or decline of East–West trade.

There are also more direct advantages to be reaped from the multinational activity of Comecon enterprises. Consumers in host countries benefit from the efforts of subsidiaries to make Comecon enterprises producing for export more responsive to external market requirements. This, in effect, has been the primary mission of many marketing subsidiaries established abroad. Their functions, as has been seen, have included not only the feedback of information to home enterprises, but they have also extended to direct product modification and servicing within the export market.

While primarily directed to the expansion of Comecon exports, Soviet and East European foreign investments serve to facilitate trade in both directions. Comecon subsidiary companies and banks abroad arrange finance, insure and transport foreign exports to East European markets. They not infrequently represent foreign exporters, and otherwise mediate in the negotiation and conclusion of contracts between foreign firms and enterprises in their home countries.

In addition to equity partnerships formed with foreign firms and individuals, the multinational enterprises of Comecon countries participate in non-equity ventures in host countries or third countries through their foreign subsidiaries. These various forms of collaboration may be presumed to be of mutual benefit to the parties concerned.

Comecon investments in the West and South tend to be in those areas in which East European enterprises have developed comparative advantages, often technological advantages. Subsidiaries abroad thus serve as a channel through which technology developed in the socialist countries is made available to users in host countries. The preceding chapters have provided a number of examples of Soviet and East European machinery and equipment marketed or manufactured by subsidaries abroad (machine tools, power generating machinery, transport and construction equipment, optical and scientific instruments) whose competitiveness is based at least in part on their technical superiority.

Comecon investments in the developing economies were seen to have served an especially wide variety of purposes. Many of these investments are identical in nature and motivation to those of Western multinational enterprises, and a few have been made in partnership with Western firms. A large number have been connected with industrial development projects in these economies, many of them in the form of joint undertakings with local partners, often national or regional development authorities in the host countries. Without a more thorough examination of the relative impact of Comecon investments in the Third World than has been possible to date, only tentative conclusions can be drawn. It would seem, however, that on the whole, the direct investments in Third World economies of Comecon state enterprises serve more as development assistance than do the investments in these economies of Western multinational enterprises. This does point to what would appear to be a significant difference between the present roles of the multinational enterprises of Comecon and Western countries in the developing economies, with a number of individual exceptions to the general case to be found on both sides.

3. Do direct investments increase Soviet and East European foreign policy leverage?

The extraterritorial reach of the state through the foreign investments of national firms, private as well as public, is an old issue in international political economy, both pre-dating and transcending the phenomenon of multinational investment activity by Soviet and East European state enterprises.[29] The United States government, to cite an important recent example, made highly publicised use in 1982 of the investments of American companies in Europe as instruments of its sanctions policies towards the Soviet Union. When they assert that East European state enterprises are not governed by the profit incentive motivating Western private firms, official representatives of the Comecon countries would seem to imply that their foreign investments are directed towards broader objectives. To what extent do these extend into the political sphere? Are foreign subsidiaries the instruments of state political, as well as economic, policy? (The security aspects of this question will be dealt with separately, in the following section.)

The institutional potential for such use would seem to be present. Foreign investment operations are analogous in this respect to Comecon foreign-trade operations. The East European state's monopoly of both trade and investment places at its disposal the organisational means to employ them in pursuit of foreign-policy objectives. The promised increase or threatened reduction of investment, as well as trade relations, could be employed to influence the policies of host governments. Ministries in the home country could direct subsidiaries to discriminate politically in the choice of customers or suppliers, to make funds available for special purposes or to lobby host governments to desired ends.[30]

In practice, however, important factors militate against such use of their foreign investments by the Comecon countries.[31] These investments have not acquired the economic force to generate effective pressure on host governments. Joint ownership, when involving significant local managerial autonomy, can also impede the employment of subsidiaries for non-commercial purposes. Moreover, Comecon assets abroad are more significant than foreign assets in the Comecon economies, where they are either forbidden or severely restricted. This asymmetry raises the vulnerability of Comecon investments to unilateral actions by host countries: operations can be shut down and assets seized without fear of reciprocity in kind.

The Comecon countries have had cause to be sensitive to their

vulnerability in this regard. In the Third World, they have witnessed
subsidiaries nationalised, or their fortunes diminished, as the result
of unexpected shifts in local politics. In the West, the risks lie more
in the changeable climate of East–West relations and its effects on
the viability of subsidiary operations.[32]

For the present, then, foreign investments offer Comecon
governments little opportunity for exerting pressure on host countries
for specific foreign policy purposes. They do contribute, if as yet
rather marginally, to the Comecon economic presence in the host
country. In the Third World, this may further the broad political
objective of counterbalancing Western influence. On the whole,
however, Comecon investments pose a far less immediate challenge
than do foreign investments from other sources to the pursuit of
independent policies by host countries.

4. *Do the foreign subsidiaries of Comecon state enterprises serve to undermine the national security of host countries?*

It is in the area of national security that the potential reach of
Comecon states through their foreign investments has prompted
more concern. Several instances of Comecon multinational
enterprises having exceeded the boundaries of host-country law in
this area have attracted public attention, and the use of Comecon
subsidiaries for intelligence purposes has grown to be a favourite
theme for the more alarmist journalistic treatments of the 'red
multinationals'. Public and official concern appears, moreover, to be
on the increase, at least in some major Western countries (most
notably the United States).

The use of foreign-controlled subsidiary companies for intelligence
purposes is the legitimate, continuing concern of security agencies in
host countries. Subsidiary operations can camouflage a variety of
intelligence-related activities. Subsidiary personnel enjoy greater
mobility and less visibility than do diplomatic personnel. Given the
widespread perception in the West of the Soviet military threat and
the atmosphere of tension and hostility characteristic of much of the
history of East–West relations, it is not surprising that in the
Western countries, in particular, concern should focus on the potential
threat to security posed by the activities of Soviet and East European
subsidiaries.

In order to assess the validity of this concern, it is useful to treat
separately two basic aspects. Comecon subsidiaries are purported to
serve as a base for general intelligence operations and for political

subversion. They are also viewed as instruments for carrying out industrial espionage and for circumvention of controls on the export of strategic goods and technology.

Although one reads general assertions that 'Moscow's multinationals . . . oversee a growing intelligence network' and that the Comecon countries' foreign marketing and manufacturing companies 'serve as havens for spies', the evidence presented in support of such sweeping statements is anecdotal and unconvincing.[33] There have, indeed, been well-known cases of the involvement of Soviet and East European countries abroad in intelligence activity, several dating as far back as the 1920s. Considering the number of companies and Comecon nationals involved more recently, however, the incidents of subsidiary personnel charged with illegal activities by host countries are relatively rare. Analysis of seventy-six instances of intelligence activities in the West involving the Soviet Union and its East European allies, reported in the Press over a twelve-year period (1970–81), revealed only eight cases where persons attached to foreign subsidiaries were implicated.[34] Seven of these instances involved Soviet-owned companies, the other a Polish company. The overwhelming majority of the incidents reported involved diplomatic, Press and other personnel assigned abroad for various ostensible purposes.

By contrast to some well-known instances involving Western private multinational enterprises, concern about which contributed to the perceived need for international guidelines and codes of behaviour, Comecon state enterprises have not been implicated in local political meddling. The single public allegation of this nature of which the author is aware was made in a book published in 1979 by a French journalist, charging that the Soviet-owned Eurobank in Paris has been used to exercise financial control over the French Communist Party.[35]

The multinational operations of Soviet and East European state enterprises are not to be confused with the business activities of local communist parties and officials, although there may be occasional business dealings between them. Neither communist parties nor their officials are prominent among the local partners in joint stock companies with Soviet and East European capital participation. In Western Europe, communist party members have not infrequently used their political connections to prosper from East–West trade, as importers or representative agents for Comecon enterprises.[36] They have generally done so through their own companies, however, rather than through equity partnerships with Comecon state enterprises. These political links played a larger role in the period immediately after World War II, and have declined in relative importance as East–West trade has expanded and entered more normal commercial channels.[37]

The relatively clear record of subsidiary companies in the West suggests that these foreign investments are of too great economic importance to the Comecon countries, especially to those among them most dependent upon foreign trade, to be placed at risk so long as alternative intelligence channels exist.[38] One of the primary purposes of these investments has been to build up the reputation of Comecon enterprises as reliable partners with whom normal business relations can be developed. There appears to have been a concerted effort to avoid spurious activities and dubious associations. As a result, these companies generally (especially those which are larger and have been longer established, with a wider range of local operations) have developed solid reputations in local business circles.

There is even less basis for the view that subsidiaries constitute an important channel for the acquisition of Western technology. Comecon foreign investments are based on the competitive advantages internationally of certain East European products and processes. With few exceptions, they are not located in the so-called high-technology sectors, and when they are, it is due to the technical strengths of the Comecon parent enterprises in these areas.[39] The net flows of technology linked to the multinational operations of Comecon enterprises are, if anything, westward rather than eastward.

Certainly, an advantage to any multinational company of a direct presence abroad is the opportunity to gain more information about foreign markets and competitors. Personnel attached to foreign subsidiaries acquire useful commercial and technical know-how in the course of their foreign assignments. For the few Comecon enterprises in high-technology industries, this could provide a channel for the transfer of technology from the host to the home country not otherwise readily available. On the other hand, technical-assistance agreements with Western firms, linked to the purchase of equipment or licences, or within the framework of co-production arrangements, are a potentially far more important means of access to Western technology for Comecon enterprises.[40]

Some subsidiaries may extend such information-gathering activity to industrial espionage. Comecon subsidiaries have not been shown to be more prone to such activity, however, than the subsidiaries of

Western firms. In the case of several recent, and much publicised, instances which occurred in the California electronics industry ('Silicon Valley'), major Japanese multinational enterprises were the principal offenders charged, although a Polish-owned company in the United States was also similarly implicated.[41]

There is little evidence either that Comecon companies in the West have been used to any significant degree to circumvent Western strategic export controls. Comecon subsidiaries are engaged principally in importing. When, more rarely, they undertake to export back to the home country, they are subject to the same export controls as other firms in the host country. Presumably any export operations which Comecon-owned companies carry out are subjected to particular scrutiny by the controlling authorities.[42] Illegal exports from West to East have tended to follow more devious and obscure routes.[43]

If the security issue raised by the growth of multinational activities by Comecon state enterprises has frequently been overstated, it is undeniable that their proliferation places an increasing burden of supervision on host-country security establishments. This must be openly recognised by policy makers as a special cost attached to the expansion of economic relations with the Comecon countries.

5. *Should foreign investments by Comecon state enterprises be subject to special regulation by host countries?*

This analysis is now sufficiently developed to address the basic question posed at its outset. Do the multinational activities of Comecon-based state enterprises require the imposition of special controls by host countries, or can they adequately be governed by existing arrangements?

As was seen in Chapter 7, regulations governing inflows of foreign direct investment vary considerably among host countries. The regulations which exist in each, however, apply without discrimination according to source. Comecon investments, therefore, are subject to the same sectoral limitations and screening procedures which apply to investments from other sources.

It is interesting to note, parenthetically, that the growth of foreign investment by state enterprises, including those in the Comecon countries, has been a factor contributing to demands for more active regulation of foreign investment in traditionally *laissez-faire* host countries. There is a trend towards a strengthened role for the state on both sides – initiative and response – of the multinational investment process. Major international investments thus increasingly involve interstate confrontation and negotiation.[44]

In less direct ways, as noted earlier, Comecon investments are effectively subject to special controls in many countries. Rules governing the application for visas restrict the residence of Comecon nationals in host countries.[45] Discriminatory laws and regulations governing commercial and financial transactions with Comecon countries further affect the climate and scope for investment.

The foreign investment activity of the Comecon countries remains, in nature and extent, in a stage of relative infancy. In neither absolute nor relative terms does it presently constitute an important economic challenge to the interests of the host country. On the contrary, it bears perhaps the best current hope for the development of a more balanced structure, and hence greater stability, in East–West trade. In the South, it has, on the whole, contributed positively – if rather marginally – to industrialisation goals.

Any potential threat to the interests of a host country from the investment activities of Comecon state enterprises comes, rather, from another quarter, and derives from the combination of two important considerations: firstly, Comecon multinational enterprises are special in the degree to which they are subject to centralised governmental control at home. Second, especially in East–West relations, fundamental differences in ideology and system, as well as recurrent tensions in the international political sphere, increase the likelihood of conflicting national objectives between host and Comecon countries. As a result of these factors, host countries can be expected to be particularly sensitive to Comecon investments in sectors regarded as being of special national importance. Investments in fishing and shipping, for example, are in support of international activities which have strategic as well as economic implications.

In these circumstances, the operational record of Comecon companies abroad is crucial. The evidence presented in this volume indicates that Comecon subsidiaries generally adhere to accepted commercial norms and in fact are principally concerned with returns on investments, perhaps better defined as gross hard-currency earnings than profits. Their operations do not appear to differ significantly from the practice of other foreign-owned firms. The publicised cases of their involvement in covert activities are rare.

Comecon claims for special treatment at the international (United Nations) level would seem to beg for special treatment at the national level. The conclusion this analysis would draw from the evidence, however, is that, for the present, there is no need for special treatment at either level. For the future, the evolutionary course of Comecon foreign investment activity must determine the nature of the policy responses to be adopted by host countries.

Reciprocity is also a factor which should be taken into account in setting policy in this area. Western firms do not enjoy the same access to the Comecon economies as do Comecon enterprises to Western economies.[46] The 1975 Helsinki agreement commits the parties to reciprocal facilitation of business activities by firms and enterprises. Certainly differences in the economic systems place serious obstacles in the path of implementation of this principle. Nevertheless, the principle should not be abandoned, and continuing efforts should be made to narrow the gap in reciprocal treatment of direct representation and investment by foreign firms.

SIGNIFICANCE AND PROSPECTS FOR COMECON FOREIGN INVESTMENT

The analysis of the preceding pages has been approached from two basic perspectives. The first has looked at the interest taken in the foreign investment activity of the Comecon countries as a new dimension in the growth and diversification of multinational activity in the world economy. This growth has also been regarded as a manifestation of the Comecon countries' desire to benefit from more intensive involvement in the international – not merely socialist – division of labour and as evidence of their commitment to the reorientation in their external economic relations which this entails.

The Soviet Union and Eastern Europe have attained a position of some world significance as a source of foreign direct investment. Available quantitative data suggest that the magnitude of investment activity by the Comecon countries is not greatly disproportionate to that of similarly involved Third World countries, when account is taken of the difference in their number.[47] Comecon investments would also appear broadly to be comparable in functional range and geographic spread to those of the developing countries.[48] In more qualitative terms, it was observed earlier that the foreign investment activity of Soviet and East European enterprises bears notable similarities to the behaviour of the multinational enterprises of Third World countries. Both in turn share many of the characteristics of Western multinational enterprises.

It is less in their form and operation abroad than in their organisation and subordination at home that Comecon multinational enterprises are distinct from multinational enterprises rooted in other socio-economic systems. If this distinction does not appear to have greatly differentiated their actual external behaviour to date it is because, as newcomers to the multinational scene, and still marginal in importance, Comecon enterprises have had to adapt to the established institutional environment. The potential for centralised state control of multinational operations nevertheless remains, and could be exercised as required in different circumstances. It is in this potential that the state-socialist countries have brought new complexity to the sphere of multinational investment, just as they have to international commerce.

Foreign investment is at the same time an important new dimension of the more active participation of the Comecon countries in the world economy. The multinational extension of national enterprise through direct investment is not, however, the only choice open to economic organisations in the planned economies or to firms based in other systems. Internationalisation of the production of goods and services can be achieved through a variety of institutional mechanisms in addition to equity investment in foreign subsidiaries and affiliates. These include turn-key projects, licensing, subcontracting, co-production, technical assistance contracts and other international, interfirm agreements for the provision of specialised services.

These alternative forms have been heavily employed by Western firms engaged in the development of productive capacity in the Comecon economies, where direct investment is severely restricted. They have also played a certain part in the activities of Comecon enterprises in the Western economies, although here far greater recourse has been made to the forms of direct investment with which the discussion has been concerned in this volume.

Comecon enterprises have sometimes used direct investment as a vehicle in one economy and interfirm contractual arrangements in another, for similar purposes.[49] The Soviet foreign trade organisation, Aviaexport, for example, established a mixed equity company to adapt and market the YAK-40 aircraft in Canada, whereas it licensed an American firm to do the same in the United States.[50] Avtoexport (USSR) has used both direct investments and franchise arrangements with local firms to market Soviet automobiles in different countries.

The direct investment channel has, relatively, been made less use of in East–South relations. The involvement of Comecon enterprises in the resource-development and manufacturing sectors of Third World economies has more often been through non-equity arrangements. The compensation format, in particular, has been the most common means by which the Comecon countries have undertaken major, long-term investments in the developing economies without establishing formal equity links.[51]

Although one of a number of alternative institutional means which enterprises in the Comecon countries may employ in their pursuit of external goals, foreign direct investment still stands as an important, seemingly permanent, new feature of the foreign trade systems of the planned economies. It has tended to strengthen the position of enterprises, increasing their relative power through the creation of multinational networks of subsidiary companies. Because a larger share of their activities now occur within a foreign market environment, less subject to planning at home, their autonomy has increased. As a result, operational decision-making in foreign trade is no longer so centralised; where subsidiaries are functioning, commercial negotiations and contracting are increasingly conducted abroad rather than in the home countries.

The multinational activities of Comecon enterprises have also helped to bridge the institutional gap between foreign trade and production in the planned economies. Their traditional separation has restricted the effective participation of the Comecon countries in the international economy. The actual transfer of manufacturing, through direct investment, to locations within foreign markets obviously serves to integrate trade and production. The development of an infrastructure abroad which combines the commercial and technical aspects of the marketing function in single foreign companies is also an important advance. Commercial and technical personnel work together in subsidiaries abroad in a way which ministerial jurisdictions at home can often make virtually impossible, or at best cumbersome and ineffective.

At the same time, growing numbers of Comecon nationals are being trained in international business through more direct experience abroad than they would obtain through assignments to official trade missions.[52] Cadres of foreign-trade personnel are receiving 'on-the-job' experience in companies which operate within a market environment and according to market norms. Many spend their careers within the multinational families of companies headed by the larger Comecon parent enterprises.[53] Cadres are being similarly trained in international banking, insurance, shipping and engineering services.

It is thus legitimate to view the phenomenon of Comecon foreign direct investment as a manifestation of change in the external economic institutions as well as in the foreign economic policies of the Comecon countries. The development of multinational operations represents a further accommodation of traditional organisations and procedures to the requirements of greater, and more effective, extraregional involvement.[54] The growth of Comecon multinational enterprise is in effect a pragmatic response to the demands of the international economic system.

As such, it is of special interest to students of the interaction of different social systems. Since it occurs outside the domestic economy, the multinational extension of enterprise activities is not contingent upon the introduction of other institutional changes. The large number of Soviet-owned companies operating abroad shows that extensive direct investment can be undertaken within the framework of a classic, largely unreformed system of centrally-planned foreign trade. Multinational operations are by no means independent of the system in which they are based, however, and it was seen that the successful performance of subsidiaries could be seriously hampered by the inadequate support of domestic organisations. (Discussion will return to this point below.)

The creation by the Comecon countries of significant assets abroad has also added a new dimension to their external capital accounts, and is of direct relevance to any assessments of their international financial position. Western estimates of the net indebtedness of these countries take into consideration their deposits in foreign banks, but typically disregard their direct investments. These would include the net worth of Comecon-owned banks and other financial companies abroad and the real assets of foreign branches, subsidiaries and affiliates to which Comecon-based enterprises have legal claim. The offsets to gross foreign indebtedness are especially important in the Soviet case. As mentioned above, accurate data on the value of such assets is extremely difficult to obtain on a systematic basis. The estimates presented in this volume furnish some conception of the orders of magnitude involved, but also point to the need for further research in this area.

The trends summarised at the outset of this chapter are all of quite recent origin. The forces that have generated them remain basically strong. At the same time, important constraints on the development of socialist multinational enterprise continue to be operative. It is these pressures which seem destined to shape its future course. All have been dealt with at various points in the preceding chapters, so they need only briefly be recalled here.

The ideological constraint is certainly not a new one. It has been overridden in most cases (the German Democratic Republic being the most notable exception) by pragmatic considerations. For all of the Comecon countries, these have been principally economic considerations. The diversification of their external relations – to which direct investment is seen to make an important contribution – also holds political attraction for the more independent-minded East European countries. For the Soviet Union, multinational enterprises afford a means of developing the relatively neglected international economic dimension of its 'superpower' aspirations through a mechanism which has been fundamental to the international economic pre-eminence and power of its rival, the United States.

Ideological principles tend to reassert themselves at times of international tension, and this has been true of the years marking the transition, in the late 1970s and early 1980s, from a period of *détente* to one of renewed confrontation. The ideological initiative this time has come from the West, led by the United States. Western ideological assertiveness has put East–West relations back on the ideological plane and makes it more difficult for the Comecon countries to adhere to a predominantly pragmatic course in their external economic relations.

The capital constraint on foreign investments has also been reinforced by recent developments. Slower growth in the Comecon countries, combined with the need to maintain levels of consumption and military spending, has sharply increased the scarcity of resources for all forms of investment. Balance of payments problems, and the related crisis of debt management in several East European countries, have curtailed the availability of foreign currency funds. It may be true, as the author was told by a senior official in one Comecon country, that a good idea can always find external financing. Certainly one of the world trends in multinational enterprise has been the shift from investment funding by the parent enterprise to financing from self-generated or local sources. Even the credit-worthiness of foreign subsidiaries has, however, been affected by the financial problems of the home countries. In the Third World, where an important link has been noted between Comecon direct investment activities and the flow of capital goods and credit, the financial bind has also grown increasingly severe.[55] Moreover, traditional East European balance-of-payments surpluses with the Third World economies have been eroded by the oil shocks of 1973–4 and 1979–80.

The international economic instability which followed the two energy crises has also constrained the growth of Comecon international enterprise. In particular, the recession of the early 1980s, and the high rates of interest associated with it, sharply reduced the demand in the West for machinery and equipment. In many developing countries, energy-related balance-of-payments problems also undermined the market for Comecon imports. These economic difficulties arose at a time when many Comecon marketing and manufacturing subsidiaries were just being established. In the circumstances, the scarcity of skilled managerial personnel on the Comecon side has been a more acute problem, contributing to investment failures and restricting investment expansion.

In addition to these cyclical problems, there are economic constraints of a more structural nature. Direct investment in foreign marketing and production may enhance competitiveness on external markets, but cannot ensure it. In the dynamic conditions of the international market-place, success – especially in manufactured exports – is dependent on the generation at home of new products and processes as well as on the development of new channels for their commercialisation abroad. Technological lags in the Comecon countries serve in this respect to inhibit both trade and investment. In the Third World, there has been a consequent trend from complementary to increasingly competitive structures between the socialist economies and the newly industrialised developing economies, encountered in the examination of the case of India. This new structural relationship creates problems not only in mutual relations but in relations on third markets, where there is increased competition in both trade and multinational investment.[56]

On the East European side, these structural problems have their roots in well-known systemic deficiencies which successive attempts at reform have in most instances failed to resolve. If, as has been argued above, foreign direct investment can be viewed as a response to some of the institutional problems traditionally faced by the Comecon countries in their extraregional economic relations, it is at best a partial solution. To be fully effective, it must be accompanied by changes in domestic institutions. In particular, it requires better integration of domestic production and marketing as well as the dismantling of the barriers which continue to separate domestic and foreign trade and investment. The experience of several East European countries, especially Hungary, but also Bulgaria and Poland, will be interesting to follow in this regard. It is in these countries where enterprises have been given the greatest incentive and scope to approach domestic and foreign operations, including investment, in an integrated fashion.

Systemic differences are likely to affect the future pattern of development of Comecon multinational enterprise in another way. Comecon-based parents tend to be monopolistic or monopsonistic in character, enjoying exclusive national rights to engage in external relations in a certain range of goods and services. Foreign subsidiaries are also often granted the exclusive rights to act on behalf of their parents in a particular foreign market. This characteristic of the economic systems of the home countries suggests that one cannot expect the proliferation of Comecon foreign subsidiaries to which competition among Western multinational enterprises gives rise. The scope does not exist for Comecon multinational enterprise to evolve through the competitive, if inevitably duplicative, processes characteristic of its Western counterpart.

The combined effect of these various factors will be to restrict the growth and slow the diversification of Comecon foreign investment activity in the foreseeable future. The Comecon countries are not likely to emerge as major multinational actors over the decade, and their foreign investment activities will remain, as in the past, of more qualitative than quantitative significance in the global context of multinational enterprises. With investment already in place in the most desirable locations, one would in any event expect further evolution to occur more within the framework of the existing network of companies.

The Comecon countries nevertheless remain under continuing pressure to improve the balance and structure of their economic relations with the rest of the world, if these relations are to continue to expand as desired. To this end they appear determined to develop their multinational investments, so that these may assume a permanent and prominent role in the process.

NOTES AND REFERENCES

1. This was a period of domestic reform and new international policy initiatives during the brief regime of Alexander Dubcek.

2. Together, the annual sales of Omnitrade, Pekao Trading and Dalimpex (see Table 7.1) grew at an average rate of 15.7 per cent over the period of eleven years, between 1966–77.

3. There is some evidence that Soviet and American parent enterprises seek to avoid joint equity ventures with foreign partners. This may be because, as continental countries, both lack the experience of their East and West European counterparts in working closely with foreign nationals.

4. *CTC Reporter*, New York, Spring 1983, p. 9. Meanwhile, both the International Chamber of Commerce, in 1972, and the OECD, in 1976, had adopted guidelines for multinational enterprise.

5. *The Impact of Multinational Corporations on Development and on International Relations*, UN E. 74 A.5 (New York: United Nations, 1974) p. 25.

6. *Multinational Corporations in World Development*, UN E. 73. II.A.11 (New York: United Nations, 1973) p. 5.

7. *Transnational Corporations in World Development: a Re-examination.*

8. *Ibid.*, p. 161.

9. *CTC Reporter*, Spring 1983, p. 9.

10. According to Press reports at the time, pressure from a senior Soviet employee of the Centre had led to the suppression of projected sections of the draft survey dealing with the Comecon-based multinational enterprises (Agence France Presse bulletin from the United Nations, New York, 24 June 1983).

11. *Transnational Corporations in World Development: Third Survey* (New York: United Nations, 1983) p. 50 *et seq*.

12. *Ibid.*, Annex p. 272 *et seq*. prepared by the Secretariat of the UN Economic Commission for Europe.

13. Draft resolution E/C.10/1983/L.4, supported by a conference room paper (E/C.10/1983/CRP.3).

14. *Revista Economica*, 11 June 1976, quoted by King in 'Romania and the Third World', *op. cit.*

15. See Valkenier, *The Soviet Union and the Third World*, *op. cit.*, Ch. 4, for a thorough discussion of the nature and evolution of the East European position on this question.

16. The most extended exposition to date in a short statement by a member of the Soviet delegation to the UN Commission on Transnational Corporations published in the bulletin of the UN Centre; V. Schetinin, 'An Alternative to TNC's', *CTC Reporter*, New York, Autumn 1983. The argument presented is largely tautological (socialist companies abroad are 'joint ventures'; transnational enterprise is a uniquely capitalist phenomenon) with no, or only selected, evidence provided in support of the assertions made.

17. See, for example, R. Mazzolini, *Government Controlled Enterprises: International Strategic and Policy Decisions* (New York: John Wiley

and Sons, 1979) and R. Vernon and Y. Ahoroni (eds), *State-owned Enterprise in the Western Economies* (New York: St Martin's Press, 1981).

18. See J. Rhodes, 'Economic Growth and Government-Owned Multinationals', *Management Review*, New York, December 1978.

19. The Japanese example has already been cited in this context. West European governments have sought to cultivate 'national champions' in priority industries, and this has inevitably involved state support of the extension of their activities to the multinational sphere. The socialist Mitterand government in France may carry the process further, through its efforts to devise a co-ordinated strategy for state-owned enterprises.

20. For a discussion of this trend in the context of the international economy, see the contributions in M. Kostecki (ed.), *State Trading in International Markets: Theory and Practice of Industrialized and Developing Countries* (New York: St Martin's Press, 1982).

21. In this respect also they are similar to other state-owned enterprises. See Rhodes, 'Economic Growth and Government-Owned Multinationals', *op. cit.*, p. 29.

22. They were couched in these terms in the annexe to the 1983 UN survey (see note 12 above).

23. See Kumar and McLeod, *Multinationals from Developing Countries, op. cit.*; L. Wells, *Third World Multinationals: the Rise of Foreign Investment from the Developing Countries* (Cambridge, Mass.: MIT Press, 1983). They are less capital-intensive than multinational enterprises from the developed Western countries; they compete more on price terms than on trademarks and advertising; they are more likely to enter into local partnerships, because they have less to protect in terms of proprietorial technology embodied in specialised products and processes.

24. The role of the state in this sphere varies widely within the heterogeneous group of countries which are the major sources of Third World foreign investment (and includes Hong Kong and Singapore as well as Brazil and India), but state-owned enterprises figure prominently among the largest multinational enterpries in the Third World. See Wells, *ibid.*

25. As do the codes and guidelines adopted by other international organisations, such as the International Labour Organisation, the International Chamber of Commerce and the OECD, which cover multinational enterprises regardless of their ownership form – private, state or mixed.

26. It will be recalled that there is some co-ordination of new investments inherent in the approval process by ministries and foreign trade banks in most countries.

27. A Polish economist, implicitly recognising this, has called for the formation of joint multinational enterprises by the Comecon countries, in order to compete effectively in the present international economy. See Zurawicki, *Multinational Enterprises in East and West, op. cit.*

28. Fishing vessels, for example, from different Comecon countries (the Soviet Union, Bulgaria, Poland) are known to have competed for

fishing grounds in North American coastal waters, with some bad feelings resulting.

29. For a recent survey of the general issue, see D. Rosenthal and W. Knighton, *National Laws and International Commerce: the Problems of Extraterritoriality* (London: Royal Institute of International Affairs, 1982).

30. See R. Vernon, 'The Fragile Foundations of East-West Trade', *Foreign Affairs*, Summer 1979.

31. Analogous constraints apply to the use of trade for political purposes. Where conditions permit (they have been most often present in relations with other socialist countries), Comecon states have shown themselves ready to use trade and investment for political purposes. The Comecon economic sanctions against Yugoslavia and China are prominent examples.

32. In 1981, there was a notable reduction in Comecon deposits in Western banks, including Comecon-owned banks in the West. The reduction was particularly marked in Soviet assets held in these banks, which the Bank for International Settlements showed as dropping by nearly $5 billion (close to 60 per cent) between December 1980 and June 1981. This shift can no doubt be explained in part by considerations of debt management, as the financial exposure of the Comecon countries grew increasingly precarious. It also appears, however, to have represented a transfer of assets to safer locations in the climate of mounting tension in East–West relations over Afghanistan and Poland, and in the aftermath of the United States government's seizure of Iranian assets in the United States in 1980.

33. D. Heenan, 'Moscow Goes Multinational', *Harvard Business Review*, May–June 1981, p. 48, and testimony to the Senate Permanent Subcommittee on Investigations, published in *Transfer of United States High Technology to the Soviet Union and Soviet Bloc Nations*, United States Senate, 97th Congress, 2nd Session, Report No. 97–664, November 15 1982, p. 11.

34. The public record no doubt understates the actual picture. If only a sample, however, there is no reason why it should be biased with regard to the share of cases involving subsidiaries.

35. J. Montaldo, *Secrets de la Banque Sovietique en France* (Paris: Ed. Albin Michel, 1979).

36. Some of the profits have, no doubt, found their way also into party coffers. Non-communist parties and officials are also reported to have at times gained financially from their part in the conclusion of large East–West commercial contracts.

37. Local Austrian communists, for example, took over several Soviet-operated companies when the period of occupation ended in 1955. Communist party officials have reportedly been direct participants in East–West trade in Italy, France and Sweden.

38. A further consideration is that, although personnel assigned to foreign subsidiaries are generally not subject to the travel restrictions applying to embassy personnel, they do not enjoy diplomatic immunity in host countries.

39. The principal examples are the three subsidiaries of the Soviet foreign trade enterprise Elektronorgtekhnika operating in the West European computer industry and the Carl Zeiss Jena (German Democratic Republic) companies abroad, which market optical equipment and scientific instruments. An incident involving one of the Elektronorgtekhnika companies was mentioned earlier, in Chapter 5.

40. See E. Zaleski and H. Wienert, *East–West Technology Transfer* (Paris: OECD Secretariat, 1980). Ch. 3.

41. See *The Economist*, 26 June 1982, p. 74; *New York Times*, 4 July 1982, p. 25.

42. Indirect ownership ties within the Comecon multinational network may not be readily apparent, however. To take a hypothetical example, the French subsidiary of a Polish company established in Sweden may well be regarded in France as a Swedish-owned company.

43. Comecon subsidiaries abroad, especially those operating in shipping and freight, may well be placed to scout out such routes, however.

44. The negotiation of the French and Bulgarian states over the size and terms of the projected investment of the Bulgarian enterprise Balkancar in France's largest fork-lift truck manufacturing firm, described in Chapter 6, is an example in the East–West context.

45. These are often determined by reciprocity. Any special restrictions have tended to be overshadowed recently by a recession-determined general tightening of resident visa regulations by host countries.

46. This asymmetry has long been recognised. See Pisar, *Coexistence and Commerce*, p. 195.

47. Wells, *Third World Multinationals*, *op. cit.*, Ch. 1, has placed the number of foreign branches and subsidiaries of firms based in 15 Third World countries at nearly 2,000 in 1980. Estimates in this analysis place those of enterprises in the 7 Comecon countries at about 700 in 1983. (While the Comecon group includes the large Soviet economy, the Third World investors prominently include India and Brazil.) Wells puts the stock of foreign direct investment from the developing countries at $5–10 billion in 1980; whereas this analysis estimates the value from the Comecon countries to be in the range of $4–6 billion in 1981–2.

48. Wells, *ibid.*, found Third World branches and subsidiaries in 125 host countries, while this analysis located Comecon equivalents in 100 countries. Investments from both sources were heavily directed to services. In the case of Third World countries, a little less than half (47 per cent) were engaged in manufacturing; in the case of Comecon countries, the share was still only about 12 per cent.

49. The two are sometimes linked when, for example, a joint equity company is established in a Western country to market the products of an East–West co-production arrangements. Thus a mixed Polish–German company, Polchemie, was established in Hamburg in 1976 to market the chemical products resulting from the co-operation of German and Polish firms.

50. This case was cited in Chapter 7.

51. The format has played an especially important role in Soviet–Third World economic relations, especially in mining and other activities

related to natural-resource development. Soviet involvement in the development of Iranian and Afghan natural gas was on this basis. See Hannigan and McMillan, 'CMEA Trade and Cooperation with the Third World in the Energy Sector', *op. cit.* (Ch. 2, n. 13, p. 26).

52. A very rough estimate, based on the partial figures available, suggests that the total number of nationals from the seven Comecon countries working in branches, subsidiaries and affiliates abroad in 1983 was in the range of 5,000–10,000.

53. The author has interviewed managers who have had a succession of assignments with their parent organisation's subsidiary companies in various parts of the world. If they advance far enough, their experience may be employed in senior posts in the responsible ministry at home.

54. Reference has earlier been made, especially in Chapter 2, to the link between the reform of foreign trade systems and the growth of extraregional relations. See also Bornstein in *East European Economies Post-Helsinki*, *op. cit.*

55. This is the major theme developed by Valkenier, *The Soviet Union and the Third World*, *op. cit.*

56. It will be recalled that India is one of the major Third World sources of foreign direct investment, and has been especially active in this regard in the African economies.

Appendix: Data and Methodology

Analysis of direct investment from the Comecon countries is severely circumscribed by lack of available data. These countries themselves provide no data on outflows of direct investment, nor do most host countries break down inflows sufficiently to enable the analyst to isolate direct investment from the countries in question. It is not possible, either, to draw on any comprehensive official listings of the foreign branches, subsidiaries and affiliates of Comecon state enterprises. A few East European countries have published partial listings in their foreign-trade directories. There are occasional references in official statements to the number of companies established abroad by national enterprises. Otherwise data are fragmented, scattered and often inconsistent.

In these circumstances, it has been necessary to develop an original data base. This base has been built up, through a research programme under the author's direction, over a period of nearly ten years. Individual files have been developed on major Comecon-based investing enterprises and on companies abroad in which they have equity holdings.

Instances of Comecon foreign direct investment have been defined as business firms, banks and other companies established abroad in which there is capital participation by Soviet and East European-based state enterprises. For the reasons described in the text, it has been assumed that in most cases investing enterprises in the Comecon countries exercise effective operational control even when their share represents a minority holding.

Included are foreign branches, subsidiaries and affiliates of Comecon-based enterprises (see Glossary). Capital participation in them may be channelled through other foreign subsidiaries or affiliates of the parent enterprises. Not included are non-equity forms of investment, such as inter-firm co-operation agreements (including compensation, or buy-back, arrangements for repayment of long-term credits), as well as the more classic forms of portfolio investment. Also excluded are the purely representational offices

abroad of East European state enterprises, banks and othe
economic organisations. It has seemed sensible, too, not to includ
the numerous contact and sales offices abroad of East Europea
state airlines and tourist agencies, except in the relatively rare even
that they have been established under local law as limited liability o
joint stock companies.[1] Lastly, the analysis does not count a
separate instances of Comecon foreign direct investment the branche
of Comecon foreign subsidiaries and affiliates.

The method for developing the data base has been as follows
Key publications in home, host and third countries have bee
searched regularly over the years for references to foreign direc
investment activity by Comecon enterprises. This effort ha
concentrated on the official economic Press in the seven Comeco
countries concerned and especially on their foreign-trade publications
In this way, individual investments have been identified and some
information on each case obtained.

Once a foreign branch, subsidiary or affiliate has tentatively bee
identified, several means have been used to validate its existenc
and extend the information base. The companies themselves an
their parent enterprises have been asked to supply basic informatio
on their organisation and activity. The response to these approache
has been good (over 50 per cent have responded in the case of firm
in the OECD countries). Business directories in host countries and
official and unofficial registries have been examined in order to
obtain further information. Finally, supervisory agencies in the
home countries and official trade missions abroad have been aske
to check this data for accuracy.

The most detailed information derived in this manner has been o
Comecon investment in the developed Western economies. It ha
even been possible, on this basis, to publish, in the form of a
business directory, information on individual companies in the Wes
with Comecon capital participation. This directory has bee
expanded and improved over a series of editions.[2] Its listings
however, cover only subsidiaries and affiliates in operation at the
time of publication.

Although every effort is made to ensure that the informatio
published in these directories is as accurate and comprehensive a
possible, some cases inevitably remain unidentified and are no
listed. Others, which are included, should not be, either becaus
Comecon equity has since been liquidated, or the company is n
longer operational, or the original identification was erroneous

Nevertheless, the coverage is estimated to be accurate to within 10 per cent (over 90 per cent complete), on the basis of comparisons with official statistics issued irregularly by the Comecon countries.

The data thus derived have gained widespread acceptance by others working in this field. They have been used by analysts in the Comecon countries and quoted in their publications.[3] They have also been incorporated in United Nations statistics and basic Western sources.[4]

The data base on Comecon direct investments in the developing countries is less comprehensive and less firmly established. Here the effort has been to develop as large a sample as possible of well-documented cases, rather than to aim for exhaustive coverage. The investments are too scattered (in some sixty-four countries) to permit broad verification of host country sources and, as yet, there has been no systematic attempt, as in the West, to approach the branches, subsidiaries and affiliates themselves. The data are based on a compilation of information gleaned from published sources, official and unofficial, from supervisory agencies in the home countries and from registries and other host-country sources whenever possible. No listing of these cases has been published, and the statistics cited are derived from the files maintained on individual cases.[5]

Given the data available, quantitative analysis of East European investments in developing countries has, for the present, been based principally on the crude measure of numbers of instances. This measure is useful as an indicator of the relative interest and involvement of Comecon countries and enterprises, and of the geographic spread, functional range and ownership structure of their multinational activities. It is weak as a measure of the absolute or comparative magnitude of their investments and, hence, of their economic significance.

It has, therefore, been deemed appropriate to supplement the basic measure with estimates of the value of Comecon foreign direct investment. Information on the value of investment and investment-supported activities (such as turnover) have been obtained for a number of companies from annual reports, host-country registries and various published sources. These have been used as the basis for calculating average values for companies engaged in similar operations. These values have, in turn, been used to estimate aggregate figures. The results give some idea of the orders of magnitude involved but, again, are more reliable for investments in the West than in the South.

A final measure, which has been used from time to time, is the employment figures for Comecon foreign subsidiaries and affiliates. As in the case of the value figures, these are ranges or averages, based on a smaller sample of known instances.

NOTES AND REFERENCES

1. These offices, found in most major Western cities, are listed in annexes to *The East–West Business Directory: a Listing of Companies in the West with Soviet and East European Capital Participation* (London: Duncan Publishing, for the East–West Project, Carleton University, 1983). Their exclusion may cause the statistics presented in Table 3.3 and elsewhere in this volume to diverge from other estimates.
2. *The East–West Business Directory*. Up to 1983, this was published directly by the East–West Project, Carleton University, Ottawa, as *Directory of Soviet and East European Companies in the West*, 1978, with revised editions in 1979, 1980 and 1981.
3. See, for example, *Contemporary Poland*, No. 7, April 1978, pp. 11–12; Bel'chuk (ed.), *op. cit.*, p. 47; Shmelev, *op. cit.*, p. 139; and Rodina, *op. cit.*, pp. 74–8.
4. *Transnational Corporations in World Development: a Re-examination, Trends in East–West Industrial Cooperation*, UN E.79.II.E.25 (Geneva: United Nations Economic Commission for Europe, 1978); *Direct Investment Abroad by Transnational Corporations of the CMEA Countries*, OECD/DAFFE/83.17 (Paris: OECD Diorectorate for Financial, Fiscal and Enterprise Affairs, March 1983); J. Stopford and J. Dunning, *Multinationals: Company Performance and Global Trends* (London: Macmillan, 1983); H. Heinen, *Ziele Multinationaler Unternehmen* (Zurich: Gabler, 1982); and E. Zaleski, 'Les Multinationales des Pays de l'Est', in A. Cotta and M. Gherman (eds), *Les Multinationales en Mutation* (Paris: Presses Universitaires de France, 1983).
5. Information on individual investments forming the basis for Tables 3.3 and 3.5 may be obtained on request from the author. The sample covers 236 individually documented instances of equity investment in the South by the CMEA countries in the period after World War II, the bulk of them made between 1965 and 1983.

Glossary

A number of terms used in this study are subject to varying interpretations in the literature on this subject. To avoid ambiguities, therefore, the following definitions are given.

Joint stock company: A business firm with a distinct juridical identity in which ownership shares define equity and legal liability. May be wholly national, wholly foreign or mixed in ownership.

Mixed (equity) company: A joint stock, or otherwise limited liability, company in which equity, and possibly management, are shared between foreign and national partners. (The literally equivalent terms in Russian, German and French (*smeshannoe obshchestvo, gemischtes Unternehmen* and *société mixte*) are sometimes used in reference to joint stock companies, even those not involving mixed ownership.)

Joint venture: A partnership with a clearly defined purpose, established between two or more business enterprises in which management, but not necessarily equity, is shared. (The Eastern European literature often employs the term 'joint venture' when referring to companies abroad in which Eastern state enterprises hold equity, even 100 per cent. The Russian term here is *sovmestnoe predpriatie.*)

Domestic firm: A juridically independent company established within the boundaries of a particular country and operating within the legal framework established for normal business activity in that country. (As opposed to 'foreign firm'.)

National firm: A domestic firm in which a controlling interest is held by nationals of the country.

Foreign affiliate: A domestic firm in which a foreign investor has equity, directly or indirectly through another company.

Foreign subsidiary: A domestic firm over which the foreign investor exercises operational control.

Foreign branch: An operational division established abroad by a foreign investor which does not have a legal identity separate from the parent and therefore is regarded as a foreign, rather than as a domestic, firm by the host country.

Agent firm: A domestic company which represents foreign clients, usually on a commission basis.

Foreign portfolio investment: Investment in a form which yields no influence over the day-to-day operation of foreign assets.

Foreign direct investment: Equity investment in new or existing assets abroad, through which the foreign investor gains operational control. Depending upon the specific circumstances, control may be associated with either a majority or a minority interest. Foreign direct investment leads to the creation of foreign branches, subsidiaries, affiliates and joint ventures.

Multinational enterprise: A national firm which pursues its international interests through direct investments in at least one foreign country. These investments may be in production or services. The United Nations employs the term transnational enterprise in place of multinational enterprise.

Bibliography

Set out below are the volumes, signed and unsigned, articles and periodicals which are referred to in the text.

AGMON, T. and KINDLEBERGER, C. (eds), *Multinationals from Small Countries* (Cambridge, Mass.: MIT Press, 1977).

ATLANTIC COUNCIL OF THE UNITED STATES, *The Soviet Merchant Marine: Economic and Strategic Challenge to the West* (Boulder, Colorado: Westview Press for the Council, 1979).

BEL'CHUK, A. I. (ed.), *Novyi Etap Ekonomicheskogo Sotrudnichestva SSSR s Razvitymi Kapitalisticheskimi Stranami* (Moscow: Izdat. Nauka, 1978).

BERGER, N., *Industrialization Policies in Nigeria* (Munich: Weltforum Verlag, 1975).

BERGMANN, T., *The Development Models of India, the Soviet Union and China* (Amsterdam: Van Gorcum, 1977).

BIERSTEKER, T., *Distortion of Development? Contending Perspectives on the Multinational Corporation* (Cambridge: MIT Press, 1978).

BORNSTEIN, M. *et al.* (eds), *East–West Relations and the Future of Eastern Europe* (London: George Allen and Unwin, 1981).

BRZEZINSKI, H., *Internationale Wirtschaftsplanung in RGW* (Paderborn: Ferdinand Schöningh, 1978).

CASSON, M., *Alternatives to the Multinational Enterprise* (London: Macmillan, 1979).

CAVES, R. E., *Multinational Enterprise and Economic Analysis* (Cambridge: Cambridge University Press, 1982).

CHOPRA, P., *Before and After the Indo–Soviet Treaty* (New Delhi: S. Chand & Co., 1971).

CLARKSON, S., *The Soviet Theory of Development: India and the Third World in Marxist–Leninist Scholarship* (Toronto: University of Toronto Press, 1978).

COTTA, A. and GHERTMAN, M. (eds), *Les Multinationales en Mutation* (Paris: Presses Universitaires de France, 1983).

CROAN, M., *East Germany: the Soviet Connection* (Beverley Hills: Sage Publications, 1976).

DATAR, A., *India's Economic Relations with the USSR and Eastern Europe* (London: Cambridge University Press, 1972).

DESAI, P., *The Bokaro Steel Plant, a Study of Soviet Economic Assistance* (Amsterdam: North Holland, 1972).

DOBOZI, I. (ed.), *Economic Cooperation between Socialist and Developing Countries* (Budapest: Hungarian Scientific Council for World Economy, 1978).

DREWNOWSKI, J. (ed.), *Crisis in the East European Economy: the Spread of the Polish Disease* (New York: St Martin's Press, 1982).

DUNNING, J., *International Production and the Multinational Enterprise* (London: George Allen and Unwin, 1981).

ENGIBAROV, A., *Smeshannye Obshchestva na Mirovom Rynke* (Moscow: Mezhdunarodnye Otnosheniia, 1976).

FRIESEN, C., *The Political Economy of East–West Trade* (New York: Praeger, 1976).

GROSSER, I. and TUITZ, G., *Structural Change in Manufacturing Industries in the European CMEA Area and Patterns of Trade in Manufactures between CMEA and Developing Countries* (Vienna: UNIDO document ID/WG 375/3, January 1982).

HANSON, P., *Trade and Technology in Soviet–Western Relations* (New York: Columbia University Press, 1981).

HEINEN, H., *Ziele Multinationaler Unternehen* (Zurich: Gabler, 1982).

HÖHMANN, H. *et al.* (eds), *The New Economic Systems of Eastern Europe* (London: Hurst, 1975).

KASER, M., *Comecon, Integration Problems of the Planned Economies* (London: Oxford University Press, 1971).

KOSTECKI, M. (ed.), *State Trading in International Markets: Theory and Practice of Industrialized and Developing Countries* (New York: St Martin's Press, 1982).

KUMAR, K. and McLEOD, M. G. (eds), *Multinationals from Developing Countries* (Lexington, Mass.: D. C. Heath and Company, 1981).

LAUTER, G. and DICKIE, P., *Multinational Corporations and East European Socialist Economies* (New York: Praeger, 1975).

LAVIGNE, M., *Le programme du Comécon et l'intégration socialiste* (Paris: Editions Cujas, 1973).

LAVIGNE, M. (ed.), *Stratégie des pays socialistes dans l'échange international* (Paris: Economica, 1980).

LENIN, V. I., *Imperialism, the Highest Stage of Capitalism* (New York: International Publishers, 1939).

LEVCIK, F. and STANKOVSKY, J., *Industrial Cooperation between East and West* (White Plains, New York: M. E. Sharpe, 1979).

LEVINSON, C., *Vodka-Kola* (Paris: Stock, 1977).

LOWENTHAL, R., *Model or Ally? The Communist Powers and the Developing Countries* (New York: Oxford University Press, 1977).

MAKSIMOVA, M., *SSSR i Mezhdunarodnoe Ekonomicheskoe Sotrudnichestvo* (Moscow: Mysl', 1977).

MAZZOLINI, R., *Government Controlled Enterprises: International Strategic and Policy Decisions* (New York: John Wiley and Sons, 1979).

McMILLAN, C. and ST CHARLES, D., *Joint Ventures in Eastern Europe, a Three-country Comparison* (Montreal: C. D. Howe Research Institute, 1974).

McMILLAN, C. (ed.), *Changing Perspectives in East–West Commerce* (Lexington, Mass.: D. C. Heath and Co., 1974).

McMILLAN, C., *Direct Soviet and East European Investment in the Industrialized Western Economies* (Ottawa: Institute of Soviet and East European Studies, Carleton University, East–West Commercial Relations Series No. 7, February, 1977).

MICHALET, C., *Le Capitalisme Mondial* (Paris: Presses Universitaire de France, 1976).

MONTALDO, J., *Secrets de la Banque Sovietique en France* (Paris: Albin Michel, 1979).

NATO ECONOMIC AND INFORMATION DIRECTORATES (eds), *CMEA: Energy, 1980–1990* (Newtonville, Mass.: Oriental Research Partners, 1981).

NAYYAR, D. (ed.), *Economic Relations between Socialist Countries and the Third World* (London: Macmillan, 1977).

NEMSHAK, F. (ed.), *World Economy and East–West Trade* (Vienna and New York: Springer-Verlag, 1976).

NEUBERGER, E. and TYSON, L. L. (eds), *The Impact of International Economic Disturbances on the Soviet Union and Eastern Europe* (New York: Pergamon Press, 1980).

NYROP, R. (ed.), *Czechoslovakia: a Country Study* (Washington: US Government Printing Office for Foreign Area Studies, The American University, 1981).

PISAR, S., *Coexistence and Commerce* (New York: McGraw-Hall, 1970).

RADU, M. (ed.), *Eastern Europe and the Third World* (New York: Praeger, 1981).

RODINA, L. A., *Sotsialisticheskaia Integratisiia i Novye Formy Sotrudnichestva, Vostok-Zapad* (Moscow: Nauka, 1983).

ROSENTHAL, D. and KNIGHTON, W., *National Laws and International Commerce: the Problem of Extraterritoriality* (London: Royal Institute of International Affairs, 1982).

SCHAETZL, L., *Industrialization in Nigeria: a Spatial Analysis* (Munich: Welforum Verlag, 1973).

SCHERBAKOV, V. V. and IUDANOV, Iu. I., *Eksport Kapitala v Usloviiakh Dal'neishego Obostreniia Obshchego Krizisa Kapitalizma* (Moscow: Vysshaiia Shkola, 1981).

SHMELEV, N., *Sotsializm i Mezhdunarodnye Ekonomicheskie Otnosheniia* (Moscow: Mezhdunarodny Otnosheniia, 1979).

SMITH, G., *Soviet Foreign Trade: Organisation, Operations and Policy, 1913–1917* (New York: Praeger, 1973).

STEGEMANN, K., *Canadian Non-Tariff Barriers to Trade* (Montreal: Private Planning Association of Canada, 1973).

STENT, A., *From Embargo to Ostpolitik, the Political Economy of West German–Soviet Relations 1955–1980* (Cambridge: Cambridge University Press, 1981).

STOPFORD, J. *et al.*, *The World Directory of Multinational Enterprises* (London: Macmillan, 1980).

STOPFORD, J. and DUNNING, J., *Multinationals: Company Performance and Global Trends* (London: Macmillan, 1983).

SURINDAR, S., *Politics and Society in India* (Calcutta: Naya Prakash, 1974).

SWEDENBORG, B., *The Multinational Operations of Swedish Firms: an Analysis of Determinants and Effects* (Stockholm: Industrial Institute for Economic and Social Research, 1979).

VALKENIER, E., *The Soviet Union and the Third World: an Economic Bind* (New York: Praeger, 1983).

VERNON, R. and AHORONI, Y. (eds), *State-owned Enterprise in the Western Economies* (New York: St Martin's Press, 1981).

WATTS, N. (ed.), *Economic Relations between East and West* (London: Macmillan, 1978).

WELLS, L., *Third World Multinationals: the Rise of Foreign Investment from the Developing Countries* (Cambridge, Mass.: MIT Press, 1983).

WILCZYNSKI, J., *The Economics and Politics of East–West Trade* (London: Macmillan, 1969).

WILCZYNSKI, J., *The Multinationals and East–West Relations* (London: Macmillan, 1976).

WILCZYNSKI, J., *Comparative Monetary Economics* (London: Macmillan, 1978).

ZEVIN, L., *Novy Tendenstii v Ekonomicheskom Sotrudnichestve Sotasialisticheskikh i Razvivaiushchikhsia Stran* (Moscow: Nauka, 1970).

ZURAWICKI, L., *Multinational Enterprises in East and West* (Alphen aan den Rijn, Netherlands: Sijthoff and Noordhoff, 1979).

ZWASS, A., *Monetary Cooperation between East and West* (White Plains, New York: International Arts and Sciences Press, 1976).

UNSIGNED VOLUMES

Bibliography on Transnational Corporations (New York: United Nations, for the Commission on Transnational Corporations, 1979).

Bulgarian Foreign Trade Organizations (Sofia: Bulgarian Chamber of Commerce and Industry, 1981).

A Comparison of Foreign Investment Controls in Canada and Australia, FIRA Paper No. 5 (Ottawa: Foreign Investment Review Agency, Government of Canada, 1979).

Comprehensive Programme for the Further Extension and Improvement of Cooperation and the Development of Socialist Economic Integration by the CMEA Member Countries (Moscow: CMEA Secretariat, 1971).

Direct Investment Abroad by Transnational Corporations of the CMEA Countries (Paris: OECD Directorate for Financial, Fiscal and Enterprise Affairs, March 1983).

East European Economic Assessment (Washington: US Government Printing Office for the Joint Economic Committee, US Congress, 1980/81).

East-European Economies Post-Helsinki (Washington: US Government Printing Office, for the Joint Economic Committee, US Congress, 1977).

East–West Business Directory, The: a Listing of Companies in the West with Soviet and East European Capital Participation (London: Duncan Publishing for the East–West Project, Carleton University, 1983).

East–West Trade: Recent Developments in Countertrade (Paris: OECD Secretariat, 1981).

East European Economics: Slow Growth in the 1980s (Washington: Government Printing Office for the Joint Economic Committee, US Congress, 1984) vol. 1.

Impact of Multinational Corporations on Development and on International Relations (New York: United Nations, 1974).

Multinational Corporations in World Development (New York: United Nations, 1973).

National Legislation Relating to Transnational Corporations (New York: United Nations, for the Centre on Transnational Corporations, 1978).

Resheniia Partii i Pravitel'stva po Khoziaistvennym Voprosam, tom 1, 1917–1928 godu (Moscow: Izdat. Politicheskoi literatury, 1967).

Soviet and East European Aid to the Third World, 1981, Department of State Publication 9345 (Washington: US Printing Office, February 1983).

Soviet Economy in a New Perspective (Washington: US Government Printing Office for the Joint Economic Committee, US Congress, 1976).

Soviet Economy in a Time of Change (Washington: US Government Printing Office, for the Joint Economic Committee, US Congress, 1979), vol. 2.

The Soviet Merchant Marine: Economic and Strategic Challenge to the West (Boulder, Colorado: Westview Press for the Atlantic Council of the United States, 1979).

Soviet Oceans Development (Washington: US Government Printing Office for the Committee on Commerce, US Congress, 1976).

Transfer of United States High Technology to the Soviet Union and Soviet Bloc Nations, Washington, United States Senate, 97th Congress, 2nd Session, Report No. 97–664, 15 November 1982.

Transnational Corporations in World Development: a Re-examination (New York: United Nations for the Commission on Transnational Corporations, 1978).

Transnational Corporations in World Development: Third Survey (New York: United Nations, for the Commission on Transnational Corporations, 1983).

UN Economic Commission for Europe, East–West Industrial Co-operation (New York: United Nations, 1979).

Vos Partenaires d'Affaires en Roumanie (Bucharest: Publicom, 1982).

ARTICLES

ADAM, GY., 'New Trends in International Business: Worldwide Sourcing and Dedomiciling', *Acta Oeconomica*, No. 3–4, 1971.

AJAYI, E., 'Nigerian–Soviet Relations 1960–68', *Nigerian Bulletin on Foreign Affairs*, January 1972.

BARTHA, F., 'Külfödi közös érdekeltségek helye Magyaroszag kereskedelempolitikajaban', *Külgazdasag*, No. 8, 1978.

CHUBIN, S., 'The Soviet Union and Iran', *Foreign Affairs*, Spring 1983.

DEMCSAK, S., 'Hungarian Entrepreneurs – Foreign Partners', *Marketing in Hungary*, No. 1, 1982.

DOBOZI, I., 'Arrangements for Mineral Development Cooperation between Socialist Countries and Developing Countries', *Natural Resources Forum*, October, 1983.

DOBOZI, I., 'Economic Interaction between East and South – the Mineral Resource Dimension', *Raw Materials Report*, No. 2, 1982.

DOBOZI, I., 'Problems of Raw Materials Supply in Eastern Europe', *The World Economy*, Vol. 1, No. 2, January 1978.

HAYMAN, C., 'Soviet Shipping', *Seatrade*, February 1976.

HEENAN, D., 'Moscow Goes Multinational', *Harvard Business Review*, May–June 1981.

HILTON, A., 'The Challenging Role of Private Foreign Investment in Nigeria', *Bulletin on Foreign Affairs*, May 1972.

JUNG, A., 'Polish Production Partnerships in Developing Countries', *Soviet and East European Foreign Trade*, Spring 1982.

KING, R. R., 'Romania and the Third World', *Orbis*, Winter 1978.

KOHLMEY, G., 'From Extensive Growth to Intensive Growth', *Czechoslovak Economic Papers*, No. 6, 1966.

KURIEN, J., 'Entry of Big Business into Fishing', *Economic and Political Weekly*, 9 September 1978.

LAPACKOVA, H., 'Development of the Forms of Relationships between Foreign Trade and Industry', *Soviet and East European Foreign Trade*, Summer 1983.

LINNAIMAA, X. and METTELIA, K., 'Ekonomicheskoe Sotrudnichestvo Findlandii co stranami-chlenami SEV', *Voprosy Ekonomiki*, No. 2, 1978.

McINNES, N., 'Ivan the Capitalist', *Barron's*, 13 December 1976.

McMILLAN, C., 'Soviet and East European Direct Investment in Canada', *Foreign Investment Review*, Spring 1979.

MITCHELL, W. and DERR, D., 'Opportunities in Canadian Banking', *Foreign Investment Review*, Spring 1981.

OGUNBADEJO, O., 'Ideology and Pragmatism: the Soviet Role in Nigeria', *Orbis*, Winter 1978.

OZAWA, T., 'Japan's Multinational Enterprise: the Political Economy of Outward Dependency', *World Politics*, July 1978.

PORTES, R., 'East Europe's Debt to the West: Interdependence is a Two-way Street', *Foreign Affairs*, July 1977.

PULAWSKI, S., 'A Method for Evaluating Polish Joint Ventures Operating Abroad', *Soviet and East European Foreign Trade*, Fall 1979.

RHODES, J., 'Economic Growth and Government-Owned Multinationals', *Management Review*, December 1978.

ROBBIE, K., 'Socialist Banks and the Origins of the Euro-currency Markets', *Moscow Narodny Bank Quarterly Review*, Winter 1975/76.

SAWICKI, H., 'Polish Firms Abroad', *Polish Foreign Trade*, No. 3, 1983.

SCHETININ, V., 'An Alternative to TNC's', *CTC Reporter*, Autumn 1983.

SCHROEDER, G., 'Soviet Economic "Reforms": a Study in Contradictions', *Soviet Studies*, July 1968.

SUZUKI, T., 'Joint Venture Corporations in Socialist Countries', *Digest of Japanese Industry and Technology*, No. 144, 1980.

TIRASPOLSKY, A., 'Les investissements occidentaux dans les pays de l'Est', *Le Courrier des Pays de l'Est*, April 1979.

TYRKA, S., 'Multinationalisation des activités bancaires des pays de l'Est', *Banque*, October 1976.

VALKENIER, E., 'The USSR, the Third World and the Global Economy', *Problems of Communism*, July–August 1979.

VANOUS, J., 'East European Economic Slowdown', *Problems of Communism*, July–August 1982.

VERNON, R., 'The Fragile Foundations of East–West Trade', *Foreign Affairs*, Summer 1979.

VLASOV, A., 'New Forms of Economic Relations of CMEA Member-Countries with Developing Nations,' *Foreign Trade*, No. 12, 1983.

WILD, G., 'La Présence Economic Soviétique en Afrique Sub-Saharienne', *Le Courrier des Pays de l'Est*, December 1979.

PERIODICALS/NEWSPAPERS

Acta Oeconomica, Budapest.
African Development, London.
Arab Economist, The, Beirut.
Banque, Paris.
Barron's, New York.
Bulgaria Today, Sofia.
Bulgarian Foreign Trade, Sofia.
Bulletin on Foreign Affairs, Lagos.
Citizen, The, Ottawa.
Contemporary Poland, Warsaw.
CTC Reporter, New York.
Courrier des Pays de l'Est, Le, Paris.
Czechoslovak Economic Papers, Prague.
Czechoslovak Foreign Trade, Prague.
Digest of Japanese Industry and Technology, Tokyo.
East European Markets, London.
Economic and Political Weekly, Bombay.
Economic Bulletin, Sofia.
Economic News of Bulgaria, Sofia.
Economist, The, London.
Financial Post, Toronto.
Financial Times, London.
Foreign Affairs, New York.
Foreign Investment Review, Ottawa.
Foreign Trade, Moscow.
Handel Zagraniczny, Warsaw.
Harvard Business Review, Cambridge, Mass.
Hungarian Foreign Trade, Budapest.
Hungaropress, Budapest.
Külgasdasag, Budapest.
Latin America, London.
Echos, Les, Paris.

Management Review, New York.
Marketing in Hungary, Budapest.
Moscow Narodny Bank Press Bulletin/Quarterly Review, London.
New Hungarian Exporter, Budapest.
New York Times, New York.
Nigerian Bulletin on Foreign Affairs, Lagos.
Orbis, Philadelphia.
Polish Economic Survey, Warsaw.
Polish Foreign Trade, Warsaw.
Problems of Communism, Washington, DC.
Quarterly Economic Review, The Economist Intelligence Unit, London.
Raw Materials Report, Stockholm.
Revista Economica, Bucharest.
Romanian Foreign Trade, Bucharest.
Rynki Zagraniczne, Warsaw.
Seatrade, Colchester, Essex, UK.
Sofia News, Sofia.
Soviet Analyst, Richmond, Surrey.
Soviet and East European Foreign Trade, New York.
Soviet Business and Trade, Washington, DC.
Soviet Export, Moscow.
Soviet Studies, Glasgow.
Statistics Canada Daily, Ottawa.
Times, The, London.
Voprosy Ekonomiki, Moscow.
West Africa, London.
World Economy, The, London.
World Politics, Princeton, New Jersey.

Index of Company Names

211

Subject Index

215